JOEL

THE ANCHOR BIBLE is a fresh approach to the world's greatest classic. Its object is to make the Bible accessible to the modern reader; its method is to arrive at the meaning of biblical literature through exact translation and extended exposition, and to reconstruct the ancient setting of the biblical story, as well as the circumstances of its transcription and the characteristics of its transcribers.

THE ANCHOR BIBLE is a project of international and interfaith scope: Protestant, Catholic, and Jewish scholars from many countries contribute individual volumes. The project is not sponsored by any ecclesiastical organization and is not intended to reflect any particular theological doctrine. Prepared under our joint supervision, THE ANCHOR BIBLE is an effort to make available all the significant historical and linguistic knowledge which bears on the interpretation of the biblical record.

THE ANCHOR BIBLE is aimed at the general reader with no special formal training in biblical studies; yet, it is written with the most exacting standards of scholarship, reflecting the highest technical accomplishment.

This project marks the beginning of a new era of co-operation among scholars in biblical research, thus forming a common body of knowledge to be shared by all.

William Foxwell Albright
David Noel Freedman
GENERAL EDITORS

THE ANCHOR BIBLE

JOEL

A New Translation
with Introduction and Commentary

JAMES L. CRENSHAW

THE ANCHOR BIBLE
Doubleday
New York London Toronto Sydney Auckland

The Anchor Bible
PUBLISHED BY DOUBLEDAY
a division of Bantam Doubleday Dell Publishing Group, Inc.
1540 Broadway, New York, New York 10036

Library of Congress Cataloging-in-Publication Data

Bible. O.T. Joel. English. Crenshaw. 1995.
Joel: a new translation with introduction and commentary / by
James L. Crenshaw.—1st ed.
p. cm.—(The Anchor Bible; v. 24C)
Includes bibliographical references and index.
1. Bible. O.T. Joel—Commentaries. I. Crenshaw, James L.
II. Title. III. Series: Bible. English. Anchor Bible. 1964; v. 24C.
BS192.2.A1 1964G3 vol. 24c
[BS1573]
224'.7077—dc20 94-34473
CIP

ISBN 0-385-41205-3

Printed in the United States of America
October 1995

First Edition

10 9 8 7 6 5 4 3 2 1

To Laura Schrader Crenshaw

A Fragile Presence

Clinging beneath a purple celosia,
the winged beauty finds shelter
from the scorching sun,
oblivious to admiring eyes.

What kind Chance
led this token of love's wonder to my flowers,
and who guards her white form,
suspended among predators
ready to devour a fragile presence?

If only my garden
were your permanent abode,
then I would not search in vain
for you another day.

Sleep, my vulnerable visitor
from heaven's door,
and these eyes will watch over you
'til your metamorphosis is complete.

Then when my spirit
breaks free from its earthly wrap
and wends its way to a distant garden,

Will the Keeper of that refuge—
on seeing a fragile presence
clinging to a leaf on the tree of life—

Be touched by its vulnerability
to unaccustomed radiance
and protect it from harm?

James L. Crenshaw
March 23, 1994

Preface and Acknowledgments

When David Noel Freedman first asked me to write a commentary on the book of Joel for The Anchor Bible I thought saying "yes" would give me an opportunity to examine the relationship between apocalyptic and wisdom. I could not have been more wrong. The oft-postulated apocalyptic influence on Joel, as well as recent claims that he was indebted to wisdom for much of his language, did not survive closer scrutiny. Thus I was left with the task of exploring the rich prophetic background for the book. This meant abandoning *for a season* the study of wisdom literature, to which I have given nearly three decades of research, in favor of my first love, prophecy. I soon discovered that I had not lost my passion for prophetic speech and religious struggle.

The last five years or so have been devoted to a tiny book in the Minor Prophets, one whose primary claim to fame for Christians rests on a single passage—the announcement of an outpouring of the divine spirit on all flesh. The author of Acts interpreted the unusual events associated with Pentecost, recorded in the second chapter of Acts, as the long-awaited fulfilment of Joel's prediction. A text in Joel that was originally restricted to the Judean populace, the contextual meaning of *kol bāśār* ("all flesh"), now takes on a universal connotation, as peoples of diverse languages and nationalities understand the speech of those who, prior to this "miracle," spoke a language that they could not grasp. Jewish readers still anticipate the outpouring of the divine spirit, yet unfulfilled, which offers a modicum of comfort to an "exiled" people.

The more I studied the language, grammar, and syntax of the book of Joel the more I was drawn to its literary artistry and passionate devotion to God. I have learned more than most people would care to know about locusts, and I have examined every secondary interpretation of the book that came to my attention over the years. The reader is spared much of this tedium, for I have tried to restrict the discussion to productive avenues of interpretation. I have also attempted to provide a translation that faithfully renders the Hebrew of the book into the modern idiom. In bringing my efforts to a close, I am painfully aware that no interpretation, however profound, ever achieves closure. The writer of a commentary does not have the luxury of postponing the end indefinitely. Knowing that every book can be improved if one works at it long enough, and believing, at least partly, with Callimachus, a contemporary of the second-century Jewish sage, Jesus Ben Sira, that "a long book is a long evil," I now have decided to submit my understandings of the book to a wider public—and to move on to other things. I do so, however, with gratitude for all those persons who have assisted me in this project.

First, David Noel Freedman. Editor extraordinaire, Noel has rendered the usual service of seeing a manuscript through its several phases, and he has called my attention to possibilities of interpretation that had previously escaped me. In his inimitable way and magnanimous spirit he has allowed me the freedom to depart from his own understanding of a text, especially in matters of translation—he prefers a more literal formal correspondence, and I opt for a dynamic equivalence. Wherever possible, I have tried to accommodate both approaches to the text.

Second, Peter Machinist and Orval Wintermute, who read part of the commentary and made many helpful suggestions. I am grateful to Peter for taking time to examine and offer a critique of my efforts at interpreting the book of Joel when he could have used those valuable hours working on his own volume on Nahum for THE ANCHOR BIBLE. I thank my colleague, Orval, for this and many other acts of collegiality.

Third, Anita Gail Chappell has typed the manuscript at every stage of its development and has done so with her usual competence and enthusiasm. Working with her on this book, as on previous ones, has been fun.

Fourth, Roberta Schaafsma, Reference Librarian at the Duke Divinity School Library, and Donald C. Polaski have helped me locate obscure references and saved much time and effort on my part. Don also prepared the Indexes.

Finally, I wish to thank Dennis Campbell, the dean of the Divinity School at Duke University, for supporting my research in various ways.

This book is dedicated to Laura Schrader Crenshaw, the wife of our older son, James Timothy. It is a small token of my gratitude to her for the joy she brings to our family.

CONTENTS

ABBREVIATIONS

AB	The Anchor Bible
ABD	*The Anchor Bible Dictionary*. 6 vols. ed. D. N. Freedman. New York, London, Toronto, Sydney, Auckland: Doubleday, 1992.
AJBI	*Annual of the Japanese Biblical Institute*
AJSL	*American Journal of Semitic Languages*
ANET	*Ancient Near Eastern Texts Relating to the Old Testament*, 3d ed. with Supplement. ed. J. B. Pritchard. Princeton: Princeton University Press, 1955, 1969.
ANETS	Ancient Near Eastern Texts and Studies
ATANT	Abhandlungen zur Theologie des Alten und Neuen Testaments
ATD	Das Alte Testament Deutsch
AUSS	*Andrews University Seminary Studies*
BASOR	*American Schools of Oriental Research Bulletin*
B.C.E.	Before the Common Era
BDB	*A Hebrew and English Lexicon of the Old Testament*. F. Brown, S. R. Driver, and C. A. Briggs. Oxford: Oxford University Press, 1907.
BEATAJ	Beiträge zur Erforschung des Alten Testament und der antiken Judentums
BETL	Bibliotheca Ephemeridum Theologicarum Lovaniensium
BHS	*Biblia Hebraica Stuttgartensia*
BHT	Beiträge zur historischen Theologie
BI	*Biblical Illustrator*
Bib	*Biblica*
BIOSCS	*Bulletin of the International Organization for Septuagint and Cognate Studies*
BJS	Brown Judaic Studies
BKAT	Biblischer Kommentar, Altes Testament
BLS	The Bible and Literature Series
BN	*Biblische Notizen*
BO	*Biblica et Orientalia*
BRT	*The Baptist Review of Theology/La Revue baptiste de théologie*
BVC	*Bible et vie chrétienne*
BZAW	Beihefte zur Zeitschrift für die alttestamentliche Wissenschaft

CAT	Commentaire de l'ancien Testament
CB	Century Bible
CBQ	*Catholic Biblical Quarterly*
CBQMS	Catholic Biblical Quarterly Monograph Series
CBSC	Cambridge Bible for Schools and Colleges
C.E.	Common Era
ConB, OT	Coniectanea Biblica, Old Testament
CQR	*Church Quarterly Review*
CTA	*Corpus des tablettes en cunéiformes alphabétiques*, ed. A. Herdner. Paris: Imprimerie Nationale, 1963.
CTM	*Concordia Theological Monthly*
CurTM	*Currents in Theology and Mission*
Di	*Dialog*
DJD	Discoveries in the Judean Desert
EC	*Ephemerides Carmeliticae*
EHPR	Études d'Histoire et de Philosophie Religieuses
ET	English Translation
ETR	*Études théologiques et religieuses*
EvT	*Evangelical Theology*
Exp	*Expositor*
ExpTim	*The Expository Times*
GKC	*Gesenius' Hebrew Grammar*, eds. E. Kautzsch and A. E. Cowley. Oxford: The Clarendon Press, 1910.
HAR	*Hebrew Annual Review*
HAT	Handbuch zum Alten Testament
HDR	Harvard Dissertations in Religion
HS	*Hebrew Studies*
HSM	Harvard Semitic Monographs
HTR	*Harvard Theological Review*
HUCA	*Hebrew Union College Annual*
IAB	Ba'al and Anat
IB	*The Interpreter's Bible*
ICC	International Critical Commentary
IDB	*The Interpreter's Dictionary of the Bible*
IDBS	*The Interpreter's Dictionary of the Bible, Supplement*
IEJ	*Israel Exploration Journal*
Int	*Interpretation*
IRT	Issues in Religion and Theology
ITC	International Theological Commentary
JBL	*Journal of Biblical Literature*
JETS	*Journal of the Evangelical Theological Society*
JQR	*Jewish Quarterly Review*

JNES	*Journal of Near Eastern Studies*
JSOT	*Journal for the Study of the Old Testament*
JSOTS	*Journal for the Study of the Old Testament Supplement*
JSS	*Journal of Semitic Studies*
JTS	*Journal of Theological Studies*
KAI	*Kanaanäische und aramäische Inschriften*. 3 vols. eds. H. Donner and W. Röllig. Wiesbaden: Otto Harrassowitz, 1964, 1966, 1968.
KAT	Kommentar zum Alten Testament
KBL	*Lexicon in Veteris Testamenti Libros*, L. Köhler and W. Baumgartner. Leiden: E. J. Brill.
KHCAT	Kurzer Handcommentar zum Alten Testament
KK	*Kurtzgefasster Kommentar zu den heiligen Schriften Alten und Neuen Testaments sowie zu den Apokryphen*, eds. H. Strack and O. Zöckler. München: C. H. Beck, 1887–1905.
KTU	*Die Keilalphabetischen Texte aus Ugarit*, eds. M. Dietrich, O. Loretz, J. Sanmartin. AOAT 24. Kevelaer: Butzon & Bercker; Neukirchen-Vluyn: Neukirchener, 1976.
Leš	*Lešonenu* (Hebrew)
MisMid	Mishna Middot
NICOT	The New International Commentary on the Old Testament
NKZ	*Neue Kirchliche Zeitschrift*
NRSV	New Revised Standard Version
NTT	*Nederlands Theologisch Tijdschrift*
OBT	Overtures to Biblical Theology
OL	*Orientalistische Literaturzeitung*
Or	*Orientalia*
OTL	Old Testament Library
OTS	*Oudtestamentische Studieen*
OTWSA	Die O. T. Werkgemeenskap in Suid-Afrika
PEQ	*Palestine Exploration Quarterly*
Pers	*Perspectives in Religious Studies*
POS	Pretoria Oriental Series
RB	*Revue Biblique*
RQ	*Restoration Quarterly*
RS	*Revue Semetique*
RSR	*Recherches de Science Religieuse*
RSV	Revised Standard Version
SB	*Semiotique et bible*
SBLDS	Society of Biblical Literature Dissertation Series
SEÅ	*Svensk Exegetisk Årsbok*
SEM	*Semitics*

SJOT	*Scandinavian Journal of the Old Testament*
SUNT	Studies zur Umwelt des Neuen Testaments
SWBA	Social World of Biblical Antiquity Series
TAuJCC	Theologische Academie uitgaande van de Johannes Calvijnstichtingtes Kampen
TBT	*The Bible Today*
TDNT	*Theological Dictionary of the New Testament*. 9 vols. eds. G. Kittel and G. Friedrich. Grand Rapids, Michigan: William B. Eerdmans, 1964–74.
TDOT	*Theological Dictionary of the Old Testament*. 6 vols. eds. G. J. Botterweck and H. Ringgren. Grand Rapids, Michigan: William B. Eerdmans, 1974–90.
TE	*Theologia Evangelica*
THAT	*Theologisches Handwörterbuch des Alten Testament*, 3d ed. 2 vols. eds. E. Jenni and C. Westermann. München: Chr. Kaiser Verlag and Zurich: Theologischer Verlag, 1978, 1979.
TLZ	*Theologische Literaturzeitung*
TOTC	Tyndale Old Testament Commentary
TRE	Theologische Realenzyklopädia
TV	*Theologia Viatorum*
TZ	*Theologische Zeitschrift*
UBL	Ugaritisch-biblische Literatur
UCPSP	University of California Publications in Semitic Philology
UF	*Ugarit Forschungen*
UT	*Ugaritic Textbook*, C. H. Gordon. Rome: Pontifical Biblical Institute, 1965.
UUÅ	*Uppsala Universitets Årsskrift*
VT	*Vetus Testamentum*
VTS	*Vetus Testamentum Supplement*
WMANT	Wissenschaftliche Monographien zum Alten und Neuen Testament
WW	*Western Watch*
ZAW	*Zeitschrift für die alttestamentliche Wissenschaft*
ZDPV	*Zeitschrift des Deutschen Palästina-Vereins*
ZNW	*Zeitschrift für die neutestamentliche Wissenschaft*
ZTK	*Zeitschrift für Theologie und Kirche*

THE BOOK OF JOEL: A TRANSLATION

THE SUPERSCRIPTION (1:1)

1:1 YHWH's word entrusted to Joel, Pethuel's son.

DIVINE JUDGMENT AGAINST JUDAH AND ITS RESPONSE (1:2–2:17)

A Summons to Lament and Return to YHWH (1:2–20)

1:2 Take heed to this, old timers,
listen, every local resident.
Has anything comparable happened in your time
or in that of your parents?

1:3 Tell it to your children;
and they to theirs,
and their children to the next generation.

1:4 What the chewer left the swarming locust consumed;
and what the swarming locust left the jumper ate;
what the jumper left the finisher devoured.

1:5 Wake up, imbibers, and weep;
sob, all who drink wine,
because of the sweet wine denied you.

1:6 For a nation has attacked my land,
one powerful and innumerable,
with leonine teeth and fangs.

1:7 It made my vineyard into a desolation,
and my fig trees into splinters,
stripping off the bark and hurling it aside,
leaving whitened cuttings.

1:8 Cry aloud like a young woman clothed in sackcloth,
over the husband of her youth.

1:9 Cereal offering and libation are withheld
from YHWH's house;
the priests mourn—
YHWH's officials.

1:10 The fields are devastated,
the ground groans;
indeed, the grain is destroyed,
the wine dried up, the oil depleted.

1:11 Be ashamed, farmers;
sob, vintners,
on account of wheat and barley;
for the harvest is ruined.

1:12 The vine has withered,
the fig is scorched,
pomegranate, date, and apple—
every tree in the orchard has wilted;
indeed, joy has utterly vanished
from the populace.

1:13 Don mourning garments and lament, priests;
sob, presiders over the altar;
come, spend the night in sackcloth,
ministers of my God;
for withheld from your God's house
are cereal offering and libation.

1:14 Arrange a sacred fast,
announce a religious assembly;
gather the elderly,
every resident of the area,
to the house of YHWH your God;
and cry out to YHWH.

1:15 That day! Horrors!
For YHWH's day is imminent,
dawning like destruction from the Destroyer.

1:16 Is food not being cut off
before our very eyes,
joy and gladness,
from the house of our God?

1:17 Seeds have shriveled under their shovels;
storage bins are desolate,
granaries ruined;
for the grain has dried out.

1:18 How the beasts moan,
the herds weep,
for lack of fodder;
even flocks of sheep are hurting.

1:19 To you, YHWH, I cry out;
for fire has consumed the pasture land,
a flame has licked all the trees in the field.

1:20 Even the beasts in the field
complain to you;
for the water sources have dried up,
and fire has devoured the pasture land.

YHWH's Efficient Army (2:1–11)

2:1 Sound the alarm in Zion,
the warning shout on my sacred mountain;
every citizen will tremble
because YHWH's day is coming—
indeed, near.

2:2 A time of darkness and murkiness,
a day of cloud and haze
like dawn engulfing mountains;
a numerous, mighty people
the like of which has never appeared,
nor will do so again
into the remote future.

2:3 Before it—fire consumed,
behind it—a flame licked;
like a garden of Eden—the land ahead of it,
like a desolate wilderness—that behind it;
nothing escapes.

2:4 Its appearance resembles horses;
it gallops like steeds;

2:5 It hurtles on mountain tops
like the rumble of chariots;

like the popping of fire
devouring stubble;
like a formidable army
organized for battle.

2:6 In its path people writhe,
every visage gathers sorrow.

2:7 They attack like soldiers;
like warriors they scale a wall,
each going in its own trail;
it does not encroach on others' paths.

2:8 One does not shove another,
each treads its own way;
they descend into a tunnel,
not breaking away.

2:9 In the city they rush about,
running on the wall,
entering houses,
going through windows
like thieves.

2:10 In its vanguard earth trembles,
sky quakes,
sun and moon are darkened,
stars gather their splendor.

2:11 Then YHWH spoke
in his army's presence;
for his encampment is particularly numerous,
mighty the one who carries out his decree;
for YHWH's day is great,
exceedingly fearful;
who can stand it?

A Call to Return to YHWH and to Lament (2:12–17)

2:12 But even now—a divine oracle—
return to me with your whole mind,
with fasting, weeping, and mourning.

2:13 Rend your inner disposition
and not just your clothes,
then return to YHWH your God;

for merciful and compassionate is he,
patient and abundantly loyal,
repenting about harm.

2:14 Perhaps he will turn and relent,
leaving a blessing in his wake;
a cereal offering and libation
for YHWH your God.

2:15 Blow the ram's horn in Zion,
inaugurate a holy fast,
announce a religious gathering.

2:16 Assemble the people,
sanctify a congregation,
bring the elderly together,
gather the infants
and those feeding on breasts;
let the bridegroom leave his room,
and the bride her chamber.

2:17 Between porch and altar
let the priests weep, YHWH's ministers;
let them say,
"Have pity, YHWH, on your people,
and do not surrender your property to reproach,
nations mocking them;
why should they say among the peoples,
'Where is their God?' "

THE RESTORATION OF JUDAH AND DIVINE JUDGMENT ON FOREIGN NATIONS

Replacing What the Locusts Consumed (2:18–27)

2:18 Then YHWH became zealous about his land
and had compassion on his people.

2:19 YHWH answered them,
"Look, I am about to send you
grain, new wine, and oil;

you will be satisfied with them;
never again will I make you
a reproach among the nations.

2:20 The Northerner
I will thrust from your midst,
driving it to a thirsty and desolate land,
his vanguard to the eastward sea,
his rearguard to the westward sea;
his stench will rise,
together with his foul odor,
for he has acted reprehensibly.

2:21 Do not fear, land,
be happy and rejoice,
for YHWH has acted mightily.

2:22 Fear not, beasts of the field,
for the pasture land has put forth lush growth;
the trees have produced their fruit,
fig and vine have yielded their produce.

2:23 Citizens of Zion, rejoice and be glad,
In YHWH your God,
for he has given you the early rain in its season,
and sent down showers for you,
both early and late, as previously.

2:24 The granaries are full of grain;
the vats spill over with new wine and oil.

2:25 I will make up for you the years
the swarming locust consumed—
the jumper, finisher, and chewer—
my mighty force that I sent against you.

2:26 You will continually consume food and always be satisfied;
you will praise the name of YHWH your God
who has worked wonderfully among you,
and my people will never again be shamed.

2:27 Then you will know
that I am in the midst of Israel,
and I, YHWH, am your God—
there is no other—
and my people will never again be shamed."

Signs and Portents (3:1–5 [2:28–32])

3:1 [2:28] Afterwards I will endow all of you with my vital force,
so that your boys and girls will speak oracles on my behalf;
your old people will discern my will through dreams,
and your young adults will become visionaries.

3:2 [2:29] On your slaves, too, both male and female,
I will bestow my vital force at that time.

3:3 [2:30] I will set portents in the sky and on earth—
blood, fire, and mushrooming smoke.

3:4 [2:31] The sun will be darkened, the moon blood-red,
before YHWH's day dawns—greatly awesome.

3:5 [2:32] Henceforth everyone who implores YHWH will avoid harm,
for on Mount Zion and in Jerusalem will be an escape
as YHWH promised,
and among survivors whom YHWH calls.

YHWH's Reasons for Judging the Nations (4:1–3 [3:1–3])

4:1 [3:1] For in those days
and at that time
when I restore the fortunes
of Judah and Jerusalem

4:2 [3:2] I will gather all nations,
making them descend to the valley of Jehoshaphat
where I will execute judgment on them
because of my people, Israel my inheritance,
whom they dispersed among the nations—
and they apportioned my land.

4:3 [3:3] Casting lots over my people—
they gave a boy for the price of a harlot,
sold a girl for wine and drank it.

Special Instances of Divine Recompense (4:4–8 [3:4–8])

4:4 [3:4] Furthermore,
what are you to me, Tyre and Sidon,
and all regions of Philistia?
Are you paying me back a recompense?
If you are working vengeance on me,
I will very quickly repay your deeds on your heads.

4:5 [3:5] Because you took my silver and gold,
and brought my priceless commodities to your palaces.

4:6 [3:6] Judeans and Jerusalemites
you sold to Ionians
to thrust them beyond their own border,

4:7 [3:7] Look, I am rousing them from the place
to which you sold them,
and I will repay your deed on your heads,

4:8 [3:8] Selling your sons and daughters
by the agency of Judeans,
and they will sell them to Sabeans,
to a distant nation;
for YHWH has spoken.

YHWH's Judgment Against the Nations (4:9–16 [3:9–16])

4:9 [3:9] Proclaim this among the nations,
"Sanctify a battle.
Rouse the mighty ones.
Let all warriors draw near and go up.

4:10 [3:10] Beat your plowtips into swords,
your pruning knives into spears;
let the weakling boast, 'I am a warrior!'

4:11 [3:11] Hurry and come,
all surrounding nations;
gather there;"
Send down your mighty ones, YHWH.

4:12 [3:12] Let the nations rouse themselves and come up
to the valley of Jehoshaphat,
for there I will sit in judgment
on all surrounding nations.

4:13 [3:13] Put forth the sickle, for the harvest is ripe;
go out and tread, for the wine press is full;
the vats overflow, for their evil deeds are copious.

4:14 [3:14] Tumult! Tumult! In the valley of decision,
for YHWH's day is near in the valley of decision.

4:15 [3:15] Sun and moon have become dark,
stars have withheld their splendor;

4:16 [3:16] then YHWH roars from Zion,
utters his voice from Jerusalem;
heaven and earth tremble,
but YHWH is a refuge for his people,
a fortress for Israelites.

JUDAH'S SECURITY IS ASSURED (4:17–21 [3:17–21])

4:17 [3:17] Then you will know that I YHWH your God
dwell in Zion, my sacred mountain;
and Jerusalem will be (a place of) holiness,
foreigners no longer traversing it.

4:18 [3:18] On that day
mountains will drip sweet wine,
hills will course with milk,
and all channels of Judah will flow with water,
a stream rushing from YHWH's house,
watering the valley of Shittim.

4:19 [3:19] Egypt will become a waste,
Edom a desolate steppe;
because of violence against Judeans,
the spilling of innocent blood in their land.

4:20 [3:20] Judah will be inhabited from now on,
Jerusalem for untold generations.

4:21 [3:21] I shall avenge their blood, yet unavenged,
and YHWH will dwell in Zion.

INTRODUCTION

AN OVERVIEW OF THE CONTENTS

The book of Joel consists of seventy-three verses. In the early thirteenth century (c. 1205) Stephen Langton divided the Vulgate text of Joel into three chapters, and in the next century the Greek text was similarly divided. The first Rabbinic Bible, edited by Felix Pratensis in 1517, adopted this practice of a tripartite division. Most subsequent editions of the Bible, including English translations, have continued to do so. The second Rabbinic Bible, edited by Jacob ben Hayyim in 1526, and most later Hebrew editions have divided the book into four chapters. Two notable English translations, those by the Jewish Publication Society and the New American Bible, follow this tradition. In the Hebrew text with which I work, *Biblia Hebraica Stuttgartensia*,[1] 3:1–5 equals 2:28–32 in English translations, and 4:1–21 equals 3:1–21. I indicate this feature of the texts by brackets, for example 3:1 [2:28] designates the first verse of chapter three in the Hebrew text and v 28 in the second chapter of English translations.

Only seven books in the Hebrew Bible have fewer verses, and all of them belong to the second division of the canon, the Prophets.[2] The other two

[1] Codex Leningradensis, which *BHS* reproduces, dates from 1008 C.E. and belongs to the textual tradition preserved by the family of ben Asher, as opposed to that of ben Naphtali.

[2] The *nebîʾîm* consists of the Former and Latter Prophets. To the first category belong the "historical" books Joshua, Judges, Samuel, and Kings—presumably because the events they record are ideologically controlled by a prophetic understanding of the effects of YHWH's word in shaping Israel's destiny. The second category is also made up of four blocks of material: Isaiah, Jeremiah, Ezekiel, and "The Twelve," the latter viewed as an entity and written on a single scroll for convenience and economy. This division of the Hebrew Bible was already intact in the early second century B.C.E., for Ben Sira refers to the three major prophets and adds: "May the bones of the twelve prophets revive from where they lie, for they comforted the people of Jacob and delivered them with confident hope" (49:10, RSV). The prologue to Sirach, composed by Ben Sira's grandson who translated the Hebrew book into Greek, acknowledges a tripartite canon by his time, c. 130, for he mentions the law, prophets, and other books. The inclusion of the literary complex Ezra-Nehemiah-Chronicles in the third division rather than the second (with the former prophets, which it resembles) and likewise Daniel (rather than with the Latter Prophets) suggests that the Former Prophets was closed by the fourth century at the latest and the Latter Prophets by the early second century. David Noel Freedman, "The Law and the Prophets," *VTS* 9 (1962) 250–65, argues for an earlier date, approximately 450–425 B.C.E.

The threefold division of the Hebrew Bible probably echoes the primary institutions in ancient divisions are the Torah, comprising Genesis, Exodus, Leviticus, Numbers, and Deuteronomy, and the Writings, made up of Psalms, Job, Proverbs, Ruth, Song of Songs, Ecclesiastes, Lamentations, Esther, Daniel, Ezra, Nehemiah, and Chronicles. The seven shorter books are Obadiah (21 verses), Haggai (38 verses), Nahum (47 verses), Jonah (48 verses), Zephaniah (53 verses), Malachi (55 verses), and Habakkuk (56 verses). Outside the prophetic canon Ruth comes closest to Joel with eighty-five verses. Scholars inclined to search for mysterious symbolism in numbers could point out that 73 is the sum of the Hebrew alphabet tripled (22 × 3 = 66), to which the perfect number seven has been added (66 + 7 = 73).[3] I find such speculation interesting but unproductive. A more precise means of comparing the length of books, facilitated by the tabulation in Francis I. Andersen and A. D. Forbes, *The Vocabulary of the Old Testament* (Rome: Pontifical Biblical Institute, 1989), results from counting the number of words in each. According to this method, the book of Joel has 957, with seven books having fewer words: Obadiah (291), Nahum (558), Haggai (600), Habakkuk (671), Jonah (688), Zephaniah (676), and Malachi (876). Using this method, the book of Ruth with 1,294 words drops out of the short list, leaving nothing in this category but those belonging to the Minor Prophets.

In 957 words the seventy-three verses tell a story about an unprecedented disaster that struck the tiny Judean countryside and its abatement through effective action by the people and their deity. In addition, the verses announce divine judgment on all nations other than Judah, singling out a few foreign powers for cruelty against Jews. The story can be outlined as follows:

I. Calamity in Judah and its Reversal 1:1–2:27
   A. An infestation of locusts and an appeal to fast and pray 1:2–20
   B. YHWH's[4] efficient army at work 2:1–11

Israel: priest, prophet, and sage. Such an understanding seems to lie behind the observation preserved in Jer 18:18 about the permanency of torah, counsel, and word. The unnamed speakers identify these three important words with priests, sages, and prophets, respectively. Even if one accepts R. N. Whybray's argument that this verse does not use *ḥākām* in a technical sense (Whybray, *The Intellectual Tradition in the Old Testament* [BZAW 135; Berlin and New York: Walter de Gruyter, 1974] 25–31), several other texts, especially in the book of Proverbs, but also in Ecclesiastes, certainly do.

[3] Such fascination with numbers has characterized the work of Patrick W. Skehan and Addison D. G. Wright, among others. Skehan applied this method to the structure of the book of Proverbs, whereas Wright used it to arrive at a structural analysis of Ecclesiastes (Skehan, *Studies in Israelite Poetry and Wisdom* [CBQMS 1; Washington, D.C.: The Catholic Biblical Association of America, 1971] 1–45, and Wright, "The Riddle of the Sphinx: The Structure of the Book of Qoheleth," *CBQ* 39 [1968] 313–34; "The Riddle of the Sphinx Revisited: Numerical Patterns in the Book of Qoheleth," *CBQ* 42 [1980] 35–51 and "Additional Numerical Patterns in Qoheleth," *CBQ* 45 [1983] 32–43).

[4] In this commentary I use the Tegragrammaton, YHWH, to designate the divine name indicated by the four Hebrew consonants *yhwh*. Although its pronunciation was obscured over the years

C. A prophetic call to turn to YHWH 2:12–17
D. The restoration of Judah and divine judgment on foreigners 2:18–27
II. Signs and Portents 3:1–5 [2:28–32]
III. Judgment of the Foreign Nations 4:1–21 [3:1–21]
A. YHWH's reasons for judging specific nations 4:1–3 [3:1–3]
B. Special instances of divine recompense 4:4–8 [3:4–8]
C. YHWH's judgment against foreign peoples 4:9–17 [3:9–17]
D. Judah's security 4:18–21 [3:18–21]

After an initial verse introducing the prophet Joel (1:1), the focus of attention falls quickly on a disaster more destructive than anything preserved in the people's collective memory. To dramatize the terrible scope of destruction Joel encourages the old people to inaugurate a chain of tradition[5] in narrative form, each generation passing the grim story along to its youth. What should they tell? The story line consists of a ruinous infestation by a swarm of locusts, one that left virtually no greenery intact. Wave upon wave of invaders chewed away at the stalks of precious grain, gnawing also on vines and leaves. The prophet effectively communicates this ongoing invasion by varying the names for locusts, giving their activity an additive character. Residents of ordinary houses felt the impact of such insatiable appetite immediately, as did persons responsible for maintaining the sacred dwelling place reserved for God. Joel compares the invaders to ravenous lions whose powerful teeth tear and splinter their victims. He thinks the scarcity of food has doubly endangered the community, for priests can no longer bring the usual cereal and drink offerings to YHWH. Such disruption of the only legitimate means of sustaining a proper relationship with God threatens the continued existence of YHWH's people. This dire circumstance evokes in Joel a poignant simile, a summons to mourn like a

---

through reluctance to pronounce the sacred name and through the use of vowels from the word "lord" (ʾ*adōnay,* a plural of majesty? "lord of all"?) once vowels were added to the Hebrew text—the Masoretes added the vocalization some time after the fifth century C.E.—scholars generally vocalize the letters as Yahweh. I leave the name unvocalized out of respect for those persons in the Jewish community for whom the sacred name is too holy to utter. Tryggve N. D. Mettinger, *In Search of God: The Meaning and Message of the Everlasting Names* (Philadelphia: Fortress Press, 1988) 11, recalls the church father, Gregorius, who thought trying "to grasp the hidden God through a study of this God's names is like trying to contain the ocean in the palm of one's hand." Mettinger goes on, nevertheless, to give a theological analysis of the different names for the One who always remains incognito.

[5]Later teachers among the Pharisees developed this concept to authenticate their views over against different interpretations promulgated by Sadducees. The Sayings of the Fathers, Pirke Aboth, states that the Pharisaic line extends in an unbroken fashion all the way back to Moses, who received Torah from God. In chapter one of the Tractate "Fathers" one reads: "Moses received Torah from Sinai and delivered it to Joshua, and Joshua to the Elders, and the Elders to the Prophets, and the Prophets delivered it to the Men of the Great Synagogue."

young woman bereft of her husband. Already the officials of the altar are in mourning, as also is the ground itself, now deprived of its participation in sustaining God's people. In short, joy has turned to mourning (1:2–12).

The prophet looks to Judah's religious leaders to institute cultic proceedings aimed at reversing the situation. Although the customary offerings are now withheld from the altar, the priests can still supplicate YHWH with words, which a liturgical text in Hos 14:3 [2] calls "oblations of the lips." Joel urges these ministers of YHWH to put on sackcloth indicating their abject humility and to tarry into the night at the holy place, possibly practicing the rite of incubation[6] in the hope of receiving a revelatory dream. Then Joel encourages them to announce a special day of fasting and to assemble the entire population for the purpose of invoking divine compassion. Ancient speculation about a wonderful day in which YHWH bestows extraordinary blessing on Judah, now reversed, prompts Joel to identify the disaster as a precursor of that dreaded day of YHWH, here heightened by means of a pun on an old name for YHWH, Shaddai.[7] Numbering himself among the suffering people, the prophet articulates the problem in a nutshell: before our very eyes food is cut off, just as rejoicing is removed from the sanctuary. It seems that Joel then describes the sorry state of granaries, which the people have neglected because they have no need for storage bins. This verse (1:17) is textually the most corrupt one in the book, otherwise remarkably free of difficulty. True to ancient thinking, Joel recognizes the comprehensive nature of suffering in Judah, the inseparability of animals and land from the destiny of the people. Cattle, both domestic and wild, wander about and moan as they search in vain for grazing places.

Suddenly, as if out of the blue, the prophet momentarily turns away from grim description and appeal to human beings. Now Joel addresses YHWH directly, although we learn nothing about the content of this cry. Instead, the text shifts to the occasion for his prayer—a surprising one indeed. No longer is the invasion by locusts the source of the trouble; now Joel introduces a new cause for dismay, a serious shortage of water. The image of fire brings together the two agents of destruction, locusts and drought. The Judean population

[6] Robert Karl Gnuse, *The Dream Theophany of Samuel* (New York et al.: University Press of America, 1983) 38, lists the following texts as possible instances of incubation: Genesis 15; 28:10–19; 46:1–4; 1 Samuel 3; 1 Kings 3. The practice is attested in Mesopotamian, Ugaritic, and Greek texts (pp. 34–38), although the actual process is not described. According to the account in 1 Kings 3, Solomon went to sleep in the shrine at Gibeon after offering sacrifices to YHWH.

[7] This text is not alone in playing on the meaning of the divine epithet *šadday*. With respect to Gen 49:25–26, Frank Moore Cross writes: "There appears to be a play on words here between *šadday* and *šadáyim*, and it is just possible that in the fertility clichés behind the present composition there is also knowledge of the epithet of ʾEl's consort *Raḥmay*. We may also draw attention to the mythological identification of the breasts of Tiamat with mountains (having gushing springs) in the creation account" (*Canaanite Myth and Hebrew Epic* [Cambridge, Massachusetts: Harvard University Press, 1973, 56]).

suffers from a widespread infestation of locusts *and* from a dry summer during which all streams have failed. Even animals' innate capacity to locate food and water avails nothing in this unfamiliar circumstance (1:13–20).

The second chapter abandons the vantage point of one who has already experienced disaster. Perhaps the admission in 1:15 that YHWH's day was *near* prompts a provocative shift in perspective, one that awaits further calamity. Traditional association of YHWH's day with warfare influences the new description of an invasion by an efficient army. Joel's language becomes decidedly martial as he urges sentinels, in YHWH's name, to sound an alarm on the sacred mountain, thus evoking dread among the populace at the thought of YHWH's day. Like the prophet Amos, Joel envisions that day as an unwelcome event; he uses the same imagery as the prophet from Tekoa, darkness rather than light. The ensuing graphic description of YHWH's army appears to combine elements of an invasion of locusts, human soldiers, and perhaps celestial beings. Drawing on language from the narrative tradition about a plague of locusts in Egypt, the prophet fixes his attention on the unique character of this new threat. Nothing quite like it has ever occurred, nor, in his view, will anything comparable to this invasion ever happen again. The great numbers of locusts obscured the source of light, yielding blackness everywhere, and the destruction of vegetation left a semblance of charred remains. Joel chooses an image from mythic tradition, the Garden of Eden,[8] to communicate the awful loss; the delightful garden is changed into a waste in the wilderness. The prophet dwells on the notions of "before" and "after" as if to emphasize the similar shift in narrative time[9] beginning in this chapter.

Having stated the inevitable consequence of such an invader, Joel proceeds to describe its approach, comparing it to that of human warriors. The comparison

[8] On the basis of a life-size statue of Had-yis i, king of Guzan, from Tell Fekheriyeh in northern Syria which contains a word cognate with Hebrew *ʿēden*, A. R. Millard concludes that the Semitic stem *ʿdn* means "abundant, lush" and calls into question a derivation of this word from Sumerian through Akkadian ("The Etymology of Eden," *VT* 34 [1984] 103–6). Jonas C. Greenfield, "A Touch of Eden," *Orientalia J. Duchesne-Guillemin Emerito Oblata*. Acta Iranica, IX 2nd Series (Leiden: E. J. Brill, 1984) 219–24, uses this inscription to clarify the meaning of Ugaritic CTA 4, V 68–71, which he translates "And moreover Baal will provide his luxuriant rain, a luxuriant . . . with overflow; will peal his thunder in the rain clouds, flashing his lightnings to the earth" (p. 221). Greenfield observes that in the Bible Eden was a well watered, luxuriant site (cf. Isa 51:3; Ezek 31:9, 16, 18; 36:25; Joel 2:3; Genesis 2, and 13:10, p. 224).

[9] Modern literary critics have mined biblical narrative with conflicting, although useful, results: e.g., Robert Alter, *The Art of Biblical Narrative* (New York: Basic Books, Inc., 1981); Mieke Bal, *Narratology* (Toronto: University of Toronto Press, 1985); Shimon Bar-Efrat, *Narrative Art in the Bible* (BLS 17; Sheffield: Almond Press, 1984); Adele Berlin, *Poetics and Interpretation of Biblical Narrative* (BLS 9; Sheffield: Almond Press, 1983); David Damrosch, *The Narrative Covenant* (San Francisco: Harper & Row, Publishers, 1987); and Meir Sternberg, *The Poetics of Biblical Narrative* (Bloomington: Indiana University Press, 1985).

with chariotry echoes widespread tradition likening the head of a locust to that of a horse, but Joel's point of reference is an invading army. Poetic license permits him to think of chariots on top of the distant mountains; the reference to flames of fire jumping about and exploding with loud bursts of energy required no flight of fantasy. Before this fire, stubble offered no resistance; an army in battle array was poised for the kill. Naturally, the vulnerable population trembled and turned ashen as the invaders climbed walls and entered windows like thieves. Nothing forced them to veer from their intended path, not even missiles hurled at them. Joel takes pains to indicate that his images refer to something other than human marauders, with whom the invaders are compared. The incidental reference to their entering windows like thieves also functions to differentiate this army from soldiers of flesh and blood. This manner of entering houses applied to invasion by locust hordes; ordinary soldiers simply knocked down doors to gain entry into houses.

The last two verses of this section (2:10–11) shift the scene of activity to the skies in the same way the earlier disaster elicited fervent prayer to YHWH. The cosmos itself joins in the attack, causing an earthquake and even shaking the heavenly realm itself. Here Joel uses ancient theophanic language associated with YHWH's self-manifestation. The divine Warrior[10] goes forth at the head of a celestial army, shouting orders all the while to an innumerable host. The thought of such majesty leads Joel to exclaim that YHWH's day is truly awesome, beyond resistance (2:1–11).

Only one thing suffices to alleviate the feeling of total helplessness before such an onslaught—divine intervention—although YHWH leads the mighty army against Judah. Nevertheless, the prophet dares to assert that timely action may still bring about a change in the heart of God, whose much-celebrated compassion offers a modicum of hope. Joel boldly attributes his message to YHWH; this use of an oracular formula, "declaration of YHWH," is one of only two instances in the book. The oracle consists of an invitation to turn to God wholeheartedly *even now*; the language recalls covenantal contexts and the expedient offer of a way out of dangerous situations invoking curses on guilty transgressors.[11] The turning must be genuine, mere external fasting, weeping, and mourning being accompanied by broken hearts. Torn clothing, a sign of repentance or abject distress, might easily mask a vicious attitude for human viewers, but not YHWH. Joel calls for inner contrition, thus emphasizing true character rather than deeds, which always require interpretation. He also

---

[10] Patrick D. Miller, Jr., *The Divine Warrior in Early Israel* (Cambridge, Massachusetts: Harvard University Press, 1973) and Gerhard von Rad, *Der Heilige Krieg im Alten Israel*, 3ᵉ ed. (Göttingen: Vandenhoeck & Ruprecht, 1958) nicely illustrate competing assessments of the divine warrior ideology.

[11] Delbert R. Hillers, *Treaty-Curses and the Old Testament Prophets* (BO 16; Rome: Pontifical Biblical Institute, 1964).

grounds all hope in the character of YHWH as announced long before to a persistent Moses who, according to tradition, wanted to see God and was granted an even greater boon, a glimpse of the divine heart (Exod 34:6–7). Because YHWH is compassionate, kind, patient, infinitely loyal, and forgiving, the momentary anger may be an anomaly. The prophet takes care not to promise too much, and thus to compromise divine freedom; therefore, he issues a cautious "Who knows?," but in doing so Joel imagines a positive response on YHWH's part. In the end the prophet even thinks of a properly functioning cultus as a sure sign of divine blessing.

Encouraged by this promising oracle, Joel once more invites someone to blow the *šôpār* in the holy city, thus calling the surrounding populace to observe a fast and to assemble before God. The entire population is invited to the solemn assembly. Unlike ancient rules governing the drafting of soldiers into YHWH's army, which provided exclusionary rights to persons belonging to certain categories—newlyweds, individuals having built houses or planted vineyards without enjoying the fruit of their labor, cowards—, Joel makes the summons all-encompassing. Aged people and infants, and everyone in between, must leave their homes and join the sacred gathering. Bride and groom, too, are ordered to forsake their place of intimacy in favor of a public gathering.

Once the congregation has assembled at Jerusalem, the priestly ministers are asked to carry out their office of mediation. With tears flowing down their cheeks, they are invited to intercede, asking YHWH to spare the people. Their fervent appeal, based on YHWH's possession of Judah as a special heritage, touches on a dire consequence of disaster in the holy city. Surrounding peoples either will rule over them or turn their misfortune into a harsh proverb. Joel concludes with a poignant question, one that made its way into Israel's psalter: "Why should they say among the nations, 'Where is their God?' " (2:12–17).

A combination of priestly intercession for a humble congregation and YHWH's compassionate nature turned the fortunes of Judah, reversing things in exquisite detail. The thought of foreign peoples taunting Judeans provoked YHWH's oft-touted zeal. The people's complete turnaround evoked a similar change in God, who promises enough grain, wine, and oil to satiate hungry appetites. Furthermore, YHWH vows to put an end to mockery of Judeans by foreigners. As for the divine army that had attacked Judah, YHWH pledges to drive the dreaded northerner into the eastern and western seas, the Dead Sea and the Mediterranean, leaving nothing but a foul stench as reminder of the northern devastation. Presumably, this mythic enemy from the north has exceeded its charge just as Assyria overstepped its assignment, according to the prophet Isaiah.

Joel then turns to those needing comfort. First, the land and its nonhuman creatures. Using traditional terminology for divine assurance throughout the ancient Near East, he allays their fear. "Do not be afraid,"[12] soil or animals, for the northerner is not the only one who has achieved great things. YHWH, too, has acted wondrously, causing earth to yield its bountiful produce.

Citizens of Zion are urged to join the land and animals in rejoicing over the return of rain in its proper time, which will assure bumper crops during the season of harvesting. The prophetic voice alternates with YHWH's in this rich resumé of assurances: "Rejoice in YHWH, who has given . . ." and "I will repay you for the years the locust consumed." YHWH does not deny responsibility for the destruction ("my powerful army which I dispatched against you"),[13] but the abundance of food now promised will enable the people to praise their Sovereign with full stomachs. The people's loss of honor will thus become a thing of the past, a never recurring event. This promise, attributed to YHWH and repeated for emphasis, concludes the singular narrative about disaster and its abatement, but not without driving home an unforgettable point—the Judeans will finally know that YHWH, the only God, has taken up residence in their midst (2:18–27).

A temporal adverb, "afterwards," places distance between the exquisite story of paradise lost and regained[14] and a divine announcement that the long-awaited outpouring of YHWH's spirit on all Israel is imminent. The hope placed in Moses' mouth and kept alive by the prophets Jeremiah and Ezekiel is here given broad scope. The outpouring of YHWH's spirit will finally turn everyone in Judah into a prophetic vessel for the divine word. The event will break normal barriers artificially imposed by society, restrictions grounded in age, sex, or social status. Moreover, this dispersal of YHWH's spirit will sanction various modes of revelation, specifically the hearing of an oracle, the dreaming of a hidden message, and the seeing of visions.

---

[12] Edgar W. Conrad, *Fear Not, Warrior: A Study of ʾal tîrāʾ Pericopes in the Hebrew Scriptures* (BJS; Atlanta: Scholars Press, 1985).

[13] The prologue to the book of Job also places blame for calamity on the deity in spite of the story line that attributes the destructive actions to the Adversary, *haśśāṭān* (Job 2:3). So long as God alone has the power to wield good or ill, such incidents of undeserved suffering cast doubt on divine benevolence, even when the harm comes indirectly—through means of an adversary. The problem of theodicy inevitably followed, being more intense in Israel than in Mesopotamia, where several examples of this literary genre flourished, precisely because of YHWH's claim of uniqueness. I have assessed the general problem in "Introduction: The Shift from Theodicy to Anthropodicy," pp. 1–16 in James L. Crenshaw, ed. *Theodicy in the Old Testament* (IRT 4; Philadelphia and London: Fortress Press and S.P.C.K., 1983). See also Crenshaw, "Theodicy," *IDBS* (Nashville: Abingdon, 1976) 895–96; "Theodicy," *ABD* VI (New York et al.: Doubleday, 1992) 444–47; and *Prophetic Conflict: Its Effect Upon Israelite Religion* (BZAW 124; Berlin and New York: Walter de Gruyter, 1971), where I discuss the Israelite understanding of YHWH as actively misleading prophetic figures and the general phenomenon of the "demonic."

[14] Northrop Frye, *The Great Code: The Bible and Literature* (San Diego, New York, London: Harcourt Brace Jovanovich Publishers, 1982) 144, lists "five bodies of imagery in the Bible: the paradisal, the pastoral, the agricultural, the urban, and the imagery of human life itself." A garden plays a significant role in both testaments, according to Frye.

Accompanying this outpouring of YHWH's spirit will be cosmic signs and portents. The language derives from ancient theophanies: blood, fire, mushrooming smoke, obscuring the sun and giving the moon a red glow.[15] Such terrifying darkness will precede the final dawning of YHWH's day, greatly awesome. Nevertheless, those persons who invoke YHWH's name will survive, particularly residents of Jerusalem, who have been promised an escape, together with individuals whom YHWH singles out for a special summons. Here Joel appeals to promissory traditions in vogue at the moment to justify the promise of special favor by the Lord of the universe who, for the time being, threatens its very existence (3:1–5 [2:28–32]).

The stage has now been set for a final judgment, a settling of old accounts. Joel adopts a traditional expression for the great assize, projecting the event into the remote future, an unspecified "in those days and at that time." Now that Judah has experienced an initial installment on the expected reward for faithful worship of YHWH, Joel ponders an even fuller payment—complete revenge against foreigners for their cruelty toward Judeans. He imagines a total gathering of the nations comparable to the earlier assembling of Judeans, but the outcome will be quite different. Because the foreign nations have deported Jews from their own homeland, YHWH will execute judgment on the offenders. They will be forced to journey to the valley of Jehoshaphat, a nonexistent place created in the prophet's imagination by a verbal play on its meaning, "YHWH has judged." Adopting the divine persona, Joel reads the indictment against the nations; the specific charges include parceling out YHWH's land, casting lots for Jewish slaves, and trading boys for prostitutes and girls for wine, drinking it down with total disregard for common decency (4:1–3 [3:1–3]).[16]

This anticipation of revenge becomes specific with regard to two enemies from premonarchical times, Phoenicians and Philistines. Again speaking for

---

[15]Theodore Hiebert, "Theophany in the Old Testament," *ABD* VI, 505–11; Jörg Jeremias, *Theophanie: Die Geschichte einer alttestamentlichen Gattung* (Neukirchen-Vluyn: Neukirchener Verlag, 1965); J. Jeremias, "Theophany in the Old Testament," *IDBS* (Nashville: Abingdon, 1976), 896–98; James Barr, "Theophany and Anthropomorphism in the Old Testament," *VTS* 7 (1960) 31–38.

[16]The eighth-century prophet Amos accused Jewish citizens in the northern kingdom of similar indecency: selling the righteous into slavery for a debt of a small sum and the defenseless for an unknown amount ("the price of sandals"), pushing the lowly aside; cohabiting (?) with a young girl (the divine Girl? a defenseless one?) who lies with both a father and his son (or the two resort to her for religious purposes); using religious expediency to get around an ancient law requiring the return of a poor person's outer garment at day's end (Exod 22:25–26 [22:26–27]); drinking wine in the temple, a drink that has been obtained through fines (Amos 2:6–8). The difficulty of determining exactly what offenses Amos has in mind is illustrated by the several interpretations of this text in Francis I. Andersen and David Noel Freedman, *Amos* (AB 24A; New York et al.: Doubleday, 1989), 306–23; Shalom M. Paul, *Amos* (Hermeneia; Minneapolis: Fortress Press, 1991) 76–87; and Hans Walter Wolff, *Joel and Amos* (Hermeneia; Philadelphia: Fortress Press, 1977) 164–68.

YHWH, the prophet asks what offense YHWH has committed against these nations that caused them to seek revenge against YHWH's heritage. Regardless of the reason for their actions, YHWH threatens to impose penalties on them promptly for confiscating valuable vessels from the temple in Jerusalem and depositing them in their own palaces and/or temples.[17] Moreover, their casual disregard for human beings will be replicated, to their dismay. For selling Judean slaves to the Greeks, who transported land-loving people to coastal areas, the Phoenicians and Philistines will watch helplessly as Judeans sell their children to Sabeans, who will remove them far from their beloved sea. Joel bases this threat of revenge on divine revelation, employing a second oracular formula. He observes, almost casually, that Judeans who were enslaved and deported will return to their homeland (4:4–8 [3:4–8]).

Returning to the idea of a huge gathering of foreigners in the valley of Jehoshaphat, Joel instructs unknown heralds to arouse the nations for warfare. Having made preparations through proper religious leaders to assure divine authorization, Joel invites the soldiers to come up and engage the enemy. Joel cites a fragment from perhaps the most profound expression of human longing in biblical tradition, the dawning of a day when nations will transform their weapons into agricultural tools, but he reverses its content, urging the peoples to forge instruments of destruction from harmless gardening implements. With lavish irony the prophet insists that persons actually incapable of fighting assume a posture of invincibility. This assembly of foreign warriors will be met by an irresistible force. At this point Joel urges YHWH to bring down his mighty army, and the commander of this host joins the prophet in urging nations to gather in the valley where YHWH will execute judgment.

In some respects harvesting grain and treading grapes resemble military activity, with its cutting down of the populace and walking in its blood.[18] This

---

[17] The later books of Daniel and 1 Esdras insert the motif of stolen vessels from the Jerusalem temple into narrative plots. According to Dan 5:1–4, Belshazzar and his subjects drank wine from the vessels brought to Babylonia by King Nebuchadnezzar, and for this sacrilege Belshazzar suffered the ultimate punishment (v 30). The reference to stolen vessels in 1 Esd 4:44, 57 occurs in the sequel to the contest over the strongest thing in the world; the winner, Zerubbabel, reminds Darius the Persian king of an oath by his father Cyrus to return all vessels taken from Jerusalem. The famous Edict of Cyrus, cited in Ezra 5:3–5, mandates that these sacred vessels fashioned from gold and silver be returned to their proper setting, the temple in Jerusalem.

[18] This metaphor has particular force when applied to deity as in Isa 63:1–6 (to which may be compared Rev 14:19–20, where an angel wields the sickle that cuts off grape clusters for trampling). Responding to a question about the cause of the red-stained clothing, YHWH admits to having trodden the wine press alone because there was no one to assist in the grim task. An Egyptian myth, "The Deliverance of Mankind from Destruction," tells about human mischief and Re's response, first through the sending of the goddess Hat-Hor to eradicate human civilization and then the sun god's act of deception that spared the people destined for destruction. This story about the spreading of a red-colored beer on a huge field where Hat-Hor planned to wreak havoc describes her as drinking this mixture, like human blood, and considering it good (*ANET*, 10–11). Similarly, the

metaphor now controls Joel's description of the events. Adopting the divine persona again, he commands the army to wield the sickle in ripe grain and to tread full wine presses until the vats spill their juice onto the ground. The abundance of grain and grapes symbolizes the vastness of the wickedness now being punished. The execution of divine recompense creates havoc, a din of noise and confusion that extends into the skies, where darkness prevails. Into this turmoil YHWH marches, shouting from the holy city, as heavens and earth reverberate. Such awesome display of power holds no terror for YHWH's people, who find in their God a refuge from the storm.

A statement of recognition, which affirms that the people will know that YHWH resides in Zion and that the city will henceforth be off limits to strangers, provides a transition from the account of YHWH's judgment and Joel's final summation of the destinies of Judah and certain foreign nations. Using technical language for a future manifestation of divine presence, Joel describes the restoration of paradise in Judah. Once more it will truly be a land of milk and sweet wine, and a perpetual stream will flow from the sanctuary to water arid wadis. No longer will Judah suffer from lack of water; however, its enemies, particularly Egypt and Edom, will become ruins in the desert because of their violence against Judeans. The prophet assures Judah that its future will be secure, but he threatens vengeance on those guilty of bloodshed. Having uttered a divine threat in the first person, the prophet ultimately returns to his own voice to assure the Judeans that YHWH has taken up residence in their midst (4:9–21 [3:9–21]). With that assurance the book of Joel comes to an end.

The Historical Setting of the Book

Nothing in the book of Joel offers a decisive clue in determining its actual historical context. The superscription refers only to the author Joel and his father Pethuel, otherwise unknown. Although Samuel had a son named Joel (1 Sam 8:2), the other references to this name occur within the Ezra-Nehemiah-Chronicles literary complex. The name Joel is associated with several tribal groups: Reuben (1 Chr 5:4, 8), Issachar (1 Chr 7:3), Gad (1 Chr 5:12), Levi (1 Chr 6:21[36]; 15:7, 11; 23:8; 26:22; 2 Chr 29:12); Manasseh (1 Chr 27:20); and Simeon (1 Chr 4:35). A brother of the prophet Nathan bore the name Joel (1 Chr 11:38), as did two individuals during the time of Ezra and Nehemiah (Ezr 10:43; Neh 11:9). If the record preserves accurate memory, this name persisted from the time of Samuel to Ezra-Nehemiah, with significant representatives during the reigns of David and Hezekiah. At the very least, the evidence

violent goddess Anat is said to have plunged "knee-deep in knights' blood, hip-deep in the gore of heroes" (*ANET*, 136), all the while laughing with abandon.

indicates the popularity of the name Joel in the late fifth and early fourth centuries.

The position of the book of Joel in the Masoretic Text does not settle the matter of date.[19] The order of the minor prophets—Hosea, Joel, Amos, Obadiah, Jonah, Micah, Nahum, Habakkuk, Zephaniah, Haggai, Zechariah, and Malachi—differs from that of the Septuagint, which has Hosea, Amos, Micah, Joel, Obadiah, Jonah, Nahum, Habakkuk, Zephaniah, Haggai, Zechariah, and Malachi. Apparently, the organizing principle of the Hebrew canon was not chronological to the degree that those individuals who arranged the books in the Greek text valued historical sequence. Instead, the literary affinities between Joel and Amos may explain their proximity to one another (Joel 4:16 [3:16] echoes Amos 1:2; cf. also Joel 4:18 [3:18] and Amos 9:13). Perhaps in Amos the initial oracles against the foreign nations, including Edom, Philistia, and Phoenicia, were understood as YHWH's judgment on these countries as announced in Joel 4 [3]. Hans Walter Wolff's hypothesis that Joel functioned as a lens through which to view the whole collection of minor prophets suffers from the book's secondary position behind Hosea.[20]

---

[19] Both chronological and thematic factors entered into the order of the Twelve. The superscriptions claim that Hosea and Amos prophesied during the eighth century when King Jeroboam ruled, Micah slightly later, Zephaniah in the time of Josiah, seventh century, Haggai and Zechariah in the sixth century. Thematic considerations link Joel and Amos, Amos and Obadiah. Moreover, these three books share a common theme, YHWH's day. The reference to Jonah ben Amittai in 2 Kings 14:23–27 as a contemporary of Jeroboam II possibly explains the position of the book of Jonah after Obadiah. Because Nahum announces the fall of Nineveh in 612 B.C.E. and Habakkuk alludes to neo-Babylonians in 1:6, these two books follow the order of the series established on the basis of chronology *and* catchwords, thus Hosea, Joel, Amos, Obadiah, Jonah, Micah, Nahum, Habakkuk. Zephaniah then follows, leaving Haggai and Zechariah (from c. 520 B.C.E.) and the final book, Malachi, to complete the collection. Why does Hosea precede Amos? Perhaps length and unwillingness to interrupt the clear connections of Joel, Amos, and Obadiah explain the priority of Hosea (James Limburg, *Jonah* [OTL; Louisville, Kentucky: Westminster/John Knox Press, 1993] 20–21). Dale A. Schneider, *The Unity of the Book of the Twelve*, Ph.D. diss., Yale University, 1979, thinks the Book of the Twelve developed in four stages: (1) an original nucleus consisting of Hosea, Amos, and Micah (linked together by literary affinities, catchword associations, and thematic/religious unity); (2) a second collection comprised of Nahum, Habakkuk, and Zephaniah and compiled by Josianic reformers; (3) the books of Joel, Obadiah, and Jonah, added to the previous six books in the exilic period; and (4) the final three, Haggai, Zechariah, and Malachi. Schneider dated the book of Joel in the seventh century partly on the basis of its position in the canon.

[20] "In all likelihood those who arranged the collection of the Twelve wished us to read Amos and the following prophets in the light of Joel's proclamation. For manifest in Joel is a comprehensive view of prophecy closely akin to that governing the prophetic corpus in its final, canonizing redaction" (Wolff, *Joel and Amos*, 4). If true, why did the persons who shaped the order of the Twelve not place Joel ahead of Hosea? Did they not want readers to view Hosea in the light of the dominant canonizing principle, whatever that may have been? In any event, Wolff's observations about the importance of interpretive comments within prophetic texts represent a move away from extravagant theories about numerous glossators (at their worst, Roland E. Wolfe, "The Editing of the Book of the Twelve," ZAW 53 [1935] 90–129). In a recent doctoral dissertation written at Duke

Chronological order does seem significant in the Septuagint, which places the three prophets from the eighth century together and then brings together three books of unknown origin, Joel, Obadiah, and Jonah, before concluding with those thought to have been associated with the late seventh and sixth centuries. The same order is found in 2 Esd 1:39–40. An interesting variant occurs in The Martyrdom and Ascension of Isaiah 4:22, where the sequence is Amos, Hosea, Micah, Joel, Nahum, Jonah, Obadiah, Habakkuk, Haggai, Zephaniah, Zechariah, and Malachi.

Internal evidence, although inconclusive, favors a late-dating of the book, perhaps fifth century.[21] A functioning cult in Jerusalem excludes the period from 586 to 516, from the destruction of the temple by the Babylonian army to its restoration under the prophetic leadership of Haggai and Zechariah.[22] The phrase, "sacred mountain," with reference to Jerusalem in an exclusive sense,

---

University, Barry A. Jones argues that the books of Joel and Obadiah were added to a prophetic "canon" consisting of nine books, and that the last book to enter the collection was Jonah. At a later time, Jones claims, the book of Jonah was transposed to its position in the Septuagint because of the literary relationships between the books of Joel and Nahum, and the Masoretic Text resulted from further juggling of the sequence of books—the insertion of the books Joel, Obadiah, and Jonah in the seams of the eighth-century prophetic collection of Hosea, Amos, and Micah (*The Formation of the Book of the Twelve: A Study in Text and Canon*, 1994). J. Nogalski, *Literary Precursors to the Book of the Twelve* (BZAW 217; Berlin and New York: Walter de Gruyter, 1993) 58–69 and *Redactional Processes in the Book of the Twelve* (BZAW 218; Berlin and New York: Walter de Gruyter, 1993) 13–22, thinks a redactor inserted catchwords into Hos 14:8[7] (*yōšebîm* ["inhabitants," the Masoretic Text has *yōšebê*]; *dāgān* ["grain"], *gepen* ["vine"], and *yāyin* ["wine"]) to link the book of Hosea with Joel, where the last three words occur in 1:10, 7, and 5, respectively. The evidence, tenuous at best, cannot support the weight of Nogalski's hypothesis.

[21] Critics have sought a plausible historical context for the book of Joel on the basis of (1) grammar, syntax, and vocabulary, (2) extra-biblical data, and (3) literary expression and/or theological ideas. The most thorough recent examination of vocabulary, Ahlström, *Joel and the Temple Cult of Jerusalem* (VTS 21, Leiden: E. J. Brill, 1971), 1–22, dismisses Aramaisms as a dialectical phenomenon (thus *hnḥt* in 4:11 [3:11], *ʾnḥ* in 1:18, *swp* in 2:20), casts doubt on the lateness of *tappûaḥ* on the basis of names of early towns—*bêt tappûaḥ* near Hebron (Josh 15:53, not 33!), *tappûaḥ* in the Shephelah (Josh 15:34) and in Ephraim (Josh 12:17; 16:8; 17:8)—and acknowledges the possible lateness of the form *weʾim* (1:2), the four hapax legomena in 1:17, the phrase "Judah and Jerusalem" in 4:1 [3:1], *benê ṣiyyôn* in 2:23, use of *bêt* instead of *hêkal* to designate the temple, and especially *min-benê* in 1:12 rather than a contracted form. Jacob M. Myers, "Some Considerations Bearing on the Date of Joel," ZAW 74 (1962) 177–95, offers an exhaustive analysis of extra-biblical data pertaining to the historical references in the book of Joel, particularly the relationships among the Phoenicians, Greeks, and Sabeans. Myers opts for a date around 520 B.C.E.

In 1987 Jehuda Jungmann completed a doctoral dissertation at Hebrew University in Jerusalem on literary expressions in the book of Joel, concluding that the stylistic literary characteristics belong to the later prophets (*Major Literary Phenomena in the Book of Joel as a Key to the Problem of its Unity and Date of Composition*, Hebrew). Jungmann thinks the "citations" in Joel from earlier prophetic literature provide literary embellishment or establish dramatic depth rather than impart major spiritual or ideological content.

[22] Carol L. and Eric M. Meyers, *Haggai, Zechariah 1–8* (AB 26B; Garden City, New York: Doubleday & Company, 1987), and David L. Petersen, *Haggai and Zechariah 1–8* (OTL;

points to a period subsequent to the Deuteronomic reform in Josiah's day. Reference to priests as YHWH's ministers who call the people to a day of fasting (1:14; 2:15) and to daily offerings of cereal and wine (1:9, 13; 2:14) imply an era when the Tamid sacrifice had come to function as a means of regulating the religious life of Judeans. The identification of Judah and Israel as one and the same (2:27; 4:2, 16 [3:2, 16]) demands a time long after the collapse of the northern kingdom to the Assyrians in 722. Mention of a wall enclosing the city of Jerusalem rules out the period between 586 and 445, for on this latter date Nehemiah and his compatriots repaired the wall demolished earlier by Babylonian forces. Possibly, however, 2:7 indicates a wall with only portions standing here and there, but such an enclosure would have offered no obstacle to an attacking army. In that case, Joel's allusion to invaders' scaling the wall would be purely rhetorical.

Both temple and wall existed prior to 586, but the references to the captivity (4:2 [3:2]) and deportation of Jewish children (4:3 [3:3]) exclude a time before the fall of Jerusalem. Furthermore, the animosity toward Edom (4:19 [3:19]) is best explained in connection with the events of 586, when fleeing Judeans were turned over to the Babylonians by neighboring Edomites. The allusion to foreigners passing through Jerusalem (4:17 [3:17]) recalls the humiliation of invading Babylonian troops who occupied the holy city. The assumption that the entire population of Judah could be assembled in Jerusalem (1:14; 2:16–17) suggests a tiny province, and the political security implicit throughout the book seems to reflect the order enforced under Persian magistrates. Although the language about a total assembly is highly rhetorical, like Jeremiah 26 and 36, it accords with the leveling of all distinctions in society based on age, gender, or status, a view paralleled only in the late apocalypse of Isaiah (24–27; cf. 24:2).

The omission of references to Assyria and Babylonia, classical enemies of the Jews, can hardly be explained as prudence growing out of fear of reprisal,[23] and the absence of specific reference to a king alongside the rulers of society indicates a time after the disappearance of the monarchy in Judah. Priests have taken over the responsibility for sanctifying a fast and assembling the people, earlier associated with royal figures (Solomon in 1 Kings 8:1; 2 Chr 5:2; Jehu in 2 Kings

---

Philadelphia: The Westminster Press, 1984), bring this period of Israelite history (521–516 B.C.E.) into sharp focus.

[23] Wilhelm Rudolph, "Wann wirkte Joel?" BZAW 105 (1967) 194–95. Given Joel's optimism about YHWH's anticipated judgment of the nations, would he have practiced caution in the form of silence about hated oppressors? Confidence in YHWH's control of world forces would surely have produced temerity rather than discreet speech. Rudolph supports a date for Joel between 597 and 587 B.C.E. and attributes 4:4–8 [3:4–8] to the prophet, although this unit was composed later than the rest of the book (195–96). Joel's reference to exiled Judeans gives Rudolph no problem for he points to 2 Chr 21:16–17 (missing in 2 Kings), which mentions an attack on Judah by Philistines and Arabs who took captive royal possessions, including wives and sons.

10:20; Hezekiah in 2 Chr 29:20). Silence about Persian authorities is natural, for they would not have been expected to join the Jews in repentance. Ambiguous attitudes toward Levites may have led to a refusal to mention this group, who seem to have been fighting an effort in the fifth and fourth centuries to diminish their power, once championed by promulgators of the Deuteronomic tradition. The failure to mention a High Priest suggests an era prior to the early fourth century, although the origin of this office remains obscure.

The allusion to collaboration between Philistines and Phoenicians in selling Jews to Sabeans, who then traded them to Greeks, could indicate any time from the seventh to fifth centuries, perhaps even later. According to Myers, Sabeans lost their lucrative trade routes to Mineans after the sixth century.[24] Sale of Jews to Greeks could easily have taken place in the sixth and fifth centuries, when Judah lay exposed to marauders seeking profitable booty from warfare. During the eighth to sixth centuries Greeks made extensive use of slaves on their ships, farms, vineyards, and in factories.[25] Phoenician participation in the sale of slaves to Greeks would have ended with the defeat of Sidon in 343 by Artaxerxes III Ochus and Tyre in 332 by Alexander. From 525, when Egypt fell to Persia, until the time of Ptolemy Soter in 312, that country was only a feeble imitation of its previous might, thus encouraging the uttering of threats like the one in Joel 4:19 [3:19].

Several other features of the book best accord with a late date. The fondness for the cult and external aspects of worship in conjunction with genuine turning to YHWH scarcely resembles anything during the prophetic activity of the eighth- or seventh-century reformers (Amos, Isaiah, Micah, Jeremiah), with the possible exception of Ezekiel. Moreover, the book of Joel marks a transition between prophecy and apocalyptic, with the emphasis still falling on prophetic eschatology despite references to cosmic signs and a final judgment. So many characteristics of apocalyptic are missing that one hesitates to label the book apocalyptic, even in its early stage. One fails to find, among others, secret messages, bizarre images of animals with symbolic meaning, divisions of history into distinct epochs, dualism, heavenly journeys, angelic interpreters.[26] Joel's

---

[24] Myers, "Some Considerations Bearing on the Date of Joel," 186. He concedes, however, that W. F. Albright gave a lower date for the Sabeans' loss of control over the trade routes. Sabean royal inscriptions continued to be composed until some time after the middle of the fourth century. Nevertheless, Myers writes: "Furthermore, Joel cannot be dated after the fifth century B.C. on the basis of the Sabean and Minean situation. The probabilities favor a date in the last decades of the sixth century or certainly not later than the early part of the fifth" (190).

[25] M. I. Rostovtzeff, *Social and Economic History of the Hellenistic World*, vol. I (Oxford: Oxford University Press, 1941) treats Greco-Palestinian and Syrian slave trade during the period from the eighth to fourth centuries B.C.E.

[26] On the characteristics of apocalyptic, see John J. Collins, *The Apocalyptic Imagination* (New York: Crossroad, 1984) and James C. VanderKam, *Enoch and the Growth of an Apocalyptic*

eschatology simply specifies disaster for foreign nations and restoration for Judah, rather than offering elaborate descriptions of divine largesse. The book's xenophobia comes closest to that of Haggai, Zechariah, Obadiah, Ezra, and Nehemiah, farthest from Jonah.

Linguistic evidence also best suits a late sixth- or fifth-century date.[27] Joel uses a few words that occur elsewhere in the Hebrew Bible only in the latest books: *haššelaḥ* ("the weapon, missile," 2:8)[28] in Job 33:18; 36:12; 2 Chr 23:10; Neh 4:11 [17], 17 [23]; *ḥûsâ* ("have compassion on," 2:17) in Neh 13:22; *ṣaḥanâ* ("stench," 2:20) in Sir 11:12; *sôp* ("rear," 2:20) in Eccles 3:11; 7:2; 2 Chr 20:16. Only Zech 14:8 contrasts the eastern and western seas the way Joel 2:20 does. Some rare words, unattested elsewhere in the Bible, probably indicate late entries into Hebrew: *ʾelî* ("to lament," 1:8), *ʿābešû* ("they shrivel"), *perudôt* ("seeds"), *megrepōtêhem* ("their clods?"), *mammegurôt* ("granaries"), all in 1:17; *yeʿabbetûn* ("they turn aside," 2:7); *min-benê* (instead of contracted *mibbenê*) in 1:12. Other expressions, not exclusively postexilic, become more common at that time: *ʾanî* (the short form of the personal pronoun "I"), *weʾim* ("or"), *bêt* ("temple," 1:9, 13–14, 16; 2:17; 4:8 [3:8]), the expression "Judah and Jerusalem" (4:1 [3:1]), *benê-ṣiyyôn* ("Zionites") in 2:23 (cf. Lam 4:2; Ps 149:2; Zech 9:13).

A distinctive characteristic of the book, its use of specific phrases from other canonical works, gives Joel the appearance of a learned interpreter.[29] Whereas

---

Tradition (CBQMS 16; Washington, D.C.: The Catholic Biblical Association of America, 1984). Collins appropriately distinguishes apocalypse as a genre, apocalypticism as a social ideology, and apocalyptic eschatology as a set of ideas and motifs also present in other genres and settings (p. 2). From the list of temporal and eschatological elements on p. 6 (cosmogony, primordial events, recollection of the past, *ex eventu* prophecy, persecution, other eschatological upheavals, judgment/destruction of the wicked, judgment/destruction of the world, judgment/destruction of other-worldly beings, cosmic transformation, resurrection, and other forms of afterlife), Joel employs only three or four—cosmogony, judgment of the wicked, and cosmic transformation (perhaps also persecution), all of which features also belong to prophecy.

[27] Wolff (*Joel and Amos*, 5) gives a concise list of vocabulary that, in his judgment, supports a date between 445 and 343 B.C.E. Other factors entering into this assessment of a late date are the defeat and exile of Judeans, the casual reference to a wall of Jerusalem, the commercial association of Phoenician cities Tyre and Sidon with Philistines, a theocratic community (with elders and priests holding the reins of leadership), the *tāmîd* offering, and Joel's dependence on several earlier prophets, especially Obadiah and Malachi.

[28] Oswald Loretz, *Regenritual und Jahwetag im Joelbuch* (UBL 4; Altenberge: CIS Verlag, 1986) 123, quotes Anton Schoors, *Ras Shamra Parallels* I (1972) 63 as follows: "Since Heb. *šlḥ* is well attested with the meaning 'javelin,' there is no reason why *šlḥ*, in an identical context, should not have the same meaning. . . . According to the Ugaritic phrase, it seems preferable to parse Heb *bʿd* as indicating the instrument and *jplw* as a hifil, thus rendering: 'And with the spear they fell.' " On the other hand, this word *šlḥ* may allude to the Siloam tunnel. Perhaps Joel chose this expression for its ambiguity and possible dual reference.

[29] Siegfried Bergler, *Joel als Schriftinterpret* (BEATAJ 16; Frankfurt am Main, Bern, New York, Paris: Verlag Peter Lang, 1988); cf. older scholars who drew attention to similarities between the book of Joel and other prophetic literature and concentrated on the problem of date, e.g., G.

earlier prophets claim to have received their words directly from YHWH, Joel frequently "cites" predecessors. In some instances he probably draws on phrases in vogue at the time, but sometimes Joel may actually quote written texts.

1:15 = Ezek 30:2	"That day! Horrors!"
1:15 = Isa 13:6; Ezek 30:3; Ob 15; Zeph 1:7	"For YHWH's day is imminent"
1:15 = Isa 13:6	"dawning like destruction from the Destroyer"
2:2 = Zeph 1:14–15	"near . . . a day of darkness and murkiness, a day of cloud and haze"
2:3b = Isa 51:3; Ezek 36:35	reversal of an image for paradise
2:6 = Nah 2:11 [10]	"every visage gathers sorrow"
2:13 = Exod 34:6; Jonah 4:2	"for merciful and compassionate is he, patient and abundantly loyal, repenting about punishment"
2:14 = Jonah 3:9	"perhaps he will turn and relent"
2:17 = Ps 79:10	"why should they say among the peoples, 'where is their God' "?
2:21 = Ps 126:3	"YHWH has acted mightily"
2:27 = Isa 45:5, 6, 18	"I, YHWH, am your God—there is no other"
3:1 [2:28] = Ezek 39:29	"I will pour out my spirit"
3:4 [2:31] = Mal 3:23 [4:5]	"before YHWH's day dawns—greatly awesome"
3:5 [2:32] = Ob 17	"for on Mount Zion and in Jerusalem will be an escape"
4:1 [3:1] = Jer 33:15; 50:4, 20	"for in those days and at that time"
4:2 [3:2] = Isa 66:18; Zech 14:2	"I will gather all nations"

Buchanan Gray, "The Parallel Passages in 'Joel' in their Bearing on the Question of Date," *Expositor* 8 [1893] 208–25. Michael Fishbane's path-breaking volume, *Biblical Interpretation in Ancient Israel* (Oxford: Clarendon Press, 1985), bristles with insights into the multifaceted manner in which canonical interpreters read the tradition and reacted to it, producing new understandings of the earlier text. Nevertheless, his reading of the ancient interpretive enterprise presupposes written texts and broad literary expertise from early times, which seems highly improbable on the basis of scholars' admittedly limited knowledge about education in Israel, on assessing which I have urged caution ("Education in Ancient Israel," *JBL* 104 [1985] 601–15).

4:4 [3:4] = Ob 15	"I will quickly repay your deeds on your heads"
4:8 [3:8] = Ob 18	"for YHWH has spoken"
4:10a [3:10a] = Isa 2:4; Mic 4:3	reversal of an image about weapons and farming tools
4:16 [3:16] = Amos 1:2	"then YHWH roars from Zion, utters his voice from Jerusalem"
4:17 [3:17] = Ezek 36:11	"then you will know that I, YHWH your God . . ."
4:18 [3:18] = Amos 9:13	"mountains will drip sweet wine, hills will ooze milk"

Establishing priority in such cases is notoriously difficult, and determining dates for insertions into older prophetic complexes seldom carries much conviction (e.g., Isa 13:6, 16; Amos 9:13). The texts under scrutiny do include some rather late postexilic entries, particularly Obadiah and Malachi.

The community depicted in the book of Joel comes closest to a theocracy,[30] with priests as YHWH's official ministers. Its modest eschatology and veneration for the cult bespeak a chastened province with minimal expectations, even when enjoying divine favor. The people long only for the return of their citizens who have been thrust far from home, and they envision a day when abundant food and water will indicate YHWH's presence in their holy city. Moreover, they dream of an era when foreigners will no longer pose any threat. Such aspirations may readily have arisen during any decade after defeat in battle and loss of inhabitants to a foreign realm.

To some extent such endeavors to establish a historical context for a biblical book constitute exercises in futility. Much of the argument moves in the realm of probability, often resting on one hypothesis after another about the development of the language and religion of the Bible. I do not think we can accurately date most books in the canon, nor do I believe it possible to determine the exact history of any Hebrew word. Even if one could fix a date for the composition of a book, Amos, for example, that would in no way establish a date for every verse, for the written text often evoked interpretive glosses and additions of various kinds.[31]

---

[30] This expression, theocracy, applied to the postexilic community by Josephus, signified a people living under YHWH's supervision as administered by priestly leaders. Viewed from another perspective, such a body could be described as a hieratically ruled entity. Otto Plöger has explored the nature of theocracy in Judah (*Theocracy and Eschatology* [Richmond: John Knox Press, 1968]).

[31] In discussing recent research on the book of Jeremiah I use the expression, "a living tradition," for the divine word constantly evoked responses that challenged, confirmed, and/or elaborated on previous understandings ("A Living Tradition: The Book of Jeremiah in Current Research,"

Furthermore, given the select and limited sampling of surviving Hebrew literature, scholars cannot adequately track a word's use. Two examples illustrate the point: *tappûaḥ* and *hanḥat*. Although the apple (1:12) may not have been cultivated until the Persian period, the word occurs in Canaanite texts and in the Bible with reference to a fruit and as a name for a village (Josh 15:33–34; Josh 12:17; 16:8; 17:8; cf. also Song of Songs 2:3, 5; 7:8; 8:5 and Prov 25:11). The rare word *hanḥat* (4:11 [3:11]) may derive from the northern kingdom (cf. Ps 18:35 [34]//2 Sam 22:35; Pss 38:3; 65:11 [10]; Job 21:13; 17:16; 2 Kings 6:8; Isa 30:3 and two texts from Ugarit, The Birth of Dawn and Dusk [52:37; pl. 52:40, 43, 47], and Baal and Anat III AB, A [68:11, 18] for the root *nḥt*).[32]

THE STRUCTURE OF THE BOOK

The unity of the book was first questioned by Maurice Vernes in 1872,[33] followed by Johann Wilhelm Rothstein[34] in 1876 and Bernhard Duhm,[35] whose 1911 article convinced most critics from that time onward. Duhm divided the book into prophetic speeches in poetic form (1:2–2:17) and speeches in prose with an apocalyptic bent dating from Maccabean times (2:18–4:21 [3:21]). That same year, 1911, Julius A. Bewer[36] argued that the sections on the day of YHWH are secondary and that the book comprises two major sections, chapters one-two and three-four. In his view, an eschatological editor added 1:15, 2:1b, 2, 6, 10–11, 2:27, 4:1, 2b–3, 14b–21 [3:1, 2b–3, 14b–21], and 4:4–8 [3:4–8] was added subsequently. The locust invasion of chapter two preceded chapter one and had no transcendent significance. At a later time, Bewer speculated, Joel wrote a second prophecy against the nations, and an eschatological editor brought them together, transforming them into a prediction of YHWH's day. In 1968, Otto Plöger[37] proposed a variant of Duhm's view; he divided the book into three parts: (1) 1:1–2:27; (2) 3:1–5 [2:28–32]; and (3) 4:1–21 [3:1–21], except for 4:4–8 [3:3–8]. Plöger considered both parts one and three postexilic, thinking

---

Interpretation 37 [1983] 117–29 and pp. 100–12 in James L. Mays and Paul J. Achtemeier, eds., *Interpreting the Prophets* [Philadelphia: Fortress Press], 1987). One of the most glaring re-interpretations of a biblical text is Eccles 12:13–14, which turns Qoheleth into an orthodox instructor of torah and contradicts his previous denial that God administers judgment against the wicked (James L. Crenshaw, *Ecclesiastes* [OTL; Philadelphia: Westminster Press, 1987] 192).

[32] Ahlström, *Joel and the Temple Cult of Jerusalem*, 1.

[33] *Le peuple d'Israël et ses espérances relatives à son avenir depuis les origines jusqu'à l'époque persane (Ve siècle avant J. C.)*. (Paris: Sandoz et Fischbacher, 1872).

[34] In Samuel Rolles Driver, *Einleitung in die Literatur des Alten Testaments*, translated and annotated by Johann Wilhelm Rothstein (Berlin: Reuther, 1896) 333–34.

[35] "Anmerkungen zu den Zwölf Propheten," ZAW 31 (1911) 161–204.

[36] *Commentary on Obadiah and Joel* (ICC; Edinburgh: T. & T. Clark, 1911) 49–56.

[37] *Theocracy and Eschatology*, 96–105.

of the latter unit as a supplement to the former. At a later time, Plöger maintained, part two corrected the third part, limiting the eschatology to "spiritual Israel."

Contemporary scholars generally accept the unity of the book, although many view 4:4–8 [3:3–8] as later than the prophet Joel. Formal resemblance between the two parts of the book has led to this rejection of Duhm's conclusion by more recent critics. For example, Arvid S. Kapelrud based his analysis of the book's structure on its use of the lament form.[38] In 1:2–2:27 he identified a lament, which he divided into two parts, 1:2–20 parallel to 2:1–17; the answer to the lament consisted of 3:1–4:21 [2:28–3:21]. Similarly, Graham S. Ogden[39] stressed the lament form, arguing that it reflects on the Babylonian attack against Jerusalem in 586. H. W. Wolff[40] emphasized the "near-perfect" symmetry in the book. He organized its contents as follows:

1:4–20	Lament over lack of food	2:21–27	End of shortage
2:1–11	Announcement of eschatological crisis	4:1–3, 9–17 [3:1–3, 9–17]	End of eschatological crisis
2:12–17	Call to return to YHWH	3:1–5 [2:28–32]	Spirit poured out

[38] *Joel Studies* (*UUÅ* 48:4; Uppsala: A. B. Lundequistska Bokhandeln; and Leipzig: Otto Harrassowitz, 1948), 4–5, 9. On p. 13 he refers to Ivan Engnell, *Studies in Divine Kingship in the Ancient Near East* (Oxford: Basil Blackwell, 1967), 159, for the claim that the book of Joel is "a revised liturgy where, according to him, the locust plague is to be understood as ranging under the traditional enumeration of misfortunes, already found in the so-called Tammuz liturgies."

[39] "Joel 4 and Prophetic Responses to National Laments," *JSOT* 26 (1983) 97–106. Ogden views the four oracles in chapter four as prophetic responses to the preceding lament ritual and identifies the four crises confronting Judah with Babylonian troops, not an invasion of locusts, a fire, or a drought. In his words, "each of the three images portrays the sweeping devastation brought by marauding foreign troops" (p. 105).

[40] *Joel and Amos*, 7 ("The Portions of the book on either side of this midpoint [2:17] form an almost perfect symmetry"). Richard G. Moulton, *The Modern Study of Literature* (Chicago: University of Chicago Press, 1915) 104, 106–7, recognizes a series of seven visions that form a perfect arch.

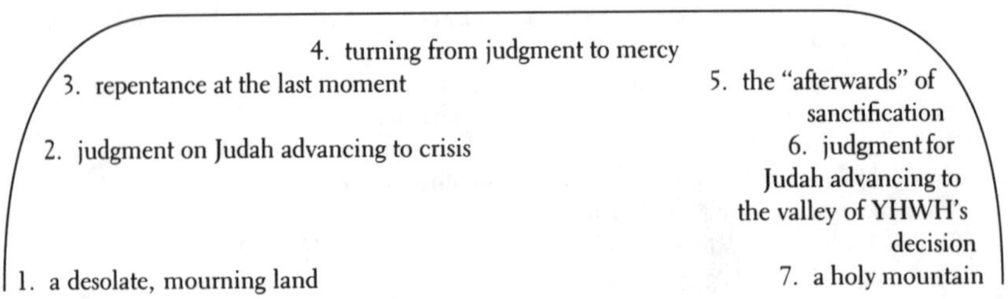

Outside the neat matching pairs were certain catchwords and glosses, particularly 4:4–8 [3:3–8] and 4:18–21 [3:18–21]. In Wolff's view, 1:13–2:17 forms the nucleus of part one, with an agricultural calamity preceding it (1:4–12) and a description of its reversal, YHWH's blessing, following it (2:21–26). He claims that 2:18–20, the proclamation of YHWH's compassionate action, was inserted into this concentric structure. Likewise, Wilhelm Rudolph[41] stressed a bipartite book with the texts dealing with YHWH's day as the unifying feature. Rudolph thought that Joel saw in the invasion by locusts and drought an indication of YHWH's day, but the actual deliverance (2:26b–27) shows that they were not harbingers of doom. This change in status therefore became the basis for promises in the final two chapters.

Willem van der Meer[42] perceives three parts in the book, which he describes as a triptych consisting of the following poetic units, from lesser to greater: foot, colon, verse, strophe, canticle, and canto. The first panel consists of cantos A (1:2–12), B (1:13–20), and C (2:1–14); the second, canto D (2:15–27); and the third, cantos E (3:1–5 [2:28–32]; 4:1–8 [3:1–8]) and F (4:9–21 [3:9–21], or 4:9–17 [3:9–17] and a sub-canto, 4:18–21 [3:18–21]. The initial panel depicts the setting (an awesome threat associated with YHWH's day concludes with a call to return to God). The correspondence between the second panel and the first shows that the situation of plenty will be restored. The final panel, which returns to the theme of YHWH's day, pictures Judah as no longer threatened, whereas foreigners are judged. The statement of recognition at the end of canto D refers back to canto C; it recurs in sub-canto F. Three phases are distinguishable, according to van der Meer, (1) a locust plague is viewed in terms of YHWH's day (1:5–20; 2:18–19, 21–24; 4:1–5 [3:1–5]); (2) Judah is threatened by enemies (1:2–4; 2:1–14, 15–17, 19–20, 25–27; 3:2, 5c [2:29, 32c]); and (3) Judah is defeated after all (4:1a, 4–8, 18–21 [3:1ac, 4–8, 18–21]). The core of the book comprises 1:5–12, 13–20, 2:18–19c, 21–24; 3:1, 3–5b [2:28, 30–32b]; it derives from the eighth or seventh century. The second phase, which shifts from locusts to enemies, comes from the late seventh to early sixth century. The third phase concretizes the reference to enemies by correlation with the destruction of Jerusalem, hence cannot date before 586. Van der Meer observes that the emphasis on YHWH's day in all three phases places a theology of YHWH's day at the center of the book.

Willem S. Prinsloo[43] finds a progression, each new state representing an

[41] *Joel-Amos-Obadja-Jona* (KAT 13/2; Gütersloh: Gütersloher Verlagshaus Gerd Mohn, 1971) 23–24. He thinks 4:4–8 [3:4–8] belonged originally after 4:21 [3:21].

[42] *Oude Woorden worden nieuw: De opbouw van het boek Joel* (TAuJCC; Kampen: Kok, 1989). I depend on an English summary (pp. 279–86) and a review by Walter A. Vogels in *CBQ* 53 (1991) 296–97. Van der Meer bases the larger units on concatenations, responsions, inclusions, internal coherence of imagery, and the Masoretic *setūmâ* and *petūḥâ*.

[43] *The Theology of the Book of Joel* (BZAW 163; Berlin & New York: Walter de Gruyter, 1985).

intensification. Nearly all the units refer back to previous ones through repetition of words and phrases, thus integrating the whole book and ultimately achieving a climax.

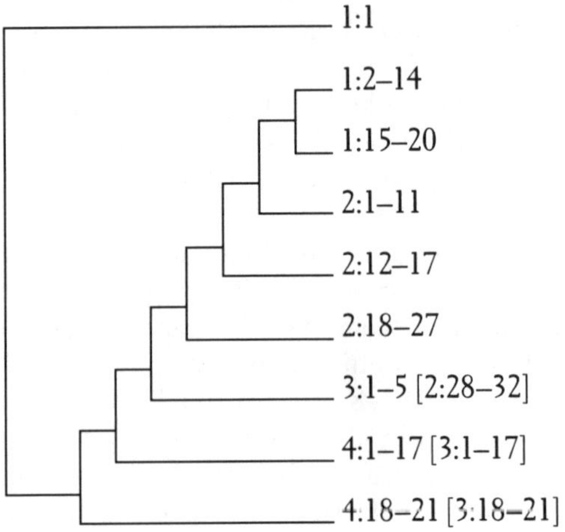

The first unit, or pericope in Prinsloo's terminology, describes the catastrophe caused by a locust plague (1:2–14). The second unit concerns an even more threatening disaster, the day of YHWH (1:15–20), and the third makes this threat more explicit (2:1–11). The next unit, 2:12–17, issues a divine call for repentance, which in turn gives way to a summons to obedient response (2:18–27). Unit six (3:1–5 [2:28–32]) announces a new era of salvation that will be characterized by an entire nation fully authorized as a medium of revelation. The seventh unit (4:1–17 [3:1–17]) describes the divine judgment of nations whose mistreatment of Judah has made them subject to YHWH's wrath. The final unit (4:18–21 [3:18–21]) contrasts promises to Judah with threats of doom for its foes. The catastrophe has been averted, and YHWH has been shown to be present as God of the covenant. The entire structure, according to Prinsloo, emphasizes YHWH's character and activity, hence is theocentric.

Duane A. Garrett[44] argues for a chiastic structure moving from punishment to forgiveness in both halves of the book.

A	(1:4–20)	Punishment by locusts
B	(2:1–11)	Punishment by an apocalyptic army

Although Prinsloo's primary interest is literary and stylistic, *in the service of theology*, he considers a postexilic date assured, specifically one after 515 B.C.E. (p. 110).

[44] "The Structure of Joel," *JETS* 28 (1985) 289–97.

C	(2:12–19)	Transition
B[1]	(2:20)	Forgiveness, the destruction of the apocalyptic army
A[1]	(2:21–27)	Forgiveness, the destruction of the locusts
A	(2:20)	Judgment on the apocalyptic army
B	(2:21–27)	Grace: the restoration of the land
B[1]	(3:1–5 [2:28–32])	Grace: the pouring out of the spirit
A[1]	(4:1–21 [3:1–21])	Judgment on the nations

J. Bourke[45] emphasizes a central core (2:2b–9) surrounded by speeches about YHWH's day. Four other motifs are associated here with the day of YHWH; they consist of penitence (1:13; 2:12–14), solemn assembly (1:14; 2:5–16), lament (1:16–20; 2:17), and blowing a trumpet in Jerusalem (2:1, 15). Bourke divides the book of Joel into two parts, 1:2–2:27 and 3:1–4:21 [2:28–3:21], which he likens to a diptych. In the second part he also thinks the day of YHWH cluster (3:1–2 [2:30–31] and 4:14–16a [3:14–16a]) is flanked by 4:9–12 [3:9–12] and 4:2–8, 13 [3:2–8, 13]. The outpouring of the spirit (3:1–5 [2:28–32]) precedes the day of YHWH, and restoration of fertility (4:18–20 [3:18–20]) follows it.

Similarly, Gosta W. Ahlström[46] views the book of Joel as correlative, everything in the first part being reversed in the second part. Ahlström emphasizes the book's liturgical characteristics but refuses to identify it as an actual lament for two reasons; first, the usual introduction is missing, and second, Joel calls on priests to lament. Ahlström thinks 1:2–2:17 shows an actual situation in which a lamentation should be performed. The turning point is 2:18, and every motif in part one is turned into its opposite in part two. Even 4:4–8 [3:3–8] belongs integrally to the book; it represents an aside like Amos 7:10–17. Ahlström claims that 2:18 may indicate that a day of penitence was held and that during the same festival 2:19–4:21 [3:21] may have been delivered.

---

[45] "Le jour de Yahvé dans Joël," *RB* 66 (1959) 5–31, 191–212 ("Les deux sections se complètent comme les deux tables d'un diptyque. Apercevoir comment elles se contrebalancent l'une l'autre, c'est la première condition pour saisir le message plus profond de Joël," p. 11). On p. 24 Bourke notes that "dans la première section, les sauterelles (un phénomène *agricole*) avaient été décrites en termes *militaires*, comme unè armée, dans la seconde section, *l'armée* des Gentils est décrite en termes *agricoles*, comme une *récolte* (iv, 13)." "The two sections complete one another like the two panels of a diptych. Recognizing the way they counterbalance one another is the primary prerequisite for understanding the profound message of Joel." . . . "in the initial section, the locusts (an *agricultural* phenomenon) were described in *military* terms, as an army; in the second section, the *army* of the Gentiles is described in *agricultural* terms, as a *harvest* (4:13)."

[46] *Joel and the Temple Cult of Jerusalem* (VTS 21. Leiden: E. J. Brill, 1971), 130–37. Ahlström considers the original form of the book to have been oral, with Joel or someone else committing it to writing at a later time (p. 137).

Carl A. Keller[47] divides the book into a dozen distinct units.

1. 1:2–4
2. 1:5–14
3. 1:15–18
4. 1:19–20
5. 2:1–11
6. 2:12–14
7. 2:15–17
8. 2:18–27
9. 3:1–5 [2:28–32]
10. 4:1–8 [3:1–8]
11. 4:9–17 [3:9–17]
12. 4:18–21 [3:18–21]

According to Oswald Loretz,[48] colometry provides the decisive clue to the book's structure. He finds eight stages in its development:

1. the core (drought and rain, 1:8–10, 11–12, 13, 14–17, 18–20; 2:12–14, 15–19, 21–24; 4:18a [3:18a])
2. locust texts strengthening the first unit and referring to foreign powers, 1:4, 5–7; 2:3b–8a, 25
3. attack by foreign powers and destruction of the northerner, 2:12–19 linked to 2:1–11a
4. judgment of the nations, 4:1–3, 9–17 [3:1–3, 9–17]
5. Jerusalem at the end time, 4:18b–21 [3:18b–21]
6. intrusive comments, 3:1–2 [2:28–29] on 2:21–27; 3:3–5 [2:29–32] on 4:1–21 [3:1–21]; 4:4–8 [3:4–8] on 4:2–3 [3:2–3]
7. passages on YHWH's day, 1:15b; 2:1b, 11b, 3:4b [2:31b] 4:14b [3:14b]
8. Israel and the nations, 2:17b, 19b, 26b, 27b

Original texts about drought are thus semanticized anew and brought to new levels by means of eschatological interpretation and symbolic transformation. This new situation corresponds to the end of kingship and prophecy. As Loretz sees it, the book bears witness to a process of actualizing the word.

[47] *Joël* (CAT XIa, 2ᵉ; Genève: Labor et Fides, 1982 [original, 1965]) 102. In Keller's view, the independent units form two groups, 1–8 and 9–12, with the day of YHWH at the center of each; liturgical reminiscences may have inspired the arrangement, although the totality is no liturgy (pp. 103 and 105).

[48] *Regenritual und Jahwetag im Joelbuch*, 140–63.

COMPOSITION AND STYLE

These attempts to arrive at a satisfactory structural analysis of the book reach different conclusions about the central problem being addressed: (1) an attack by locusts or by an army, (2) the imminence of YHWH's day, (3) drought. Kathleen Sarah Nash[49] identifies the fundamental problem as failure of the agricultural cycle due to a harsh sirocco that prevented the coming of rain at its appropriate time. The failed crops were subsequently ruined by a severe invasion of locusts, with the grain failing in the spring. Joel understands these past disasters as harbingers of the day of YHWH, the sirocco. He urges a penitential assembly and announces a flourishing agricultural harvest (chapters one and two). In chapters three and four [2:32–3:21] he looks to another fall interchange period in the unknown future when another fall sirocco, the day of YHWH, will annihilate Judah's enemies. In 4:18–21 [3:18–21] Joel reverses the agricultural cycle, guaranteeing a new and permanent stream from the sanctuary. In 3:1–2 [2:28–29] YHWH sends the west wind with early rains; in 3:3–4 [2:30–31], he sends the east wind of YHWH's day. Consequently, Nash argues, 3:1–5 [2:28–32] is a summary of 4:1–3 + 9–21 [3:1–3 + 9–21].

Seigfried Bergler[50] also identifies drought as the direct occasion of the book; this original core consists of a five-strophe poem on nature, humanity, and animals (1:5, 9–13, 17–20). This poem then was made liturgical by the addition of a speaking prayer (1:15–16) and reference to the temple (1:14). The prayer linked the drought with YHWH's day, divine judgment according to Ezek 30:2. The call to reflect looks backward (1:2–4) to the plagues associated with the Exodus, and this threat in turn is linked with Jeremiah's mythic threat of enemies from the north and with Isa 13:6. The language of the enemy mixes metaphors and concrete reality (fruit trees, grain, waste, fire); locusts "burn" the landscape, as in Exodus 10, and enter houses. This advancing foe is identified with the dawning of YHWH's day; all Joel's speeches about YHWH's day derive from previous prophecy. Joel realizes that the day can be turned away (2:12–14); he grounds this hope in YHWH's compassion (2:13b, 14a//Jonah 4:2b; 3:9a). The quotation of Isa 13:9, 13 indicates that wrath has given way to blessing (2:14ab). The return to YHWH is not *from evil* as in Jonah 3:8b. Joel calls for a national lament over drought, and he addresses YHWH directly in 2:17b. Comparison with Jer 14:15–19 confirms two phases in moving from drought to a future foe. Whereas Jeremiah offered a negative divine response, Joel gives a positive answer (1:14; 2:15–17a, 19ff.). The middle of the book, 2:18 and 2:19aα, is confirmed by later self-citations of 1:2–2:17.

---

[49] *The Palestinian Agricultural Year and the Book of Joel* (Ph.D. diss., The Catholic University of America, 1989).

[50] *Joel als Schriftinterpret*, passim.

For Bergler, part two begins with an oracle of salvation (2:21–24, 26a), northerner (2:20), plagues (2:23aα, 25, 26aγ, 27), and possibly the day of YHWH (2:20bβ, 21bβ, 25bα). The drought is the teacher of righteousness, a sign. In Egypt YHWH has already acted wondrously. The community now lives in the eschatological era, spiritual blessings corresponding to material ones, the fulfillment of Moses' wish (Num 12:29). The cosmic dimensions of the plagues associated with the Exodus no longer present any danger for a repentant Judah. The citations of promises describe a second exodus, and Joel now explains a new calamity, YHWH's judgment on the nations. The punishment of Phoenicians and Philistines contrasts with rewards for Judah. A conclusion (4:4–8 [3:4–8]) and an epilogue (4:18–21 [3:18–21]) assure a theocracy. The book is therefore, according to Bergler, a literary unity, everything going back to Joel except the drought liturgy, appeal to elders, and enemy from the north.

The most striking stylistic feature of the book is its anthological quality.[51] It seems that Joel was thoroughly familiar with a wide range of sacred tradition, either oral floating traditions or written texts. His use of words and phrases from this rich repertoire resembles that of a learned scribe, a teacher of preserved religious tradition. He draws on the ancient account of the Exodus, particularly the plagues, the theophanic language, and the divine declaration to Moses of YHWH's essential attributes. He echoes the terminology of Deuteronomic threats linked to the covenant, and he is thoroughly at home in the language of holy war.

His use of prophetic themes appears almost limitless. Drawing on the notion of a mythic enemy from the north,[52] he effectively uses the concept of a holy mountain and even cites the statement of recognition, which Ezekiel employed again and again.[53] Joel reverses the twice-used promise of universal peace, and

[51] André Robert, "Les attaches littéraires bibliques des Prov. I–IX," *RB* 43 (1934) 42–68, 172–204, 374–84 and 44 (1935) 344–65, 502–25, employs this term in studying the phenomenon of intertextuality in canonical wisdom. Robert examines the way authors spliced fragments of earlier texts into their compositions, turning them into a virtual anthology of sacred literature. This practice differs from mere allusion, the "tacit reference to another literary work, to another art, to history, to contemporary figures, or the like" (Earl Miner, "Allusion," p. 10 in Arthur Preminger, ed. *The Princeton Handbook of Poetic Terms* [Princeton: Princeton University Press, 1986]). Herbert Marks, "The Twelve Prophets," in Robert Alter and Frank Kermode, eds., *The Literary Guide to the Bible*, (Cambridge: The Belknap Press of Harvard University, 1987) 230, remarks on Joel's use of allusion: "The allusive texture is probably densest in the late Book of Joel, sometimes called the 'learned prophet.' "

[52] Brevard S. Childs, "The Enemy from the North and the Chaos Tradition," *JBL* 78 (1959) 187–98; D. J. Reimer, "The 'Foe' and the 'North' in Jeremiah," ZAW 101 (1989) 223–32.

[53] Walther Zimmerli's exhaustive analysis of this "formula" arrives at a fundamental insight, in his view, that knowledge of God cannot emerge "darkly from interior human meditation, from an existential analysis of human beings and the world, or from speculation," for it depends wholly on divine acts which nourish it ("Knowledge of God According to the Book of Ezekiel," *I Am Yahweh* [Atlanta: John Knox Press, 1982] 64). More accurately, one can only conclude that the biblical authors under discussion believed divine initiative alone made knowledge of God possible.

he demonstrates a knowledge of utopian visions[54] elsewhere attested in the concluding sections of Amos and Zechariah. Joel adopts the terminology for Zion's special place in YHWH's scheme of things, and the prophet remembers the long-announced expectation of a special outpouring of YHWH's spirit.

The ancient story about a garden of Eden provides a simile for Joel, and the notion of YHWH's day functions as a theme unifying the divine threats against Judah and the nations. Even mocking language that found its way into the psalter did not escape Joel's keen eye. His knowledge of cultic terminology and practice includes ritual shouts, sounds of alarm, fixed petitions, and titles for priestly officials. This fondness for anthological discourse is remarkably similar to that of Ben Sira, a teacher of sapiential tradition in the early second century, c. 180 B.C.E.

Repetition, another notable characteristic of Joel's style, gives the book the semblance of a mirror, the second half reversing the first in minute detail. Such repetition functions in various ways:[55] (1) to conclude sections (1:20; 2:27; 4:21 [3:21], cf. 1:19, 2:26, 4:17 [3:17]), (2) to achieve climax (1:15; 2:1, 11; 3:4 [2:31], 4:14 [3:14]); and (3) to provide ironic contrast (4:4, 7 [3:4, 7] "arouse"; 4:9, 12 [3:9, 12] "come up"). The frequent use of the same verbal stem in description, for example, *ybš* ("to dry up") and *bʾš* (to be ashamed"), demonstrates the prophet's skill with repetition. The reader can attain an appreciation of this phenomenon by following the treatment within the commentary proper.

---

[54] I examine biblical descriptions of a future era of peace in "Freeing the Imagination; The Conclusion to the Book of Joel," forthcoming in *Semeia*.

[55] John A. Thompson, "The Use of Repetition in the Prophecy of Joel," pp. 101–10 in Matthew Black and W. Smalley, eds., *On Language, Culture and Religion: In Honor of Eugene A. Nida* (The Hague: Mouton, 1974). In "Nonrecurring Doublets in the Book of Joel," *CBQ* 56 (1994) 56–57, David Marcus isolates forty-seven phrases of two words or more that occur only twice in the book of Joel. Marcus distinguishes seven varieties of these doublets: (1) the two are exactly alike; (2) the second is slightly modified; (3) the parts of the phrases are reversed; (4) both occurrences have strict parallelistic form; (5) a doublet in parallelism is followed by one in syndetic parataxis; (6) a doublet in parallelism is followed by one in asyndetic parataxis; and (7) doublet phrases are broken apart. He stresses their function to emphasize, to reverse the first use, and to link sections through allusion. In addition, Marcus believes the doublets serve as a corrective and guide for text criticism (e.g., to retain *welōʾ yēbōšû ʿammî leʿôlām* in 2:26, *hakkōhanîm mešāratê* YHWH in 1:9, and *wayyištû* in 4:3 [3:3]). Finally, he argues that the interlinking doublets from chapter to chapter imply unitary authorship. These two theoretical applications of his findings do not take into account the likelihood of editorial additions to the book by one who imitated the style of the original author(s). Besides providing a complete list of the forty-seven nonrecurring doublets in the book of Joel, Marcus identifies the following key words: (1) "all the inhabitants of the land" (*kōl yôšĕbê hāʾāreṣ*) in 1:2, 14; 2:1; (2) "the nearness" (*kî qārôb*) in 1:15; 2:1; 4:14 [3:14]; (3) of the "day of the Lord" (*yôm YHWH*) in 1:15; 2:1, 11; 3:4 [2:31]; 4:14 [3:14]; (4) the "cutting off" (*nikrat*) in 1:5, 16, and (*hokrat*) in 1:9, and the "drying up" (*yābešû/hôbîš/hôbîšâ*) in 1:10, 12 (twice), 17 of "offerings and libations" (*minḥâ wānesek*) in 1:9, 13; 2:14 in the "House of the Lord" (*bêt YHWH*) in 1:9, 14; 4:18 (3:18), (*bêt ʾelōhêkem*) in 1:13, (*bêt ʾelōhênû*) in 1:16.

The book is rich in simile and metaphor. The invasion by locusts conjures up various images—horses, chariots, fire, the ruining of a lush garden, an army, a thief, a lamenting "virgin." These comparisons of locusts with dreaded foes of various kinds enhance the concrete details of the description. Likewise, the metaphors widen the semantic range of discourse, to some degree personalizing the attack. Locusts are called a "people," and the stricken inhabitants of Judah are admonished to rend their hearts rather than their garments. The vast scope of Judah's fear is addressed in a single word, "northerner," and the judgment of the foreign nations is pictured as a harvest. YHWH, who sits in judgment on the nations, is both a refuge and a fortress for the Zionites whose names are known to their protector. The place of judgment is a valley of decision, the valley of Jehoshaphat ("YHWH has judged").

Extensive reference to specific details reinforces such use of simile and metaphor. Joel employs four different words for locusts, lists various kinds of plants affected by the voracious appetite of locusts and the accompanying drought, mentions the different ages of people summoned to an assembly, specifies the social classes, sexual distinctions, and age differentials involved in the outpouring of YHWH's spirit. The prophet refers to grain, wine, and oil; he singles out the fig, pomegranate, apple, and palm. His references to animals include domesticated and wild ones, large and small. He mentions sun, moon, stars, heaven, and earth. Both the eastern and the western seas receive equal notice, as do early and latter rains, mountains and hills, fountains and wadis. Joel invokes the names YHWH, *ʾelōhîm* and *šadday*; he also refers to word, visions, and dreams, the three prophetic means of receiving a divine oracle, and he envisions YHWH's bountiful provisions on the sacred mountain as encompassing wine, milk, and water.

Of the numerous rhetorical devices in the book, the following examples provide a representative sample:

hendiadys: "mushrooming smoke" (3:3 [2:30]); "greatly awesome" (3:4 [2:31])

merism: "old people and infants" (2:16), "early and latter rain" (2:23), "sons and daughters, old and young, male and female slaves" (3:1–2 [2:28–29]).

hyperbole: "multitudes, multitudes" (4:14 [3:14])

onomatopoeia: *hamônîm hamônîm* (4:14 [3:14])

personification: "a people" (1:6)

alliteration: "and like destruction from Shaddai" *ûkešōd mišadday* (1:15)

rhetorical question: "are you paying me back?" (4:4 [3:4]); "who knows?" (2:14) chiasm: of the vowels "o" and "i," *hôbîš tîrôš* (1:10b); of a verb, *weʾîš bidrākāyw yēlēkûn . . . geber bimsillātô yēlēkûn* (2:7b–8a)

inclusio: 2:27a and 4:21 [3:21]

The abundance of imperatives, and thus the frequency of direct address, marks the urgency of Joel's message and suggests oral presentation. His minimal appeal to prophetic formulae for authentication (*nᵉʾum YHWH,*[56] 2:12; *kî YHWH dibbēr,* 4:8 [3:8]) contrasts mightily with the weighty language from religious tradition. When speaking in the divine persona, he often shifts into that of the spokesperson, making it difficult to distinguish between what is meant to be divine and human speech. The rhythm, by no means clear, shifts to create different moods. According to John A. Thompson,[57] two stresses occur in descriptions (1:4, 9b–11, 19–20; 2:9) and commands (1:14; 2:15b–16; 4:9–13 [3:9–13]); four stresses appear in solemn indictment (4:4–6 [3:4–6]. The prose-like section in 4:4–8 [3:4–8] and to a lesser extent 3:1–5 [2:28–32] stand out from the rest of the book.

RELIGIOUS VIEWS

Recent critical theorists have recognized the political nature of a given text,[58] insisting that critics cannot legitimately make a direct correlation between the ideas expressed and the actual situation of the author. I am fully aware of the difficulty involved in moving from a text to historical context, but I am not entirely skeptical about the possibility of imagining a reasonable setting for Joel. To be sure, the text of Joel is a literary construct, but one can plausibly contextualize his teachings. In my view, interpreters who consider every prophetic text tenuous have seized a correct insight and carried it to an indefensible extreme. I do not believe religious bias discolored Joel's teachings to the extent that one cannot, with care, reconstruct some of the forces that prompted him to say what he did in the manner he did. Nevertheless, I readily admit that he could easily have constructed a world that did not correspond at all with the one in which he found himself, and for that reason I offer the following description of Joel's religious views only as indirect evidence. I understand the following as elucidating the thought world of the author, not necessarily or exclusively the real world in which he lived.

Above all else, Joel thinks of YHWH as the sole means of escaping the

[56] Friedrich Baumgärtel, "Die Formel *nᵉʾum jahwe,*" ZAW 73 (1961) 277–90.

[57] "The Book of Joel," *IB* 6 (Nashville: 1956) 730.

[58] Peter J. Rabinowitz, *Before Reading: Narrative Conventions and the Politics of Interpretation* (Ithaca, New York: Cornell University, 1987).

full consequences of the locusts and the dreaded day they presage. This acknowledgment of YHWH's sovereignty over invading insects, drought, and ominous events in the heavens implies divine complicity in the calamity that has struck the inhabitants of Judah.[59] At the same time, Joel accuses the locusts of invading YHWH's land, as if to exonerate the deity of all responsibility. Furthermore, the prophet depicts YHWH as leading an army against Jerusalem and even has the deity state the matter in no uncertain terms ("my powerful army that I dispatched against you," 2:25b). Nowhere does Joel mention the reason for his disaster.

Modern critics have more than compensated for the prophet's silence in this regard. They have accused the unfortunate victims of committing the following offenses: syncretistic worship,[60] hubris,[61] emphasis on external ritual,[62] priestly abdication of leadership,[63] breach of covenant,[64] and refusal to be known as a follower of an impotent deity, i.e., one defeated in battle.[65] Evidence for all these claims, solely inferential, begins with an unproven assumption of guilt. The reasoning, often specious, ignores the complexity of the issue. The fervent appeal to turn to YHWH applies to sinners and to innocent victims like Job; the

---

[59] Frederik Lindström, *God and the Origin of Evil* (ConB, OT 21; Lund: C.W.K. Gleerup, 1983) illustrates the complexity of attributing blame for evil on the basis of biblical texts. As the parallel accounts of David's census demonstrate (2 Sam 24:1–17; 1 Chr 21:1–17) by the substitution of Satan for God as the one who provoked the king to number the people for military service, later Israelites were troubled by the attribution of evil to YHWH. H. Shapiro, "Joel," in D. Rosenberg, ed., *Congregation: Contemporary Writers Read the Jewish Bible* (San Diego: Harcourt Brace Jovanovich, 1987) 201, caustically identifies Joel's God as a megalomaniac.

[60] Ahlström, *Joel and the Temple Cult of Jerusalem*, 26 and passim. In his view, the phrase *šubû ʿāday* ("return to me") implies worship of other gods by the people.

[61] Wolff, *Joel and Amos*, 48–53.

[62] Gunther Wanke, "Prophecy and Psalms in the Persian Period," p. 177 in W. D. Davies and L. Finkelstein, eds., *The Cambridge History of Judaism*, vol. I (Cambridge: Cambridge University, 1984).

[63] Paul L. Redditt, "The Book of Joel and Peripheral Prophecy," *CBQ* 48 (1986) 240, claims that Joel's accusations against leaders of the cult eventually thrust him and his followers to the periphery of society, thus limiting his effectiveness and nullifying the cult. The categories "central prophecy" and "peripheral prophecy" appear prominently in Robert R. Wilson, *Prophecy and Society in Ancient Israel* (Philadelphia: Fortress Press, 1980).

[64] Leslie C. Allen, *The Books of Joel, Obadiah, Jonah and Micah* (NICOT; Grand Rapids: William B. Eerdmans Publishing Co., 1976) 77–84, thinks the covenant people have "evidently strayed from their Shepherd, turning to their own way" and that "it is evidently left to the people and priests to search their own hearts and habits for evidence of the sin that God's reaction proved to be there" (78–79). Curiously, in Allen's view, Joel does not use the normal place in the rhetoric of 2:12 to mention the community's offense.

[65] Ronald Simkins, *Yahweh's Activity in History and Nature in the Book of Joel* (ANETS 10; Lewiston; Queenston, Lampeter: The Edwin Mellen Press, 1991). In " 'Return to Yahweh': Honor and Shame in Joel," forthcoming in *Semeia*, he revises this charge against the people, based on a covenant model, and replaces it with an interpretation based on the honor/shame model, one that labels the book of Joel a theodicy for innocent worshipers of YHWH.

verb *šûb* by itself does not necessarily imply guilt, although it has that connotation in some texts where the transgression is clearly stated (Amos 4:6–12;[66] contrast Isa 44:22, where a pardoned nation is encouraged to turn to YHWH). The insistence that the people rend their hearts rather than their garments does not necessarily imply that their repentance merely touched the surface. It may be a piece of religious instruction entirely unrelated to the present state of repentance. Joel's encouragement of ritualistic acts leaves no doubt that he valued such conduct when accompanied by genuine contrition. The urging of priests to intercede hardly indicates a failed leadership, for they certainly mourned the loss of a functioning cult. Despite ancient promises associated with covenants, not every incident of calamity grew directly out of a broken treaty. Moreover, YHWH's apparent defeat at the hands of Babylonian deities and the resulting mockery of Jews did not always turn the conquered people into loyal devotees of strange gods (cf. Psalm 137 for the resolute faithfulness of the exiled community in the face of ridicule). The assumption of guilt whenever disaster struck indicates a calculating morality that obscures the ambiguity of human existence and a perceived ambiguity in the deity as well.[67]

The combination of a resolute mind and external ritual characterizes Israel's turning to YHWH who is *raḥûm* (Deut 4:30–31; 30:2–3). Outside Joel 2:12b, only Esth 4:3 has a triple manifestation of remorse (*weṣôm ûbekî ûmispēd*), although Joel's fourfold use of the preposition *be* differs strikingly from the language in Esther. Joel's emphasis on external manifestation proves that he values visible expressions of an inner state. The wedding of inner and outer did not compromise divine freedom, according to the story about David's intercession for his dying child (2 Sam 12:15b–23). Jewish thinkers waged considerable debate over the value of fasting (Zech 7:3, 5; Isa 58:3–9), and in their eagerness to defend YHWH's compassion they sometimes caused the pendulum to swing to the opposite end of the spectrum from justice (2 Chr 30:9b). At rare moments, a text such as Mal 3:6–7 actually juxtaposes divine constancy and turning on the part of both humans and YHWH.

Although Joel's assessment of YHWH's essential character belongs to an ancient confessional statement (Exod 34:6–7; cf. 33:19),[68] he goes his own way.

---

[66] James L. Crenshaw, "A Liturgy of Wasted Opportunity: Am. 4:6–12; Isa. 9:7–10:4; 5:25–29," *Semitics* 1 (1971) 27–37.

[67] Mettinger, *In Search of God*, 175–200, discusses competing views of god in the book of Job, the supreme biblical example of divine ambiguity. As my entry on the book of Job in the *Anchor Bible Dictionary* indicates ("Job, Book of," *ABD* III [New York: Doubleday, 1992] 858–68), interpreters find this work irresistible (cf. Katharine J. Dell, *The Book of Job as Sceptical Literature* [BZAW 197; Berlin & New York: Walter de Gruyter, 1991]).

[68] Scholars have examined this pregnant text at great length: Joseph Scharbert, "Formgeschichte und Exegese von Ex 34,6f. und seiner Parallelen," *Bib* 38 (1957) 130–50; Robert C. Dentan, "The Literary Affinities of Exodus XXXIV 6f.," *VT* 13 (1963) 34–41; Phyllis Trible, *God and the Rhetoric of Sexuality* (OBT 2; Philadelphia: Fortress Press, 1978) 1–5; Ludwig Schmidt, *"De Deo": Studien*

Like all later uses of this statement, he omits the attributes emphasizing punishment (v 7). The sequence *ḥannûn weraḥûm* accords with Exod 33:19, although the verbal form differs. Joel omits the attribute of truthfulness (*we'emet*), and the four character traits he lists occur in entirely different syntax. Moreover, he concludes the statement with a new element, "and repents of evil" (*weniḥām ʿal-hārāʿâ*). This exact expression in connection with the four attributes from Joel 2:13 occurs elsewhere only in Jonah 4:2, except for the direct address, "you, God" (*'attâ-'ēl*).[69] The kinship between these two texts is heightened by comparison of Joel 2:14 and Jonah 3:9, "who knows whether he may turn and relent?" (*mî yôdēaʿ yāšûb weniḥām*).[70] Both prophets use this rhetorical question in the sense of "perhaps." The specification God (*hā'elōhîm*) in Jonah accords with narrative custom, which does not permit foreigners to speak YHWH's name.

Elsewhere Joel focuses on YHWH's actions, whether sending locusts and a celestial army against Jerusalem or removing all threat to this people. Everything is subject to YHWH's will, whether insects, the cycle of rain, meteorological phenomena, or foreign nations. YHWH's zeal and pity transform woe into weal for the people of Judah, while promising ruin for their ancient and present enemies. Joel uses traditional concepts to describe YHWH's deeds—theophanies, the day of YHWH, the foe from the north, the sacred mountain, the outpouring of the spirit, the statement recognizing YHWH's uniqueness[71] and presence in Zion, and the notion of mockery of YHWH's people. Total

---

zur Literaturkritik und Theologie des Buches Jona, des Gesprächs zwischen Abraham und Jahwe in Gen 18,22ff. und Hi 1 (BZAW, 143; Berlin & New York: Walter de Gruyter, 1976); G. Vanoni, *Das Buch Jona* (St. Ottilien: Eos, 1978) 138–41; David Noel Freedman, "God Compassionate and Gracious," *Western Watch* 6 (1955) 6–24; Thomas B. Dozeman, "Inner-Biblical Interpretation of Yahweh's Gracious and Compassionate Character," *JBL* 108 (1989) 207–23; Jack M. Sasson, *Jonah* (AB 24B; New York et al.: Doubleday, 1990) 279–82; and above all, Michael Fishbane, *Biblical Interpretation in Ancient Israel*, 335–50. I treat this literature in "Who Knows What YHWH Will Do? The Character of God in the Book of Joel," forthcoming in Andrew H. Bartelt, et al., eds., *Fortunate the Eyes That See. Essays in Honor of David Noel Freedman in Celebration of his Seventieth Birthday* (Grand Rapids: William B. Eerdmans Publishing Company, 1994).

[69] In assessing the matter of priority, Vanoni writes that if Joel wished to quote, he would probably have cited the intercessory prayer of Moses, not the king of Nineveh (*Das Buch Jona*, 140). Actually, Joel "quotes" from the king of Nineveh *and* from Jonah. To this latter text, which originally derives from Exod 34:6, Jonah added a clause about the God who repents about evil (4:2). The other citation expresses the king's hope that YHWH may repent—"Who knows, God may relent and change his mind . . . ?" (Jonah 3:9). Jonathan Magonet, *Form and Meaning: Studies in Literary Techniques in the Book of Jonah* (BLS 8; Sheffield: Almond Press, 1983) 78–79, argues that Joel borrows from Jonah.

[70] On this phrase, see my article entitled "The Expression *mî yôdēaʿ* in the Hebrew Bible," VT 36 (1986) 274–88.

[71] C. J. Labuschagne, *The Incomparability of Yahweh in the Old Testament* (POS 5; Leiden: E. J. Brill, 1966).

control over nature's forces and human beings entitled YHWH to a claim of uniqueness.

Unfortunately, Joel's experience presented him with incidents not easily woven into this beautiful tapestry of providential care. The disparity between confessional statements and the reality confronting Joel must have driven him to an almost untenable position, silence representing a refusal to place blame on innocent citizens and equal conviction that the one causing the dismay also possessed the inclination and the power to dispel it. Where Joel seems to have found comfort, the pathetic figure Jonah could discover only further justification for condemning a deity whose concept of justice[72] differed from his. The decisive difference, however, throws light on Joel's restricted vision, for he never achieved the broader notion of YHWH's compassion for all creatures on earth that enabled the unknown author of the book of Jonah to indict the sulking prophet in spite of scrupulous faithfulness where the divine attributes proclaimed in Exod 34:6–7 were concerned.

Instead of expanding the breadth of YHWH's compassion to embrace all humankind and animals, Joel restricts the blessing and spirit to citizens of Judah and particularly residents of Jerusalem. In his vocabulary, even the old designation "Israel" is synonymous with Judah. Moreover, the phrase *kol bāśār* ("all flesh") actually has a restrictive sense in 3:1 [2:28], as the subsequent pronominal suffixes demonstrate. The prophet only envisions the divine dispersal of the spirit on inhabitants of Judah. The fate of foreigners will be determined solely on the basis of guilt or innocence, and Joel condemns them as a group. Old wrongs will be set right, in his view, and all peoples who have mistreated Jews will pay dearly. Perhaps one should not be altogether surprised when the deity who insists on exact vengeance—after all, the book closes on this note—also keeps a careful record of offenses and then replicates the crimes for which the nations stand indicted, this time, however, making them unwilling victims.

Although the concept of a sacred mountain and temple can coincide with universalistic theology, YHWH's cult does not achieve that goal in the book of Joel. The small sanctuary presided over by priestly officials performed a limited, albeit significant, function comparable no doubt to the role of rival sanctuaries, some of which even displayed items of gold and silver that once rested in Jerusalem's temple. In this cultic world sacrifices and fasting brought pleasure to YHWH, as did rites such as incubation. This world was most accurately symbolized by *śimḥâ wâgîl*, "joy and exultation."[73] In Joel's eyes the change of

[72]Terence E. Fretheim, "Jonah and Theodicy," ZAW 90 (1978) 227–37 and *The Message of Jonah: A Theological Commentary* (Minneapolis: Augsburg Publishing Company, 1977).

[73]Gary A. Anderson, *A Time to Mourn, A Time to Dance: The Expression of Grief and Joy in Israelite Religion* (University Park, Pennsylvania: The Pennsylvania State University Press, 1991), uses rabbinic sources instead of depending exclusively on ancient Near Eastern literature to

fortune, the direct result of prayer,[74] would bring with it not only YHWH's blessing (*berākâ*, 2:14) but also renewed daily offerings "for YHWH your God" (*laYHWH ʾelōhêkem*). The people's well-being would at the same time benefit their God. In the midst of a particularistic cult, a claim to uniqueness and, hence, exclusive obedience was not really that unusual, for worshipers of various gods praised their own deity as the only god, i.e., the only one who mattered in their lives.

What does the book of Joel say about people? First, the Jews. We can infer that Joel addresses a struggling agrarian society in a tiny province including Jerusalem and its environs. The only professions mentioned are farmers, vintners, and priests, but these are precisely those necessitated by the plot. If other professional guilds existed alongside agriculturalists and religious leaders,[75] their subsistence was threatened along with that of providers of food and sacral order. Joel characterizes daily life as joyless; he also points to painful memories of foreign soldiers in the holy city and of exiled Jews, some of whom suffered doubly from servitude and nostalgia for a more favorable place of residence. Second, foreigners. Joel's thoughts about them are as merciless as their slave traders, for he remembers the pain inflicted through mockery and he shares YHWH's zeal in announcing a day of judgment on all foreign nations. In

---

reconstruct the emotional world view of biblical Israel. Relying on Clifford Geertz's *The Interpretation of Cultures* (New York: Basic Books, Inc., 1973), Anderson understands religion as a producer of experience, a template for reality in which "the inner experiences of religious believers are generated by the external forms of their religious traditions" (p. 7). He also stresses the connection between joy and sex in the Bible and rabbinic Judaism (pp. 27–37). See also Y. Muffs, "Joy and Love as Metaphorical Expressions of Willingness and Spontaneity in Cuneiform, Ancient Hebrew, and Related Literatures: Divine Investitures in the Midrash and in the Light of Neo-Babylonian Royal Grants," pp. 1–36 in Jacob Neusner, ed., *Christianity, Judaism, and Other Greco-Roman Cults* III (Leiden: E. J. Brill, 1975).

[74] Interest in biblical prayer has surged during the last decade or so: Ronald E. Clements, *In Spirit and in Truth: Insights from Biblical Prayers* (Atlanta: John Knox Press, 1985); Erhard Gerstenberger, *Der bittende Mensch* (Neukirchen: Neukirchener Verlag, 1980); Moshe Greenberg, *Biblical Prose Prayer As a Window to the Popular Religion of Ancient Israel* (Berkeley, Los Angeles, and London: University of California Press, 1983); Henning Graf Reventlow, *Gebet im Alten Testament* (Stuttgart: Kohlhammer, 1986); A. Aejmelaeus, *The Traditional Prayer in the Psalms* (BZAW 167; Berlin and New York: Walter de Gruyter, 1986); Samuel E. Balentine, *Prayer in the Hebrew Bible: The Drama of Divine-Human Dialogue* (OBT; Minneapolis: Fortress Press, 1993); and James L. Crenshaw, "The Restraint of Reason, the Humility of Prayer," forthcoming in a Festschrift for Lou H. Silberman.

[75] The Egyptian "Satire on the Trades" mentions metal workers, carpenters, jewel smiths, barbers, merchants, building contractors, brick masons, farmers, weavers, arrow-makers, couriers, embalmers, cobblers, laundry persons, hunters, persons engaged in fishing for a living, and first and foremost in significance, scribes (*ANET*, 432–34). A shorter listing occurs in Sir 38:24–39:11, where one finds reference to farmers, craftspersons, smiths, potters, and scribes. Despite the negative comparison between all these other professions and scribes, Ben Sira makes a remarkable concession about the indispensability of the "inferior" trades: "but they keep stable the fabric of the world, and their prayer is in the practice of their trade" (38:34, RSV).

his view, only Jews will survive the ominous portents accompanying this universal judgment.

Joel's vision of a better day for the Jews makes use of a wealth of ideas that occur elsewhere, particularly in Amos 9:11–15; Mic 4:1–4; Isa 2:2–4; 11:6–9; Ezek 47:1–12; Zech 14:1–21; Mal 3:19–21 [4:1–3]; and Gen 49:10–12. Three major themes characterize these texts: (1) nature's transformation; (2) the restoration of the greatness of the Davidic dynasty; and (3) the inauguration of an era of peace. Joel's silence about the Davidic dynasty may derive from the dominance of the priests at the time and the dismal experience under the leadership of Haggai and Zechariah, when messianic impulses surfaced only to be squelched decisively by Persian authorities. The sole reminiscence of Amos 9:11–15 and Gen 49:10–12 occurs in the image of fabulous fertility, for Joel mentions milk and sweet wine flowing from the hills; however, the former concept could derive from the ancient phrase describing Israel as a land of milk and honey. Both Amos 9:11–15 and Ezekiel 47:1–12 surpass Joel 4:17–21 [3:17–21] in describing the scope of fertility, for they mention overlapping sowing and reaping, together with prolific plants that mature in a month. If he knew the exuberant depiction of abundance in Hos 14:5–7 [4–7], Joel chose not to articulate it.

The reference to YHWH's summoning of the nations in Joel has nothing in common with their pilgrimage to Judah for religious instruction as chronicled in Mic 4:1–4 and Isa 2:2–4. Joel does think in terms of universal judgment ushering in an era of peace, but he reverses the sentiment about beating swords into plow tips and spears into pruning shears. The notion of healing in Ezek 47:1–12 and Mal 3:19–21 [4:1–3] does not appear in Joel's account, although the life-bestowing stream does. This extraordinary river that flows from the sanctuary in Jerusalem plays a major role in Ezek 47:1–12[76] and Zech 14:1–21, running both east and west in the latter text. Perhaps priestly interest in Joel prompted him to prefer texts from Ezekiel and Zechariah over the exquisite images in Hos 14:5–7 [4–7]; Isa 11:6–9; Isa 8:23–9:6 [9:1–7]; and Mic 4:1–4 = Isa 2:2–4.

The most striking feature of Joel's description of the future is its restraint. If one is going to dream, why not dream big? It remains a mystery that this text modestly envisions nothing more than YHWH's presence to assure a holy place; an ample supply of wine, milk, and water; revenge on enemies for the spilling of innocent blood; and a permanent title to the Judean hills. Other dreamers in the Hebrew Bible certainly set their sights higher, judging from their robust language. The beauty of Joel 4:17–21 [3:17–21] lies in its response to suffering occasioned by calamity and the resulting soul-searching. No wonder the inclusio in this unit concentrates on YHWH's residence in Zion. The prophet believed

[76]On this stream flowing from underneath the temple in Jerusalem, see Walther Zimmerli, *Ezechiel* (BKAT 13/15; Neukirchen-Vluyn: Neukirchener Verlag, 1968), 1186–1201.

that divine presence guaranteed safety. The inclusio, "You will know that I YHWH dwell in your midst," corresponds to the ecstatic shout concluding the book of Ezekiel: "YHWH is there" (*YHWH šammâ*).[77] In Joel's view, where YHWH resides, one need not fear locusts, drought, fire, portents, or armies.

ECHOES OF A CULT OF BAAL

Several critics have insisted that Joel preserves features from the earlier cult of Baal. In 1938 Flemming Friis Hvidberg wrote: "The distress over which the prophet laments originally had nothing to do with swarms of locusts but was connected with the effects of the fire of the summer sun. It corresponds to the distress which in ancient Canaan was due to the fact that Ba'al descended into the mouth of Mot and the olive tree was burnt off. . . ."[78] Hvidberg did not deny that Joel 1–2 also dealt with weeping before YHWH, but the texts, he insisted, occasionally used motifs from the cult of Baal. In particular, he thought the reference to the weeping virgin in 1:8 echoed Anat's lament over her dead brother, Baal.

Oswald Loretz's examination of texts in Joel illuminated by Ugaritic literature concludes that these similarities nevertheless indicate a late postexilic date for the book.[79] He isolates the following similarities: (1) the reference to a spear in 2:8 (cf. KTU 1:14 I 20); (2) the idea of honey flowing in streams in 4:18 [3:18] (cf. KTU 1.6 III 7); (3) the locusts in 1:4 (cf. KTU 1.14 II 50 = III 1, IV 29–30 and 1.3 II 10; 1.14 II 50–III 1; IV 29–30); (4) the lament of the virgin in 1:8; (5) the festivals of New Year and Succoth; (6) individual pairs[80] of words; (7) rain-

---

[77] This expression, *YHWH šammâ*, may consciously echo the ancient doxological formula, *YHWH ṣebā'ôt šemô*, which I have analyzed in *Hymnic Affirmation of Divine Justice. The Doxologies of Amos and Related Texts in the Old Testament* (SBLDS 24; Missoula, Montana: Scholars Press, 1975) and "*YHWH ṣebā'ôt šemô*: A Form-Critical Analysis," ZAW 81 (1969) 156–75.

[78] *Weeping and Laughter in the Old Testament* (Kobenhaven: Nyt Nordisk Forlag, A. Busck, & Leiden: E. J. Brill, 1962).

[79] *Regenritual und Jahwetag im Joelbuch*, 117–39.

[80] On pages 127–28 Loretz compiles the following list:

irby // ḥsn   *'rbh // ḥsyl*
ym // ym
ʿwlm // dwr dwr
pnym // 'ḥrym
'rṣ // šmm
šmš yrḥ // kwkbym
dgn // tyrwš // yṣhr
šd / śdh // (n'wt) mdbr
šmh/śmḥ // gl / gyl
hr(y̆m) // gbʿwt
ʿsys // ḥlb

making rituals; (8) mourning rites and fasts; (9) an oracle of salvation within a vegetative cult; and (10) the designation for rain in Joel 2:23. B. Margalit has written that "*yôreh* is the initial fertilizing/impregnating agency of the newly ploughed, 'opened up' and 'seeded' earth of early winter."[81] Loretz concurred, observing that "hardly any possibility exists for a better understanding of *môreh* in Joel 2:23 than from Ugaritic."[82]

Although opting for a much earlier date for Joel, Arvid S. Kapelrud reached a similar conclusion about strong influence on the prophet from the cult of Baal.[83] He noted that the verb *yll*, "to lament," occurs frequently with reference to mourning rites and that "sweet wine," *ʿāsîs*, corresponds to a noun in Ugaritic for a similar drink. These and other instances of possibly older motifs notwithstanding, Kapelrud considered the powerful influence of teachings from the book of Jeremiah decisive in dating Joel's activity to a period between 609 B.C.E. and 598, thus c. 600. Like Loretz, then, Kapelrud understood the resemblances between the book of Joel and Ugaritic texts as surviving motifs in a syncretistic religion. G. W. Ahlström arrived at a similar conclusion: that the Jewish cult in Joel's day had become highly syncretistic, with echoes of the cult of Baal permeating the prophet's message.[84]

The Day of YHWH in the Book

"Das Joelbuch kreist von Beginn bis Ende um ein einzoges Thema, das seit dem Beginn der klassichen Prophetie gelaufig war: den Tag Jahwes?"[85] This observation by Jörg Jeremias can hardly be faulted, although it leaves open the crucial issue: the origin and nature of YHWH's day in prophetic literature. Theories about its origin range from the cultic to the natural, from specific ritual to general theophany, from holy war to activating curses associated with treaties.[86] From the eighth century onward, that is, after Amos released the

---

[81] Cited from Loretz, *Regenritual und Jahwetag im Joelbuch*, 136.

[82] *Regenritual und Jahwetag im Joelbuch*, 137. ("Es besteht deshalb kaum eine Möglichkeit, *môreh* in Joel 2,23 vom Ug. her besser zu verstehen").

[83] *Joel Studies*, 23 ("The whole chain of ideas in vv. 8–12 points to the fact that the background of the Prophet's speech is the wailing and mourning over Baal when he descended into the earth, and grass and trees perished").

[84] *Joel and the Temple Cult of Jerusalem*, 27–34.

[85] Jörg Jeremias, "Joel/Joelbuch," TRE 17 (1987) 94 ("From beginning to end the book of Joel revolves around a single theme, one that was common since the beginning of classical prophecy: the 'day of YHWH' ").

[86] Sigmund Mowinckel, *He That Cometh* (Nashville: Abingdon Press, 1954) 132–33, identifies the day of YHWH as an expected theophany during the New Year's Enthronement Festival. In the view of K. D. Schunck, the day had two fundamental lines of development, an eschatological era of supernatural abundance and a noneschatological day of vindication ("Strukturlinien in der

"bombshell" in 5:18–20, the essential meaning of the idea was an unveiling of divine wrath and an implementing of judgment on YHWH's enemies, Jewish or non-Israelite.[87]

The earliest Jewish interpreters of the Bible did not understand *yôm YHWH* as a technical expression: Targum Jonathan, followed by Rashi, Ibn Ezra, and Maimonides. Modern critics have disagreed with these scholars, for the most part, although they differ among themselves on relevant texts and which ones to use as a point of departure in studying the concept. If one restricts oneself to the term *yôm YHWH*, for which exact parallels exist such as "the day of Midian," "the day of Jezreel," "the day of Jerusalem," and "the day of Egypt," one chooses to ignore many related expressions: e.g., "the day of YHWH's vengeance," "a day belonging to YHWH of hosts," "the day of YHWH's wrath," "the day of his fierce anger," "the day of his anger," "the day of tumult, confusion, and trampling belonging to YHWH," "that day is YHWH God's," "in that day," "in that day and at that time."[88]

Although not all interpreters agree, Amos apparently used the term in such a manner as to presuppose an existing concept, at least among some of his listeners, one that he completely reversed, turning anticipated deliverance into destruction. The most important texts for understanding the *yôm YHWH* cover several centuries and a wide geographical expanse: Isa 13:6, 9; Ezek 13:5; Joel 1:15; 2:1, 11; 3:4 [2:31]; 4:14 [3:14]; Amos 5:18; Ob 15; and Zeph 1:7, 14–16. Its association with a theophany suggests the reason for the term's ambiguity;

Entwicklung der Vorstellung vom 'Tag Jahwes,' " *VT* 14 [1964] 319–30). Gerhard von Rad stressed the origins of the concept in holy war, a view endorsed and expanded by Patrick D. Miller, Jr. to include the divine council and cosmic wars of YHWH (Rad, "The Origin of the Concept of the Day of Yahweh," *JSS* 4 [1959] 97–108 and Miller, *The Divine Warrior in Early Israel*, Cambridge, Massachusetts: Harvard University Press, 1973). The concept originated in political threats connected with Hittite and Assyrian treaties, according to F. C. Fensham, "A Possible Origin of the Concept of the Day of the Lord," *Biblical Essays* (OTWSA 9, 1966, 90–97). Meir Weiss thinks the idea arose in regard to theophany and was not a technical term in Amos' day ("The Origin of the 'Day of the Lord' Reconsidered," *HUCA* 37 [1966] 29–72). Yair Hoffmann recognizes a metamorphosis in the term from a nontechnical and vague idea in Amos' day to a technical term in the book of Zephaniah where the thirteen uses of YHWH in 1:1–14 and twelve uses of "day" in 1:14–3:2 bring the two ideas together ("The Day of the Lord as a Concept and a Term in the Prophetic Literature," ZAW 93 [1981] 37–50). A bifurcation into a local and a cosmic day, an historical and a supernatural event, best describes YHWH's day for J. Bourke, "Le jour de Yahvé dans Joel," *RB* 66 [1959] 5–31, 191–212. At least one scholar, Ferdinand E. Deist, considers Joel's use of the idea as purely literary, a theological construct ("Parallels and Reinterpretation in the Book of Joel: A Theology of the Yom Yahweh?" in W. Claassen, ed., *Text and Context: Old Testament and Semitic Studies for F. C. Fensham* [JSOTS 48; Sheffield: JSOT Press, 1988] 63–79).

[87] Ernst Kutsch, "Heuschreckenplage und Tag Jahwes in Joel 1 und 2," *TZ* 18 (1962) 81–94, especially 89.

[88] A. J. Everson, "The Days of Yahweh," *JBL* 93 (1974) 329–37, uses six expressions to describe the day of YHWH, one of which is *yôm YHWH*.

YHWH's self-manifestation portends either blessing or curse, depending on whether the deity comes in favor or wrath. For Joel, dialogue between a humbled Jewish community and YHWH contrasts with a militant foreign encampment arrayed for battle against YHWH, bringing the ambiguity of the *yôm YHWH* into sharp focus. In the words of J. Bourke, "The dialogue between Israel and YHWH constitutes the principal difference between the day of Judah and that of the Gentiles. . . . It is not given to the Gentiles, as it was granted to Israel, to understand the voice and respond to it."[89] Unlike Zephaniah, who favors emotional terms in association with *yôm YHWH*, Joel prefers visual images.[90]

The old tradition about an enemy from the north, the avenger of broken covenants in Deuteronomy, unites with the *yôm YHWH* in Joel. The two passages in chapter two that mention YHWH's day form an inclusio around the threat of an attack by YHWH's great army of locusts: 2:1b–2a and 2:10–11. The symmetry between a repentant Jewish community that receives YHWH's salvation and a warlike foreign nation that generates divine judgment communicates Joel's message dramatically. Sensing the power of the unknown mystery from afar in the book, Bourke aptly calls Joel a prophet of the numinous,[91] which seems ill at home among such controlled symmetry. This balancing of polarities extends further to include the initial description of locusts (four terms corresponding to four cultic rites—weeping, tearing garments, putting on sackcloth, beating the breast),[92] which signifies the approach of YHWH's day.

Is the *yôm YHWH* past or future in the book of Joel? Deist interprets the "afterwards" in 3:1 [2:28] as implying that the *waw* consecutives in 2:18 refer to the future. The ambiguity with regard to the actual time involved is heightened by the predicate adjective *qārôb* (2:1), suggesting nearness, an approaching threat.[93] Perhaps one should think in terms of several levels of interpretation, the *yôm YHWH* in the book of Joel being (1) apocalyptic, (2) eschatological, (3) theophanic and judgmental, and (4) anti-Canaanite.[94] This way of viewing the ancient concept does not imply that Joel was "merely creating a *literary* world

---

[89] Bourke, "Le jour de Yahvé dans Joel," 28 ("C'est ce dialogue entre Israël et Yahvé qui constitue la différence principale entre le Jour de Juda et le Jour des Gentils . . . Il n'est pas donné aux Gentils, comme il était donné à Israël, de comprendre la Voix et d'y répondre").

[90] Bourke, "Le jour de Yahvé dans Joel," 29.

[91] Ibid., 210.

[92] Kutsch, "Heuschreckenplage und Tag Jahwes in Joel 1 und 2," 81. The text does not mention beating the breast, although such practice normally accompanied the other three acts. This may be a case of breaking up a symmetrical structure by balancing only three points on one side with four on the other side.

[93] "Parallels and Reinterpretation in the Book of Joel: A Theology of the Yom Yahweh," 70. He recognizes three parallel passages: 1:2–20 // 2:18–27; 1:2–20 // 2:1–17; 2:10–11 // 4:14–17 [3:14–17] (p. 74).

[94] Deist, "Parallels and Reinterpretation in the Book of Joel: A Theology of the Yom Yahweh," 75.

of calamities to serve as metaphors describing the character of the Day of the Lord."[95] Instead, the prophet interpreted a natural catastrophe in Judah, a severe infestation of locusts and a severe drought, in terms of the dreaded day of YHWH's visitation in wrath, only to transfer this divine manifestation to foreign nations after the Jewish community turned to YHWH and became fortunate recipients of divine compassion.

THE TRANSLATION

Every translator who takes the task seriously understands the dilemma attributed to Rabbi Eliezer, to wit that whoever renders a text literally prevaricates and whoever translates freely is guilty of blasphemy. Whether to adhere strictly to the text being put into a target language or to add new features required by the character of the modern language—that is the choice facing every translator. The type of translation depends largely on which end of the spectrum it represents. Those translations opting for literal renditions, for example the New Revised Standard Version, fall into the general category of formal correspondence, whereas freer translations such as the New English Bible follow the principle of "dynamic equivalence." The first type runs the risk of using substandard English (German, French, or whatever the target language may be), and the second type risks paraphrase. Why? Because in translations opting for formal correspondence the effort to retain the exact grammatical and syntactical features of Hebrew, for example, creates unnatural structures in the target language. Similarly, translations based on dynamic equivalence surrender interesting and sometimes vital features of Hebrew in the search for appropriate idioms in English, French, German, or whatever language.

The most thoroughgoing endeavor to replicate exactly every single feature of ancient Hebrew was that by Martin Buber and Franz Rosenzweig,[96] who tried to translate the Bible into German. The result was inevitably a failure, for it invented an artificial language. The same judgment applies to Everett Fox's effort to employ the Buber/Rosenzweig principles in translating the Bible into English.[97] At the same time, this approach has made a valuable contribution by focusing on distinctive rhetorical, syntactic, grammatical, and etymological characteristics of the Hebrew language. In English, the comparable translation

[95] Ibid., 64.

[96] *Die Schrift: Die hebräische Bibel. Das Alte Testament*, Vol. 1–5 (Heidelberg: Verlag Lambert Schneider, 1979 7e).

[97] *In the Beginning: A New English Rendition of the Book of Genesis* (New York: Schocken Books, 1983) and *Now These Are the Names: A New English Rendition of the Book of Exodus* (New York: Schocken Books, 1986).

on the other end of the spectrum is The Good News Bible published by the United Bible Society.

To some degree, every translator makes a decisive turn—converting, perverting, inverting, reversing, subverting, controverting—so that Douglas Robertson aptly entitles his insightful volume on this subject *The Translator's Turn.*[98] Ideally, I suppose, the translator remains invisible, functioning like a window, thus allowing viewers on each side to see clearly. In reality, a translator builds a bridge connecting two different countries,[99] and visitors cross in either direction. This journey between two quite distinct lands seeks to familiarize foreigners with every hill and valley from one end of the country to the other. No single trail accomplishes the goal; instead, one travels along the path of etymology, the winding road of idiom, the avenue of context, the cul-de-sac of sound, the street of signs. Furthermore, one needs to be alert to the politics inherent to the translator's task, whether overt or covert. However innocuous windows and bridges appear to be at first glance, they conceal conscious decisions at every turn, for translators inevitably interpret. Like interpretation, translation demands art and artifice.

The natural redundancy in a given language poses a problem; Hebrew poetry therefore presents an almost insurmountable obstacle, above and beyond rhythmic scansion.[100] Parallelism, a constitutive element of Hebrew poetry, overloads the diction in all modern tongues. Likewise, paratactic *waw* in prose yields far too many connective "ands," making it imperative to determine exactly when a *waw* must be represented in English. Whether one follows Augustine in viewing a word's meaning as objective and thus requiring an exact equivalence, or one prefers Ferdinand de Saussure's understanding of words as arbitrary signs, a further fact cannot be avoided: language operates on at least two levels, those of *parole* and *langue*. Moreover, words have a somatic quality, both taste and feeling, in addition to forming a deep linguistic system. They also

---

[98] *The Translator's Turn* (Baltimore: Johns Hopkins University Press, 1991).

[99] Marcia Falk, *The Song of Songs: A New Translation and Interpretation* (San Francisco: Harper San Francisco, 1990) 91–98, understands translation as a journey. I agree with her that the literal level of a text is no more than a hypothetical concept (p. 91) and that "fidelity means being close, not clinging to surfaces" (p. 92). In Falk's words, "the process of translation is a to-and-fro voyage, toward and away from the shores of the text, until finally one embarks on new land" (91–92).

[100] Four basic types of poetic scansion are currently in vogue among biblical scholars: (1) syllabic, (2) accentual, (3) accentual-syllabic, and (4) quantitative. I do not claim any expertise in scanning poetic meter; one must certainly allow for considerable freedom and variety (see David Noel Freedman, "Another Look at Biblical Hebrew Poetry," in Elaine R. Follis, ed., *Directions in Biblical Hebrew Poetry* [JSOTS 40; Sheffield: JSOT Press, 1987] 11–27, and David W. Cotter, *A Study of Job 4–5 in the Light of Contemporary Literary Theory* (SBLDS 124; Atlanta: Scholars Press, 1992) 48–96. Cotter concludes that the attempts to understand biblical meter have produced chaos: "Accentual, quantitative, word-counting, syllable-counting, letter-counting, constraint-counting welter of confusion that it is . . ." (p. 73).

function as drama, often conveying an emphatic "no" to every attempt at discovering meaning.

Acquiring the right linguistic register for an intended audience is not easy, for one must eschew both the colloquial and the elite, the common and the over-refined, so as to protect the general reader from boredom or bafflement. At times, however, translators may be called on to introduce coarse language into the discourse for its shock value in order to communicate the impact of an Ezekiel's scandalous stories about two sisters, who represent the capital cities of the kingdom of Israel and Judah. Even after completing the appropriate amount of atomistic lexicography and componential analysis, translators cannot successfully reproduce every weight and measure, metaphor, syntactic feature, ambiguity and infelicity. Since they navigate in limbo, translators must create their own gyroscope or compass. In this endeavor nothing compensates for *Sprachgefühl*, a sense or feel for the language—not even good intentions.

In translating the book of Joel I have tried to navigate in treacherous waters, steering between the Scylla of literalism and the Charybdis of paraphrase. Sometimes this strategy has obscured familiar vocabulary, although I have sought in the commentary to call attention to more traditional renderings. For example, whenever the Hebrew text uses the word *lēb* ("heart") in a cognitive sense, I translate accordingly ("mind"). In the most significant such text, 3:1–5 [2:28–32], I dispense with the customary translation of *rûaḥ* ("spirit") in favor of "vital force," for that seems best to convey the meaning in context. Preserving the external form of the ancient language carries no special virtue in my eyes.[101]

Although I do not assume that one should adhere to the Hebrew text for religious reasons, as a matter of principle I translate the text that has been transmitted to today's religious communities, rather than emending it on the basis of ancient translations. In the commentary I try to assess variants insofar as possible, but the excellent state of the Hebrew text except for 1:17 has made the Greek and Latin witnesses less helpful than in some other biblical books. I also refuse to alter the sequence of verses or to delete outright repetitions, knowing

---

[101] To illustrate the point I offer an alternative rendering of the passage in which Joel announces the divine dispersal of the power to prophesy, 3:1–5 [2:28–32]:

> 3:1 [2:28] And it will be afterwards that I shall pour out my spirit on all flesh; your sons and daughters will prophesy, your old people will dream dreams, your young men will see visions. 3:2 [2:29] Also on the male servants and female servants I shall pour out my spirit in those days. 3:3 [2:30] And I shall set portents in the heavens and on earth—blood, fire, and columns of smoke. 3:4 [2:31] The sun will be turned to darkness and the moon to blood before the day of YHWH arrives, terrifyingly great. 3:5 [2:32] And it will be that all who call on YHWH's name will escape, for on Mount Zion and in Jerusalem there will be an escape just as YHWH said, and among survivors whom YHWH calls.

Although staying close to the surface of this significant text, such a translation is inferior, in my judgment, to the one given elsewhere in this commentary.

that repetitions function rhetorically and that not everyone consistently thinks according to modern ideas of logical progression.

ANCIENT TEXTS

Recent discoveries in the Judean desert have yielded a scroll of the Minor Prophets from the era of the second Jewish revolt. This scroll from the Wadi Murabba'at has portions of Joel 2:20–4:21 [3:21].[102] Fragments of the book of Joel have also turned up at Qumran; this text (4 QXII[c]) has tiny segments of 1:11–2:1; 2:8–23; and 4:6–21 [3:6–21]. According to Russell Earl Fuller, it is closer to G than to the Masoretic Text.[103] An unedited manuscript from Qumran Cave IV (4QXIIg) contains portions of Hosea, Joel, Amos, Zephaniah, and Jonah.

Shawn Smith's analysis of the Greek translation of the book of Joel concludes that it is highly consistent in its rendering of specific vocabulary for which parallelism provides a check.[104] A summary of his findings illustrates the point nicely. Nearly 40 percent of the nouns occur more than once. Of the thirty-four nouns occurring twice, twenty-nine are translated identically or have the same root. In four instances that deviate from this practice, the translator sought to avoid confusion or repetition (4:14 [3:14], *ēchoi ex ēchēsan* for *hamônîm hamônîm*; 4:13 [3:13], *hypogēnia* instead of *lēnoi* for *yeqābîm*; 2:23, *brōmata* and *proimon* for *môreh*; and 1:18, *boukolia* and *poimnia* for *ʿedrê*). Only *ʿāsîs* in 1:5 and 4:18 [3:18] cannot be explained this way, suggesting that the translator may not have been familiar with this word in Hebrew for "sweet wine." Of thirty-five words occurring between three and five times in the Hebrew text of Joel, consistency reigns in the Greek, with three exceptions: (1) *en autois* in 1:18 for *behēmâ*, the result of a different dividing of the letters into the preposition *be* plus the plural pronoun *hemmâ*; *pedia* in 2:22 for *neʾôt*; *ischuō* in 4:10 [3:10] for *gibbôr* and *katabarunomenoi* in 2:8. Nouns occurring over five times are translated consistently with two exceptions: *śādeh* (*pedia* in 1:10, 20, and 2:22; *agros* in 1:11, 12, and 19); *bēn* (*teknon* in 1:3 [four times] and 2:23 but *huios* in 1:12, 3:1 [2:28], 4:6 [3:6, three times], 4:8 [3:8, two times], 4:16 [3:16], and 4:19

[102] This second century C.E. scroll, *Murabbaʾat* 88, was discovered in 1955 and published in P. Benoit, J. T. Milik, R. de Vaux, *Les Grottes de Murabba'at* (DJD 2; Oxford: Clarendon Press, 1961) 181–208 (*Texte*), 55–73 (*Planches*).

[103] *The Minor Prophets Manuscripts from Qumran, Cave IV* (Ph.D. diss., Harvard University, 1988), 154.

[104] "The Greek Translation of Joel," an unpublished paper prepared for Professor Melvin Peters at Duke University, January 19, 1987. C. Robert Harrison, Jr., "The Unity of the Minor Prophets in the Septuagint," *BIOSCS* 21 (1988) 55–72, rejected the reigning hypothesis of a single translator of the Minor Prophets in the Septuagint, but Takamitsu Muraoka quickly came to its defense ("In Defense of the Unity of the Septuagint Minor Prophets," *AJBI* 15 [1989] 25–36).

[3:19]). To avoid repetition *ʿām* in 2:17 is rendered *ethnesi.* Such consistency suggests that the translator consulted a text very similar to the present Masoretic Text.

All of the twenty-eight Hebrew imperatives in the book are translated as such in Greek, and only once is a perfect rendered as an imperative. In this instance, *pentheîte* ("mourn") in 1:9 for *ʾābelû* may be correct, given the frequency of imperatives surrounding it. In the Hebrew *Vorlage* the word would have read *ʾblw,* which could have been interpreted as an imperative or a perfect verb. The Masoretes made a mistake reading it as perfect. As for divine names, in thirty of the thirty-three occurrences of YHWH the translator uses *kyrios.* The exceptions are 1:9 where *mešārетê YHWH* is rendered *leitourgountes thusiasterio* ("servants of the altar"); 1:14, where *bêt YHWH ʾelōhêkem* is translated by *oikon theou humōn* ("house of your God"); and 4:11 [3:11], where *estō* ("let . . . become") renders a verb *yihyeh* instead of YHWH. The divine name *ʾelōhîm* always occurs (ten times) as *theos* (in 2:12 the Greek adds *ho theos humōn* ["your God"] to YHWH). In 1:15 the Greek translator probably missed the pun on the name Shaddai, rendering *hōs talaipōria ek talaipōrias* ("as trouble upon trouble") for Hebrew *ûkešōd mišadday.*

According to Benjamin Kedar-Kopfstein, Jerome's translation of the prophetic literature is rather literal, but inconsistent.[105] His commentary on Joel followed the translation by almost fifteen years (c. 392 and 407). In only two places do the editors of *BHS* cite the Vulgate as textual witness for the book of Joel (1:15; 2:23); both times the Vulgate supports the Septuagint. Kedar-Kopfstein notes that the Vulgate's *a a a* in 1:15 "is not a triple exclamation as *BHS* interprets it," but the usual way of translating the Hebrew interjection *ʾahâ* (mirroring it graphically and phonetically).[106] In 2:23 the reliable manuscripts and the lemma to Jerome's commentary lack *sicut,* thus confirming the Masoretic Text. However, he read the future tense *weyorid* instead of completed action (*way-yôred*).

[105] "The Hebrew Text of Joel as Reflected in the Vulgate," *Textus* 9 (1981) 16–35, especially 16–17.

[106] Ibid., 18.

BIBLIOGRAPHY

COMMENTARIES AND MONOGRAPHS ON THE BOOK OF JOEL

Ahlström, G. W. *Joel and the Temple Cult of Jerusalem*. VTS 21. Leiden: E. J. Brill, 1971.

Allen, L. C. *The Books of Joel, Obadiah, Jonah and Micah*. NICOT 13/2. Grand Rapids: William B. Eerdmans Publishing Company, 1976.

Bergler, S. *Joel als Schriftinterpret*. BEATAJ 16. Frankfurt am Main, Bern, New York, Paris: Verlag Peter Lang, 1988.

Bewer, J. A. *Commentary on Obadiah and Joel*. ICC. Edinburgh: T. & T. Clark, 1911 (pp. 49–146 in J. M. P. Smith, W. H. Ward, and J. A. Bewer, A *Critical and Exegetical Commentary on Micah, Zephaniah, Nahum, Habakkuk, Obadiah and Joel*).

Bic, M. *Das Buch Joel*. Berlin: Evangelische Verlagsanstalt, 1960.

Driver, S. R. *The Books of Joel and Amos*. CBSC. Cambridge: University Press, 1907.

Horton, R. F. *The Minor Prophets: Hosea, Joel, Amos, Obadiah, Jonah, and Micah*. CB. Edinburgh: T. C. & E. C. Jack, n.d.

Hubbard, D. A. *Joel & Amos: an Introduction & Commentary*. TOTC. Downers Grove, Illinois, and Leicester, England: Inter-Varsity Press, 1989.

Jungmann, J. *Major Literary Phenomena in the Book of Joel as a Key to the Problem of its Unity and the Date of its Composition*. Ph.D. diss., Hebrew University, Jerusalem, 1987.

Kapelrud, A. S. *Joel Studies*. *UUÅ* 48:4; Uppsala: A. B. Lundequistska Bokhandeln; and Leipzig: Otto Harrassowitz, 1948.

Keller, C. A. *Joël* (pp. 99–155 in E. Jacob, C. A. Keller, and S. Amsler, *Osée Joël Amos Abdias Jonas*). CAT XIa. 2e. Genève: Labor et Fides, 1982 (original 1965).

Loretz, O. *Regenritual und Jahwetag im Joelbuch*. UBL 4. Altenberge: CIS Verlag, 1986.

Marti, K. *Das Dodekapropheton*. KHCAT XIII. Tübingen: Verlag von J. C. B. Mohr (Paul Siebeck), 1904.

Meer, W. van der. *Oude woorden worden nieuw. De opbouw van het boek Joel.* TAuJcc. Kampen: Kok, 1989.

Merx, E. O. A. *Die Prophetie des Joel und ihre Ausleger von den ältesten Zeiten.* Halle: Weisenhaus, 1879.

Nash, K. S. *The Palestinian Agricultural Year and the Book of Joel.* Ph.D. diss., The Catholic University of America, 1989.

Nowack, W. *Die Kleinen Propheten übersetzt und erklärt.* HAT III, 4[3e]. Göttingen: Vandenhoeck & Ruprecht, 1922.

Ogden, G. S. *Joel & Malachi: A Promise of Hope. A Call to Obedience.* ITC. Edinburgh: The Handsel Press Ltd. and Grand Rapids: William B. Eerdmans Publishing Company, 1987.

Orelli, C. von *Die Zwölf Kleinen Propheten.* KK 5/2. München, 1908.

Prinsloo, W. S. *The Theology of the Book of Joel.* BZAW 163. Berlin and New York: Walter de Gruyter, 1985.

Robinson, T. H., and F. Horst *Die zwölf Kleinen Propheten.* HAT XIV 3[e]. Tübingen: *J. C. B. Mohr (Paul Siebeck), 1964.*

Rudolph, W. *Joel-Amos-Obadja-Jona.* KAT XIII. 2. Gütersloh: Gütersloher Verlagshaus Gerd Mohn, 1971.

Sellin, E. *Das Zwölfprophetenbuch.* KAT XII, 2. 3[e]. Leipzig: A. Deichertsche, 1929.

Simkins, R. *Yahweh's Activity in History and Nature in the Book of Joel.* ANETS 10. Lewiston, Queenston, Lampeter: The Edwin Mellen Press, 1991.

Watts, J. D. W. *The Books of Joel, Obadiah, Jonah, Nahum, Habakkuk and Zephaniah.* CBC. Cambridge: Cambridge University Press, 1975.

Weiser, A. *Das Buch der Zwölf Kleinen Propheten.* ATD, 24, 1. 3[e]. Göttingen: Vandenhoeck & Ruprecht, 1959.

Wellhausen, J. *Die Kleinen Propheten: übersetzt und erklärt.* 4[e]. Berlin: Walter de Gruyter, 1898 [1963].

Widmer, G. *Die Kommentare von Raschi, Ibn Esra, Radaq zu Joel: Text, Übersetzung und Erläuterung, ein Einführung in die rabbinische Bibelexegese.* Basil: Volksdruckerei, 1945.

Wolff, H. W. *Joel and Amos: A Commentary on the Books of the Prophets Joel and Amos.* Philadelphia: Fortress Press, 1977 (original, *Dodekapropheton 2 Joel und Amos.* BKAT XIV, 2. 2[e], 1975).

ARTICLES ON THE BOOK OF JOEL AND GENERAL BIBLIOGRAPHY

Aejmelaeus, A.

1986 *The Traditional Prayer in the Psalms.* BZAW 167. Berlin and New York: Walter de Gruyter.

Albertz, R., and C. Westermann
1979a "*Rûaḥ Geist*," *THAT* II:726–53.
1979b "*plʾ ni.* wunderbar sein," *THAT* II:413–20.
Albrekston, B.
1967 *History and the Gods.* Coniectanea Biblica, *OTS* 1. Lund: C. W. K. Gleerup.
Alter, R.
1981 *The Art of Biblical Narrative.* New York: Basic Books, Inc.
Alter, R., and F. Kermode
1987 *The Literary Guide to the Bible.* Cambridge, Massachusetts: The Belknap Press of Harvard University Press.
Andersen, F. I., and D. N. Freedman
1989 *Amos.* AB 24A. New York et al.: Doubleday.
Anderson, G. A.
1989 "Celibacy or Consummation in the Garden. Reflections on Early Jewish and Christian Interpretations of the Garden of Eden," *HTR* 82:121–48.
1991 *A Time to Mourn, a Time to Dance.* University Park, Pennsylvania: The Pennsylvania State University Press.
Andiñach, P. R.
1992 "The Locusts in the Message of Joel," *VT* 42:433–41.
Bach, R.
1962 *Die Aufforderungen zur Flucht und zum Kampf im alttestamentlichen Prophetenspruch.* WMANT 9. Neukirchen-Vluyn: Neukirchener Verlag.
Bal, M.
1985 *Narratology.* Toronto: University of Toronto Press.
Balentine, S. E.
1993 *Prayer in the Hebrew Bible: The Drama of Divine-Human Dialogue.* OBT. Minneapolis: Fortress Press.
Bar-Efrat, S.
1984 *Narrative Art in the Bible.* BLS 17. Sheffield: Almond Press.
Barr, J.
1985 " 'Why?' in Biblical Hebrew," *JTS* 36:1–33.
1960 "Theophany and Anthropomorphism in the Old Testament," *VTS* 7:31–38.
Barstad, H. M.
1984 *The Religious Polemics of Amos.* *VTS* 34. Leiden: E. J. Brill.
Bartlet, V.
1893/4 "Is Joel a Unity?" *ExpTim* 5:567–68.
Bartlett, J.
1989 *Edom and the Edomites.* *JSOTS* 77. Sheffield: JSOT Press.
1982 "Edom and the Fall of Jerusalem, 587 B.C.," *PEQ* 114:13–24.

Baumann, E.
1929 "*twb. bw.* Eine exegetische Untersuchung," ZAW 47:17–44.
Baumgärtel, F.
1961 "Die Formel *nᵉʾum jahwe*," ZAW 73:277–90.
Baumgartner, W.
1920 "Joel 1 und 2," pp. 10–19 in *Karl Budde zum siebsigsten Geburtstag*, ed. K. Marti. BZAW 34. Giessen: Töpelmann.
Begrich, J.
1936 "Die priesterliche Tora," pp. 63–88 in *Werden und Wesen des Alten Testaments*, eds. Paul Volz, Friedrich Stummer, and Johannes Hempel. BZAW 66. Berlin: A. Töpelmann.
Bergman, J., H. Ringgren, and M. Tsevat
1975 "*betûlâ, betûlîm*," *TDOT* 2:338–43.
Berlin, A.
1983 *Poetics and Interpretation of Biblical Narrative*. BLS 9. Sheffield: Almond Press.
Bickerman, E.
1967 *Four Strange Books of the Bible*. New York: Schocken.
Bourke, J.
1959 "Le jour de Yahvé dans Joel," *RB* 66:5–31, 191–212.
Boyce, R. N.
1988 *The Cry to God in the Old Testament*. SBLDS 103. Atlanta: Scholars.
Bracke, J. M.
1985 "*šûb šebût*: A Reappraisal," ZAW 97:233–44.
Brongers, H. A.
1963 "Der Eifer des Herrn Zebaoth," *VT* 13:269–84.
1965 "Bemerken zum Gebrauch des adverbialen *weʿattāh* im Alten Testament," *VT* 15:289–99.
1977 "Fasting in Israel in Biblical and Post-Biblical Times," pp. 1–21 in *Instruction and Interpretation*, ed. A. S. van der Woude. *OTS* 20. Leiden: E. J. Brill.
Buber, M. and F. Rosenzweig
1979 *Die Schrift: Die Hebräische Bibel, Das Alte Testament*, Vol. 1–5. Heidelberg: Verlag Lambert Schneider, 7ᵉ.
Budde, K.
1919a "Der Umschwung in Joel 2," *OL* 22:104–10.
1919b " 'Der von Norden' in Joel 2:20," *OL* 22:1–5.
1922 "Eine folgenschwere Redaktion des Zwölfprophetenbuchs," ZAW 39:218–29.
Cannon, W. W.
1926 " 'The Day of the Lord' in Joel," *CQR* 103:32–63.

Caquot, A.
1978 *"debaš," TDOT* 3:128–31.
Carroll, R.
1982 "Eschatological Delay in the Prophetic Tradition," ZAW 94:47–58.
Centre pour l'Analyse du Discours Religieux
1977 "Prophetie et manipulation: Analyse du livre de Joël," *SB* 7:7–29.
Černy, L.
1948 *The Day of Yahweh and Some Relevant Problems.* Prague: Nakladem Filosoficke Faculty University Karlovy.
Chary, Theophane
1955 *Les prophètes et le culte à partir de l'exil autour du Second Temple. L'ideal cultuel des prophètes exiliens et postexiliens.* Bibliothèque de Théologie 3/3. Tournai: Desclée & Cie.
Childs, B. S.
1959 "The Enemy from the North and the Chaos Tradition," *JBL* 78:187–98.
1974 *The Book of Exodus.* OTL. Philadelphia: Westminster Press.
Christensen, D. L.
1975 *Transformations of the War Oracle in Old Testament Prophecy.* HDR 3. Missoula, Montana: Scholars Press.
Clements, R. E.
1977 "Patterns in the Prophetic Canon," pp. 43–56 in *Canon and Authority,* eds. G. W. Coats and B. O. Long. Philadelphia: Fortress Press.
1985 *In Spirit and in Truth: Insights from Biblical Prayers.* Atlanta: John Knox Press.
Clifford, R. J.
1972 *The Cosmic Mountain in Canaan and the Old Testament.* HSM 4. Cambridge: Harvard University Press.
Clines, D. J. A.
1987 "The Parallelism of Greater Precision," pp. 77–100 in *Directions in Biblical Hebrew Poetry,* ed. E. Follis. *JSOTS* 40. Sheffield: JSOT Press.
1992 "Was There an *ʾBL* II 'Be Dry' in Classical Hebrew?" *VT* 42:1–10.
Collins, J. J.
1984 *The Apocalyptic Imagination.* New York: Crossroads.
Collins, T.
1971 "The Physiology of Tears in the OT," *CBQ* 33:18–38, 195–97.
Conrad, E. W.
1985 *Fear Not, Warrior: A Study of ʾal tîrāʾ Pericopes in the Hebrew Scriptures.* BJS. Atlanta: Scholars Press.

Cotter, D. W.
1992 *A Study of Job 4–5 in the Light of Contemporary Literary Theory*. SBLDS 124. Atlanta: Scholars Press.

Crenshaw, J. L.
1969 "*YHWH ṣebāʾôt šemô*: A Form-Critical Analysis," ZAW 81:156–75.
1971a *Prophetic Conflict: Its Effect Upon Israelite Religion*. BZAW 124. Berlin and New York: Walter de Gruyter.
1971b "A Liturgy of Wasted Opportunity: Am. 4:6–12; Isa. 9:7–10:4; 5:25–29," *Sem* 1:27–37.
1975 *Hymnic Affirmation of Divine Justice. The Doxologies of Amos and Related Texts in the Old Testament*. SBLDS 24. Missoula, Montana: Scholars Press.
1976 "Theodicy," *IDBS*, 895–96.
1981 "The Contest of Darius' Guards in I Esdras 3:1–5:3," pp. 74–88, 119–20 in *Images of Man and God: The Old Testament Short Story in Literary Focus*, ed. B. Long. Sheffield: Almond Press.
1983a "Introduction: The Shift from Theodicy to Anthropodicy," pp. 1–16 in *Theodicy in the Old Testament*. IRT 4. Philadelphia and London: Fortress Press and S.P.C.K.
1983b "A Living Tradition: The Book of Jeremiah in Current Research," *Int* 37:117–29 (100–12 in *Interpreting the Prophets*, eds. J. L. Mays and P. J. Achtemeier. Philadelphia: Fortress Press, 1987).
1985 "Education in Ancient Israel," *JBL* 104:601–15.
1986 "The Expression *mî yôdēaʿ* in the Hebrew Bible," *VT* 36:274–88.
1987 *Ecclesiastes*. OTL. Philadelphia: Westminster Press.
1992a "Theodicy," *ABD* VI:444–47. New York et al.: Doubleday.
1992b "Job, Book of," *ABD* III:858–68.
1994a "Who Knows What Yahweh Will Do? The Character of God in the Book of Joel," pp. 197–209 in *Fortunate the Eyes That See. Essays in Honor of David Noel Freedman in Celebration of his Seventieth Birthday*, ed. A. H. Bartlett et al. Grand Rapids: William B. Eerdmans Publishing Company.
Forthcoming
"The Restraint of Reason, the Humility of Prayer," forthcoming in *Origins: Early Judaism and Christianity in Historical and Ecumenical Perspective (Festschrift for L. H. Silberman)*, part of the Brown Judaic Studies series.
Forthcoming
"Freeing the Imagination: The Conclusion to the Book of Joel," forthcoming in a volume of *Semeia*.

Cresson, B.
1972 "The Condemnation of Edom in Post-Exilic Judaism," pp. 125–48 in *The Use of the Old Testament in the New and Other Essays*, ed. J. M. Efird. Durham: Duke University.
Cross, F. M., Jr.
1973 *Canaanite Myth and Hebrew Epic*. Cambridge, Massachusetts: Harvard University Press.
Dahood, M.
1971 "The Four Cardinal Points in Ps 75,7 and Joel 2,20," *Bib* 52:397.
1977 "Hebrew *tamrûrîm* and *tîmarôt*," *Or* 46:385.
Damrosch, D.
1987 *The Narrative Covenant*. San Francisco: Harper & Row, Publishers.
Deist, F. E.
1988 "Parallels and Reinterpretation in the Book of Joel: A Theology of the Yom Yahweh," pp. 63–79 in *Text and Context: Old Testament and Semitic Studies for F. C. Fensham*, ed. W. Claassen. *JSOTS* 48. Sheffield: JSOT Press.
Dell, K. J.
1991 *The Book of Job as Sceptical Literature*. BZAW 197. Berlin and New York: Walter de Gruyter.
Dennefeld, L.
1924–26 "Les problèmes du livre de Joel," *RSR* 4:555–75; 5:35–37, 591–608, 6:26–49.
Dentan, R. C.
1963 "The Literary Affinities of Exodus XXXIV 6f.," *VT* 13:34–51.
Dommershausen, W.
1975 *"gôrāl," TDOT* 2:450–56.
Dozeman, T. B.
1989 "Inner-Biblical Interpretation of Yahweh's Gracious and Compassionate Character," *JBL* 108:207–23.
Dressler, H. H. P.
1975 "Is the Bow of Aqhat a Symbol of Virility? Ugaritic UZR and Joel 1:13," *UF* 7:221–25.
Driver, G. R.
1938 "Linguistic and Textual Problems: Minor Prophets. III. Joel," *JTS* 39:400–2.
1933 "Studies in the Vocabulary of the Old Testament VI," *JTS* 34:378.
Driver, S. R.
1896 *Einleitung in die Literatur des Alten Testaments*, trans. J. W. Rothstein. Berlin: Reuther.

Duhm, B.
1875 *Die Theologie der Propheten als Grundlage für die innere Entwicklungsgeschichte der israelitischen Religion.* Bonn: Marcus.
1911 "Anmerkungen zu den zwölf Propheten," ZAW 31:161–204.
1922 *Israels Propheten.* Tübingen: Verlag J. C. B. Mohr (Paul Siebeck), 1992, 2[e].
Ellul, D.
1979 "Introduction au livre de Joel," *ETR* 54:426–37.
Engnell, I.
1967 *Studies in Divine Kingship in the Ancient Near East.* Oxford: Basil Blackwell.
Eslinger, L.
1992 "Inner-Biblical Exegesis and Inner-Biblical Allusion: The Question of Category," *VT* 42:47–58.
Evans, C.
1983 "The Prophetic Setting of the Pentecost Sermon," *ZNW* 74:148–50.
Everson, A. J.
1974 "The Days of Yahweh," *JBL* 93:329–37.
Eybers, I. H.
1973 "Dating Joel's Prophecies," *TE* 6:199–223.
Falk, M.
1990 *The Song of Songs: A New Translation and Interpretation.* San Francisco: Harper San Francisco.
Fensham, F. C.
1966 "A Possible Origin of the Concept of the Day of the Lord," pp. 90–97 in *Biblical Essays.* OTWSA 9.
Fishbane, M.
1985 *Biblical Interpretation in Ancient Israel.* Oxford: Clarendon Press.
Fleer, D.
1983 "Exegesis of Joel 2:1–11," *RQ* 26:149–60.
Fohrer, G.
"Zion-Jerusalem in the Old Testament," *TDNT* 7:293–319.
Fowler, H. T.
1897 "The Chronological Position of Joel among the Prophets," *JBL* 16:146–54.
Fox, E.
1983 *In the Beginning: A New English Rendition of the Book of Genesis.* New York: Schocken Books.
1986 *Now These Are the Names: A New English Rendition of the Book of Exodus.* New York: Schocken Books.

Fox, M. V.
1980 "The Identification of Quotations in Biblical Literature," ZAW 92:416–31.
Frankfort, Thérèse
1960 "Le *kî* de Joël 1:12," *VT* 10:445–48.
Fredricksson, H.
1945 *Jahwe als Krieger: Studien zum alttestamentlichen Gottesbild.* Lund: C. W. K. Gleerup.
Freedman, D. N.
1955 "God Compassionate and Gracious," *WW* 6:6–24.
1962 "The Law and the Prophets," *VTS* 9:250–65.
1987a "Another Look at Biblical Hebrew Poetry," pp. 11–27 in *Directions in Biblical Hebrew Poetry,* ed. E. R. Follis, *JSOTS* 40. Sheffield: JSOT Press.
1987b "Headings in the Books of the Eighth-Century Prophets," *AUSS* 25:9–26.
Frerichs, W. W.
1984 "Joel 2:28–9 (and Acts 2 [Pentecost])," *Di* 23:93–96.
Fretheim, T.
1977 *The Message of Jonah: A Theological Commentary.* Minneapolis: Augsburg Publishing Company.
1978 "Jonah and Theodicy," ZAW 90:227–37.
1987 "The Repentance of God: A Study of Jeremiah 18:7–10," *HAR* 11:81–92.
1988 "The Repentance of God: A Key to Evaluating Old Testament God-Talk," *Horizons of Biblical Theology* 10:47–70.
Frye, N.
1982 *The Great Code: The Bible and Literature.* San Diego, New York, London: Harcourt Brace Jovanovich Publishers.
Fuller, R. E.
1988 *The Minor Prophet Manuscripts from Qumran, Cave IV.* Ph.D. diss., Harvard University.
Gamberoni, J.
1974 "Die Geistbegabung im Alten Testament, besonders nach Joel 3,1–5," pp. 9–32 in *Die Gabe Gottes,* ed. P. Nordhues. Paderborn: Bonifacius-Druckerei.
Garrett, D. A.
1985 "The Structure of Joel," *JETS* 28:289–97.
Geertz, C.
1973 *The Interpretation of Cultures.* New York: Basic Books, Inc.
Gelin, A.
1959 "L'annonce de la Pentecôte (Joël 3:1–5)," *BVC* 27:15–19.

Gelston, A.
1987 *The Peshitta of the Twelve Prophets*. Oxford: Clarendon Press.
Gerstenberger, E.
1980 *Der bittende Mensch*. Neukirchen: Neukirchener Verlag.
Gnuse, R. K.
1983 *The Dream Theophany of Samuel*. New York et al.: University Press of America.
Görg, M.
1978 "Eine formelhafte Metapher bei Joel und Nahum," *BN* 6:12–14.
Gray, G. B.
1893 "The Parallel Passages in 'Joel' in Their Bearing on the Question of Date," *Exp* 8:208–25.
Gray, J. A.
1974 "The Day of Yahweh in Cultic Experience and Eschatological Prospect," *SEÅ* 39:5–37.
Greenberg, M.
1983 *Biblical Prose Prayer as a Window to the Popular Religion of Ancient Israel*. Berkeley, Los Angeles, and London: University of California Press.
Greenfield, J. C.
1984 "A Touch of Eden," pp. 219–24 in *Orientalia J. Duchesne-Guillemin Emerito Oblata*, ed. Jacques Duchesne-Guillemin. Acta Iranica, IX, 2nd Series. Leiden: E. J. Brill.
Gunkel, H.
1928 "The Close of Micah: A Prophetic Liturgy," pp. 115–40 in *What Remains of the Old Testament and Other Essays*. New York: Macmillan.
Gunn, D.
1982 "The 'Hardening of Pharaoh's Heart': Plot, Character and Theology in Exodus 1–14," pp. 72–96 in *Art and Meaning: Rhetoric in Biblical Literature*, eds. D. J. A. Clines, D. M. Gunn, and A. J. Hauser. *JSOTS* 19. Sheffield: JSOT Press.
Halévy, J.
1908 "Recherches bibliques, le livre de Joël," *RS* 16:274–84.
Hamp, V.
1975 "*bākhāh*," *TDOT* 2:116–20.
1977a "*ʾeš*," *TDOT* 1:418–28.
1977b "*bārar*," *TDOT* 2:308–12.
Harrison, C. R., Jr.
1988 "The Unity of the Minor Prophets in the Septuagint," *BIOSCS* 21:55–72.

Hasel, G.
1980 "*zā*ᶜ*aq, ze*ᶜ*āqâ, ṣā*ᶜ*aq, ṣe*ᶜ*āqâ,*" *TDOT* 4:112–22.
Héléwa, F. J.
1964 "L'origine du concept prophétique du 'Jour de Yahvé,'" *EC* 15:3–36.
Hiebert, T.
1992a "Joel, Book of," *ABD* III:873–80. New York et al.: Doubleday.
1992b "Theophany in the Old Testament," *ABD* VI:505–11.
Hillers, D. R.
1985 "Analyzing the Abominable: Our Understanding of Canaanite Religion," *JQR* 75:253–69.
1964 *Treaty-Curses and the Old Testament Prophets. BO* 16. Rome: Pontifical Biblical Institute.
1965 "A Convention in Hebrew Literature: The Reaction to Bad News," ZAW 77:86–90.
Hoffmann, Y.
1981 "The Day of the Lord as a Concept and a Term in Prophetic Literature," ZAW 93:37–50.
Holladay, W. L.
1958 *The Root šûbh in the Old Testament*. Leiden: E. J. Brill.
Hölscher, G.
Die Profeten. Untersuchungen zur Religionsgeschichte Israels. Leipzig: J. C. Hinrichs, 1914.
Holzinger, H.
1889 "Sprachcharakter und Abfassungszeit des Buches Joel," ZAW 9:89–131.
Honeyman, A. M.
1952 "Merismus in Biblical Hebrew," *JBL* 71:11–18.
Hopkins, D. C.
1985 *The Highlands of Canaan*. SWBA 3. Sheffield: Almond Press.
Horst, F.
1961 "Zwei Begriffe für Eigentum (Besitz): *naḥalâ* und ᵓ*aḥuzzâ*," pp. 135–56 in *Verbannung und Heimkehr: Beiträge zur Geschichte und Theologie Israels im 6. und 5. Jahrhundert v. Chr.* (*Festschrift für Wilhelm Rudolph*), ed. A. Kuschke. Tübingen: J. C. B. Mohr.
Hosch, H.
1972 "The Concept of Prophetic Time in the Book of Joel," *JETS* 15:31–38.
Hulst, A. R.
1958 "*Kol bāśār* in der priesterlichen Fluterzählung," pp. 28–66 in *Studies on the Book of Genesis, OTS* 12. Leiden: E. J. Brill.

Humbert, P.
1946 *La "Terouᶜa". Analyse d'un rite biblique.* Neuchâtel: Secrétariat de l'Université.
1958 "La formule hebräique en *hineni* suivi d'un participe" pp. 54–59 in *Opuscules d'un Hebräisant.* Mémories de l'Université de Neuchâtel 26. Neuchâtel: Secrétariat de l'Université.
Hurowitz, V. A.
1993 "Joel's Locust Plague in Light of Sargon II's Hymn to Nanaya," *JBL* 112:597–603.
Hvidberg, F. F.
1962 *Weeping and Laughter in the Old Testament.* Nyt Nordisk Forlag, A. Busck, & Leiden: E. J. Brill.
Hyatt, J. P.
1940 "The Peril from the North in Jeremiah," *JBL* 59:499–513.
Jacobs-Hornig, B.
1978 "*gan*," *TDOT* 3:34–39.
Jacobsen, T.
1987 *The Harps That Once . . .* New Haven and London: Yale University Press.
Janzen, W.
1972 *Mourning Cry and Woe Oracle.* BZAW 125. Berlin: Walter de Gruyter.
Jenni, E.
1975 "*yom* Tag," *THAT* 1:707–26.
Jensen, K.
1941 "Indledningsspørgsmaal: Joels Bog," *DTT* 4:98–112.
Jeppesen, K.
1988 "The Day of Yahweh in Mowinckel's Conception Reviewed," *SJOT* 2:42–55.
Jepsen, A.
1938 "Kleine Beiträge zum Zwölfprophetenbuch," ZAW 56:86–96.
Jeremias, G.
1963 *Der Lehrer der Gerechtigkeit.* SUNT 2. Göttingen: Vandenhoeck & Ruprecht.
Jeremias, J.
1965 *Theophanie: Die Geschichte einer alttestamentliche Gattung.* Neukirchen-Vluyn: Neukirchener Verlag.
1987 "Joel/Joelbuch," TRE 17:91–97.
Jerome
1969 "Commentorium in Joelem Prophetam ad Pammachium," pp. 159–209 in *S. Hieronymi Presbyteri Opera*, Pt. 1, Vol. 5.

Corpus Christiana Series Latina, Vol. 76. Turnholt: Editores Pontificii.

Jones, B. A.
1994 *The Formation of the Book of the Twelve: A Study in Text and Canon*, Ph.D. diss., Duke University.

Joüon, P.
1929 "Notes philologiques sur le texte hébreu de Osée 2,7,11; Joel 1,7;1,15 (=Is. 13,6); Jonas 1,8; Habacuc 2,2; Aggee 2,11–14; Zacharie 1,5;3,9; Malachie 1,14," *Bib* 10:417–20.

Karp, L. A. G.
1974 "A Comparative Analysis of Stylistic Embellishment in the Speeches of Hosea and Joel," pp. 55–67 in *Biblical Literature, 1974 Proceedings*, ed. J. D. Francis. Tallahassee: American Academy of Religion.

Katzenstein, J.
1973 *The History of Tyre*. Jerusalem: The Schocken Institute for Jewish Research.

Kedar-Kopfstein, B.
1981 "The Hebrew Text of Joel as Reflected in the Vulgate," *Textus* 9:16–35.

Kennedy, J. M.
1987 "The Root GʿR in the Light of Semantic Analysis," *JBL* 106:47–64.

Kerrigan, A.
1959 "The 'sensus plenior' of Joel III, 1–5 in Acts II, 14–36," pp. 295–313 in *Sacra Pagina. Miscellanea biblica congressus internationalis catholicide re biblica*. BETL 13, ed. J. Coppens et al. Gemblous: Editions J. Duculot.

Klein, R. W.
1968 "Day of the Lord," *CTM* 39:517–25.

Klopfenstein, M. A.
1972 *Scham und Schande nach dem Alten Testament*. ATANT 62. Zurich: Theologischer Verlag.

Koch, K.
1976 "*ṣdq, gemeinschafstren/heilvoll sein*," *THAT* II:507–30.

Köhler, L.
1926 "Die Bezeichnungen der Hauschrecke im AT," *ZDPV* 49:328–33.

Kuhl, C.
1952 "Die 'Wiederaufnahme'—ein literakritisches Prinzip?", ZAW 64:1–11.

Kuschke, A.
1951 "Die Lagervorstellung der priesterschriftlichen Erzählung. Eine überlieferungsgeschichtliche Studie," ZAW 63:84–86.

Kutsch, E.
1952 "Die Wurzel ʿṣr im Hebräischen," *VT* 2:57–69.
1962 "Heuschreckenplage und Tag Jahwes in Joel 1 und 2," *TZ* 18:81–94.

Labuschagne, C. J.
1966 *The Incomparability of Yahweh in the Old Testament*. POS 5. Leiden: E. J. Brill.

Lambert, W. L.
1972 "Destiny and Divine Intervention in Babylon and Israel," pp. 65–72 in *The Witness of Tradition*. *OTS* 17, ed. A. S. van der Woude. Leiden: E. J. Brill.

Largement, R., and H. Lemaitre
1959 "Le jour de Yahweh dans le contexte oriental," pp. 259–66 in *Sacra Pagina*. BETL 12, eds. J. Coppens, A. Descamps, and É. Massaux. Paris: Gabalda; and Gembloux: J. Duculot.

Lattimore, R. E.
1951 *The Date of Joel*. Th.D. diss., Southern Baptist Theological Seminary.

Launderville, D.
1989 "Joel: Prophet and Visionary," *TBT* 27:81–86.

Leibel, D.
1959–60 "On *yeʿabbetun* (Joel:2:7)," *Leš* 24:253.

Levenson, J.
1988 *Creation and the Persistence of Evil*. New York: Harper & Row.

Limburg, J.
1993 *Jonah*. OTL. Louisville, Ky.: Westminster/John Knox Press.

Lindblom, J.
1962 *Prophecy in Ancient Israel*. Philadelphia: Fortress Press.
1965 "Wolff, Hans Walter: Dodekapropheton. Joel," *TLZ* 90:423–24.

Lindsay, J.
1976 "The Babylonian Kings and Edom," *PEQ* 108:23–29.

Lindström, F.
1983 *God and the Origin of Evil*. Coniectanea Biblica, *OTS* 21. Lund: C. W. K. Gleerup.

Loewenstamm, S. E.
1959–60 "*yeʿabbetun = yeʿawwetun*," *Leš* 24:107–8.

Loretz, O.
1986 *Regenritual und Jahwetag in Joelbuch*. UBL 4. Altenberge: CIS Verlag.

Lys, D.
1962 "*Rûach*," *Le souffle dans l'Ancien Testament. Enquête anthropoli-*

gique à travers l'histoire théologique d'Israël. EHPR 56. Paris: Universitaires de France.

van Leeuwen, C.

1974 "The Prophecy of the Yom YHWH in Amos v. 18–20," pp. 113–34 in *Language and Meaning. OTS* 19, ed. J. Barr et al. Leiden: E. J. Brill.

1988 "Tekst, structuur en betekenis van Joel 2:1–11," *NTT* 42:89–98.

Magonet, J.

1983 *Form and Meaning: Studies in Literary Techniques in the Book of Jonah.* BLS 8. Sheffield: Almond Press.

Malamat, A.

1955 "Doctrines of Causality in Hittite and Biblical Historiography: A Parallel," *VT* 5:1–12.

Mallon, E. D.

1983 "A Stylistic Analysis of Joel 1:10–12," *CBQ* 45:537–48.

Mann, T. W.

1971 "The Pillar of Cloud in the Reed Sea Narrative," *JBL* 90:15–30.

Mariès, L.

1950 "A propos de récentes études sur Joël," *RSR* 37:121–24.

Mariottini, F. C.

1987 "Joel 3:10 [H 4:10]. 'Beat Your Plowshares into Swords,'" *Pers* 14:125–30.

McHatten, M. T.

1979 *The Day of Yahweh: A Study of the Concept Yom Yahweh in the Old Testament.* Ph.D. diss., University of Ottawa.

Mettinger, T. N. D.

1988 *In Search of God: The Meaning and Message of the Everlasting Names.* Philadelphia: Fortress Press.

Meyers, C. L. and E. M.

1987 *Haggai, Zechariah 1–8.* AB 26B. Garden City, New York: Doubleday & Company.

Milik, J. T., R. de Vaux, and P. Benoit

1961 *Les Grottes de Murabbaʿat.* DJD 2. Oxford: Clarendon Press.

Millard, A. R.

1984 "The Etymology of Eden," *VT* 34:103–6.

Miller, P. D., Jr.

1965 "Fire in the Mythology of Canaan and Israel," *CBQ* 27:256–61.

1968 "The Divine Council and the Prophetic Call to War," *VT* 18:100–7.

1973 *The Divine Warrior in Early Israel.* Cambridge, Massachusetts: Harvard University Press.

1980 "Studies in Hebrew Word Patterns," *HTR* 73:79–89.

Miner, E.
1986 "Allusion," p. 10 in *The Princeton Handbook of Poetic Terms,* ed. A. Preminger. Princeton: Princeton University Press.

Moldenke, H. N. and A. L.
1952 *Plants of the Bible.* Cambridge: Chronica Botanica.

Moore, M. S.
1987 "Yahweh's Day," *RQ* 29:193–208.

Moulton, R. G.
1915 *The Modern Study of Literature.* Chicago: University of Chicago Press.

Mowinckel, S.
1934 "The 'Spirit' and the 'Word' in the Pre-exilic Reforming Prophets," *JBL* 53:199–227.
1954 *He That Cometh.* Nashville: Abingdon Press.

Muffs, Y.
1975 "Joy and Love as Metaphorical Expressions of Willingness and Spontaneity in Cuneiform, Ancient Hebrew, and Related Literatures: Divine Investitures in the Midrash and in the Light of Neo-Babylonian Royal Grants," pp. 1–36 in *Christianity, Judaism, and Other Greco-Roman Cults* III, ed. J. Neusner, Leiden: E. J. Brill.

Müller, H. P.
1966 "Prophetie und Apokalyptik bei Joel," *TV* 10:231–52.

Munch, P. A.
1936 *The Expression Bayyôm hahūʾ. Is It an Eschatological Terminus Technicus.* Avhandlinger Uttgitt av Det Norske Videnskaps-Akademi i Oslo II. Hist. Filos. Klasse, 2. Oslo: Jacob Dybwab.

Muraoka, T.
1989 "In Defense of the Unity of the Septuagint Minor Prophets," *AJBI* 15:25–36.

Myers, J. M.
1962 "Some Considerations Bearing on the Date of Joel," ZAW 74:177–95.

Nash, K. S.
1989 "The Cycle of Seasons in Joel," *TBT* 27:74–80.

Neil, W.
1962 "Joel, Book of," *IDB* 2:926–29.

Nestle, E.
1900 "Miscellen: 1. Joel 1,17," ZAW 20:164–65.
1904 "Miscellen. 1. Zur Kapiteleinteilung in Joel," ZAW 24:122–27.

Nogalski, J.
1993 *Literary Precursors to the Book of the Twelve.* BZAW 217. Berlin and New York: Walter de Gruyter.

1993 *Redactional Processes in the Book of the Twelve*. BZAW 218. Berlin and New York: Walter de Gruyter.

Ogden, G. S.

1983 "Joel 4 and Prophetic Responses to National Laments," *JSOT* 26:97–106.

Palmoni, J.

1962 "Locust," *IDB* 3:144–48.

Paul, S. M.

1991 *Amos*. Hermeneia. Minneapolis: Fortress Press.

Pelli, Moshe

1979–80 "The Literary Art of Jonah," *HS* 20/21:18–28.

Petersen, D. L.

1984 *Haggai and Zechariah 1–8*, OTL. Philadelphia: Westminster Press.

Plath, M.

1929 "Joel 1:5–20," ZAW 47:159–60.

Plöger, O.

1968 *Theocracy and Eschatology*. Richmond: John Knox Press.

Preminger, A., and E. L. Greenstein, eds.

1986 *The Hebrew Bible in Literary Criticism*. New York: Ungar.

Preuschen, E.

1895 " 'Die Bedeutung von *šûb šebût* im Alten Testaments. Eine alte Controverse," ZAW 15:1–74.

Prinsloo, W. S.

1985 *The Theology of the Book of Joel*. BZAW 163. Berlin & New York: Walter de Gruyter.

1992 "The Unity of the Book of Joel," ZAW 104:66–81.

van der Ploeg, J. P. M.

1972 "Eschatology in the Old Testament," pp. 89–99 in *The Witness of Tradition*. *OTS* 17, ed. A. S. van der Woude. Leiden: E. J. Brill.

Rabinowitz, I.

1958 "The Guide of Righteousness," *VT* 8:391–404.

Rabinowitz, P. J.

1987 *Before Reading: Narrative Conventions and the Politics of Interpretation*. Ithaca, New York: Cornell University.

Rad, G. von

1958 *Der Heilige Krieg im Alten Israel*. 3[e] Göttingen: Vandenhoeck & Ruprecht. (English translation, *Holy War in Ancient Israel*. Trans. Marva J. Dawn. Grand Rapids: William B. Eerdmans Publishing Co., 1991.)

1959 "The Origin of the Concept of the Day of Yahweh," *JSS* 4:97–108.

1965 *Old Testament Theology*, I–II. New York: Harper & Row.

Raitt, T. M.
1971 "The Prophetic Summons to Repentance," ZAW 83:30–49.
Redditt, P. L.
1986 "The Book of Joel and Peripheral Prophecy," *CBQ* 48:225–40.
1989 "The Book of Joel: An Overview," *TBT* 27:69–73.
Reicke, B.
1967 "Liturgical Traditions in Mic. 7," *HTR* 60:349–67.
Reimer, D. J.
1989 "The 'Foe' and the 'North' in Jeremiah," ZAW 101:223–32.
Rendtorff, R.
1968 "*nabîʾ* in the Old Testament," *TDNT* 6:796–812.
Reventlow, H. G.
1986 *Gebet im Alten Testament*. Stuttgart: Kohlhammer.
Reymond, P.
1958 *L'eau, sa vie, et sa signification dans l'AT*. *VTS* 6. Leiden: E. J. Brill.
Rimbach, J. A.
1981 "Those Lively Prophets: Joel ben Pethuel," *CTM* 8:302–4.
Ringgren, H.
1963 "Einige Schilderungen des göttlichen Zorns," pp. 107–13 in *Tradition und Situation*, eds. E. Würthwein and Otto Kaiser. Göttingen: Vandenhoeck & Ruprecht.
Robert, A.
1934/35 "Les attaches littéraires bibliques des Prov. I–IX," *RB* 43:42–68, 172–204, 374–84, and 44:344–65, 502–25.
Robinson, D.
1991 *The Translator's Turn*. Baltimore: Johns Hopkins University Press.
Romerowski, S.
1993 "Joel et le Culte," *BRT* 3:18–35.
Rostovtzeff, M.
1941 *Social and Economic History of the Hellenistic World*. Oxford: Oxford University Press.
Roth, C.
1963 "The Teacher of Righteousness and the Prophecy of Joel," VT 13:91–95.
Rudolph, W.
1967a "Ein Beitrag zum hebräischen Lexikon aus dem Joelbuch," VTS 16:244–50.
1967b "Wann wirkte Joel?" pp. 193–98 in *Das Ferne und nahe Wort*, ed. F. Maass. BZAW 105. Berlin: Töpelmann.
Saebo, M.
1979 "*sōd*" *Geheimnis*," *THAT* II:144–48.

Sakenfeld, K.
1985 *Faithfulness in Action: Loyalty in Biblical Perspective.* OBT. Philadelphia: Fortress.

Sasson, J. M.
1990 *Jonah.* AB 24B. New York et al.: Doubleday.

Scharbert, J.
1957 "Formgeschichte und Exegese von Ex 34,6f und seiner Parallelen," *Bib* 38:130–50.

Schmid, H. H.
1968 *Gerechtigkeit als Weltordnung.* BHT 40. Tübingen: Mohr.

Schmidt, L.
1976 *"De Deo": Studien zur literaturkritik und Theologie des Buches Jona, des Gesprächs zwischen Abraham und Jahwe in Gen 18, 22ff. und Hi 1.* BZAW 143. Berlin and New York: Walter de Gruyter.

Schmidt, W.
1963 "*miškān* als Ausdruck Jerusalemer Kultsprache," ZAW 75:91–92.

Schmidt, W. H.
1976 "*ṣāfôn* Norden," *THAT* II:575–82.

Schneider, D. A.
1979 *The Unity of the Book of the Twelve.* Ph.D. diss., Yale University.

Schnutenhaus, F.
1964 "Das Kommen und Erscheinen Gottes im Alten Testament," ZAW 76:1–21.

Schunck, K. D.
1964 "Strukturlinien in der Entwicklung der Vorstellung vom 'Tag Jahwes,' " *VT* 14:319–30.

Schungel, P. H.
1968 "Noch einmal zu *qbṣw pʾrwr* Jo 2,6 und Nah 2,11," *BN* 7:29–31.

Scott, R. B. Y.
1952 "Meteorological Phenomena and Terminology in the Old Testament," ZAW 64:11–25.

Sellers, O. R.
1935–36 "Stages of Locust in Joel," *AJSL* 52:81–85.
1955 "A Possible Old Testament Reference to the Teacher of Righteousness," *IEJ* 5:93–95.

Seybold, K.
1978 "*gāmal; gāmûl; gemûl; gemûlâ; taghmûl,*" *TDOT* 3:23–33.

Shapiro, H.
1979/80 "Joel," pp. 197–209 in *Congregation: Contemporary Writers Read the Jewish Bible*, ed. D. Rosenberg. San Diego: Harcourt Brace Jovanovich.

Simkins, R.
Forthcoming
"'Return to Yahweh': Honor and Shame in Joel," forthcoming in a volume of *Semeia*.

Skehan, P. W.
1971 *Studies in Israelite Poetry and Wisdom*. CBQMS 1. Washington: The Catholic Biblical Association of America.

Smelik, K. A. D.
1986 "The Meaning of Amos 5:18–20," *VT* 36:246–48.

Smith, J. Z.
1975 "Wisdom and Apocalyptic," pp. 131–56 in *Religious Syncretism in Antiquity*, ed. B. Pearson. Missoula, Montana: Scholars Press.
1978 "Sacred Persistence: Towards a Redescription of Canon," pp. 11–28 in *Approaches to Ancient Judaism*, Vol. 1, ed. W. S. Green. Missoula, Montana: Scholars Press.

Smith, M.
1972 *Palestinian Parties that Shaped the Old Testament*. New York: Columbia University Press.

Smith, P. J.
1982/83 "A Discourse-Analytical Discussion of Joel 1.1–2.17," pp. 150–62 in *The Exilic Period—Aspects of Apocalypticism*, ed. W. C. van Wyk. OTWSA 25/26.

Smith, S.
1987 "The Greek Translation of Joel," unpublished paper presented to Professor Melvin Peters, Duke University.

Soggin, J. A.
1976 "*šûb* zuruckkehren," *THAT* II:886–88.

Sprengling, M.
1919 "Joel 1:17A," *JBL* 38:129–41.

Stähli, H. P.
1978 "*yrʾ* furchten," *THAT* I:765–78.

Stephensen, F. R.
1961 "The Date of the Book of Joel," *VT* 19:224–29.

Sternberg, M.
1985 *The Poetics of Biblical Narrative*. Bloomington: Indiana University Press.

Stocks, H. H. D.
1908 "Der 'Nordliche' und die Komposition des Buches Joel," *NKZ* 19:725–50.

Stoebe, H. J.
1979 "*rḥm* pi-sich erbarmen," in *THAT* II:762–68.

Stolz, F.
1978 "*boš* zuschanden werden," *THAT* I:269–72.
Stuart, D.
1976 "The Sovereign's Day of Conquest," *BASOR* 221:159–64.
Taylor, A.
1951 "A Riddle for a Locust," pp. 429–32 in *Semitic and Oriental Studies: A Volume Presented to William Popper*, ed. W. J. Fischel. UCPSP II. Berkeley: University of California Press.
Thompson, J. A.
1955 "Joel's Locusts in Light of Near Eastern Parallels," *JNES* 14:52–55.
1956 "The Book of Joel," *IB* 6:729–60.
1974 "The Use of Repetition in the Prophecy of Joel," pp. 101–10 in *On Language, Culture and Religion: In Honor of Eugene A. Nida*, eds. M. Black and W. Smalley. Approaches to Semiotics 56; The Hague: Mouton.
1974 "The Date of Joel," pp. 453–64 in *A Light unto My Path. Old Testament Studies in Honor of J. M. Myers*, eds. H. N. Bream et al. Philadelphia: Temple University.
Tobias, H.
1986 "Joel: His Life and Times," *BI* 12:56–59.
Treves, M.
1957 "The Date of Joel," *VT* 7:149–56.
Trible, P.
1978 *God and the Rhetoric of Sexuality.* OBT 2. Philadelphia: Fortress Press.
Uvarov, B. P.
1928 *Locust and Grasshoppers*, I–II. London: Imperial Institute of Entomology.
Van Leeuwen, C.
1979 "*nqh* ni. schuldlos sein," *THAT* II:101–6.
Vanderkam, J. C.
1984 *Enoch and the Growth of an Apocalyptic Tradition.* CBQMS 16. Washington, D.C.: The Catholic Biblical Association of America.
Vanoni, G.
1978 *Das Buch Jona.* St. Ottilien: Eos.
Vernes, M.
1872 *Le peuple d'Israël et ses espérances relative à son avenir depuis les origines jusqu'à l'epoque persane* (V[e]*siècle avant J. C.*). Paris: Sandoz et Fischbacher.
Vetter, D.
1979 "*neʾum* Ausspruch," *THAT* II:2–3.

Vogels, W. A.
1991 Review of Willem van der Meer, *Oude woorden worden nieuw* (Theologische Academic uitgaande van de Johannes Calvignstichting te Kampen; Kampen: Kok, 1989) *CBQ* 53:296–97.

Vriezen, Th. C.
1953 "Prophecy and Eschatology," pp. 199–229 in *Congress Volume: Copenhagen, 1953*. *VTS* 1. Leiden: E. J. Brill.

Wagner, S.
1990 "*yārâ*ʾ II; *yôreh; môreh*," *TDOT* 6:336–39.

Wanke, G.
1979 "*naḥala* Besitzanteil," *THAT* II:55–59.
1984 "Prophecy and Psalms in the Persian Period," pp. 174–77 in *The Cambridge History of Judaism*, eds. W. D. Davies and L. Finkelstein, vol. 1. Cambridge: Cambridge University Press.

Weingren, J.
1961 "The Title *môreh ṣedek*," *JSS* 6:162–74.

Weippert, M.
1979 "*šadday* Gottesname," *THAT* II:873–81.

Weise, M.
1957–65 "Joelbuch," pp. 800–2 in *Die Religion in Geschichte und Gegenwart*, 3, ed. K. Galling. Tübingen: J. C. B. Mohr (P. Siebeck).

Weiss, M.
1966 "The Origin of the 'Day of the Lord' Reconsidered," *HUCA* 37:29–72.

Welch, A.
1920 "Joel and the Post-exilic Community," *Exp* 20:161–80.

Wenham, G. J.
1972 "*Betûlāh*. 'A girl of Marriageable Age,' " *VT* 22:326–48.

Whiting, J. D.
1915 "Jerusalem's Locust Plague," *National Geographic* 28:512–50.

Whitley, C. F.
1984 "*ʿbt* in Joel 2,7," *Bib* 65:101–2.

Whybray, R. N.
1974 *The Intellectual Tradition in the Old Testament*. BZAW 135. Berlin and New York: Walter de Gruyter.

Wilson, R.
1980 *Prophecy and Society in Ancient Israel*. Philadelphia: Fortress Press.

Wolfe, R. E.
1935 "The Editing of the Book of the Twelve," ZAW 53:90–129.

Wolff, H. W.
1951 "Das Theme 'Umkehr' in der alttestamentlichen Prophetie," ZTK 48:129–48.

1977 *Joel and Amos*. Hermeneia. Philadelphia: Fortress Press.
1984 "Schwerter zu Pflugscharen—Missbrauch eines Prophetenwortes," *EvT* 44:280–92.
1985 "Swords into Plowshares: Misuse of a Word of Prophecy (Joel 3; Isa 2, Mic 4)," *CurTM* 12:133–47.

Wood, G. E.
1968 "Joel, Obadiah," pp. 439–45 in *The Jerome Biblical Commentary*, ed. R. E. Brown et al. Englewood Cliffs, New Jersey: Prentice Hall.

Wright, A. D. G.
1968 "The Riddle of the Sphinx: The Structure of the Book of Qoheleth," *CBQ* 39:313–34.
1980 "The Riddle of the Sphinx Revisited: Numerical Patterns in the Book of Qoheleth," *CBQ* 42:35–51.
1983 "Additional Numerical Patterns in Qoheleth," *CBQ* 45:32–43.

Zimmerli, W.
1963 "Erkenntnis Gottes nach dem Buch Ezechiel," pp. 41–119 in *Gottes Offenbarung*. München: Chr. Kaiser Verlag. E.T. "Knowledge of God According to the Book of Ezekiel," pp. 29–98 in *I Am Yahweh*. Atlanta: John Knox Press, 1982.
1968 *Ezechiel*. BKAT 13/15. Neukirchen-Vluyn: Neukirchener Verlag.

Zimmerman, Frank
1954 "Some Textual Studies in Genesis," *JBL* 73:97–101.

Zobel, J.-J.
1990 "*yiśrāʾēl*," *TDOT* 6:397–420.

NOTES AND COMMENTS

THE SUPERSCRIPTION (1:1)

1:1 YHWH's word entrusted to Joel, Pethuel's son.

NOTES

1:1 In the Book of the Twelve only the headings in Joel and Jonah limit the information to the prophet's name and to that of his father ("when YHWH's word came to Jonah, Amittai's son," Jonah 1:1). The superscription to the book of Jonah differs from Joel, however, in two essentials. First, the verb *wayehi* stands in the initial position, as in Ruth 1:1, introducing a circumstantial clause modifying another verb, and second, *lēʾmōr*, an ancient equivalent of quotation marks (M. V. Fox 1980:416–31), concludes the sentence (cf. Hag 1:1; Zech 1:1). Formally closer to Joel's biographical heading, therefore, are the introductions to Hosea, Micah, and Zephaniah. In two of these books the title begins with acknowledgment that YHWH's message was granted to a prophet whose name and that of his father are given; Micah substitutes his place of residence (cf. Nah 1:1). These superscriptions also offer additional information—the names of four kings in Judah and one king in Israel during Hosea's activity, the names of three kings in Judah during Micah's time, and the name of only one king in Judah during Zephaniah's prophetic ministry. The heading in Micah also adds an observation about the presumed audience for whom the divine message was made available to the prophet ("Yahweh's word . . . that he saw concerning Samaria and Jerusalem," the capital cities of the two kingdoms, Israel and Judah, serving as *pars pro toto* and thus communicating the vast sweep of Micah's interest). Among these headings, only Zeph 1:1 includes the names of the prophet's grandfather (Gedaliah), great-grandfather (Amariah), and great-great-grandfather (Hezekiah). In all the prophetic inscriptions, only one king of Israel is mentioned, Jeroboam II (Hos 1:1; Amos 1:1; cf. D. N. Freedman 1987b:9–26).

entrusted (lit., "was" = "came"). The verb *hāyâ*, when linked with a prophet's name by *ʾel*, carries the nuance of commissioning. The prophet is designated as an envoy in divine service, Joel having been granted YHWH's message to Judeans. The singular word of YHWH, as opposed to human words, came to

Joel, whose responsibility was to interpret it faithfully in light of his understanding of the tradition. The complete revelatory event included (1) the initial word or vision, (2) the prophet's reflection on its meaning, (3) the poetic articulation of that message in the language of the people, (4) the addition of reasons, threats, or admonitions, and (5) the actual delivery of the prophetic message, accompanied by gestures and intonations no longer accessible to readers of the written account of that event. The antecedent of *ʾašer*, not represented in the translation, is *debar* rather than YHWH; the alternative rendering, "The word of YHWH who came to Joel the son of Pethuel," while syntactically possible, misses the sense of the formulation.

Joel. Except for 1 Sam 8:2, the name Joel occurs elsewhere only in the Chronicler's genealogical lists (1 Chr 4:35; 5:4, 8, 12; 6:18 [33], 21 [36]; 7:3; 11:38; 15:7, 11, 17; 23:8; 26:22; 27:20; 2 Chr 29:12; Ezra 10:43; Neh 11:9). The extensive Levitical connections (1 Chr 6:21 [36]; 15:7, 11, 17; 23:8; 26:22; 2 Chr 29:12) and the association of the name with various tribal ancestors—Simeon, Reuben, Gad, Issachar, Manasseh—are noteworthy. The name Joel was therefore common during the time of the Chronicler but not before then, according to the biblical record.

Pethuel. The Greek *bathouel* identifies the name with that of Rebekah's father, Bethuel, in Gen 22:22–23; 24:15, 24, 47, 50, which occurs elsewhere only in Josh 19:4 and 1 Chr 4:30. Support for this reading appears in the Peshitta and Vetus Latina, but Greek 86, Targum, and Vulgate follow the Masoretic Text. The possibility cannot be ruled out that both the names Joel and Pethuel are symbolic. Abraham Kuenen believed that Joel was the result of reversing the name Elijah (see J. A. Bewer 1911:75); similarly, Pethuel could mean "The One Seduced by God." The book of Joel certainly uses at least one symbolic name, the valley of Jehoshaphat ("YHWH has rendered judgment") in which YHWH will enter into judgment (4:12 [3:12]), to which may be compared *beʿēmeq heḥārûṣ* ("in the valley of decision," 4:14 [3:14]).

SUPERSCRIPTIONS IN THE BOOK OF THE TWELVE

Hos 1:1	*debar-YHWH*	*ʾašer hāyâ*	*ʾel-hôšēaʿ*	*ben-beʾērî*	*bîmê. . . .*
Joel 1:1	*debar YHWH*	*ʾašer hāyâ*	*ʾel-yôʾēl*	*ben-petûʾēl*	
Amos 1:1	*diḇrê ʾāmôs*	*ʾašer-hāyâ*	*bannōqedîm . . .ʾašer ḥāzâ*		*bîmê. . . .**
Ob 1	*ḥazôn ʿobadyâ*				
Jonah 1:1	*wayehî debar-YHWH*		*ʾel-yônâ*	*ben-ʾamittai lēʾmōr*	
Mic 1:1	*debar-YHWH*	*ʾašer hāyâ*	*ʾel-mikâ hammōraštî*		*bîmê. . . .*†
Nah 1:1	*maśśāʾ nînevēh śēper* *ḥāzôn naḥûm haʾelqōšî*				

Hab 1:1	*hammaśśāʾ*	*ʾăšer ḥāzâ habaqqûq hannābîʾ*			
Zeph 1:1	*debar-YHWH*	*ʾăšer hāyâ*	*ʾel-ṣepanyâ*	*ben kûšî . . .*	*bîmê. . . .*
Hag 1:1	*bišnat štayîm ledāryāweš . . . hāyâ debar-YHWH*		*beyad-haggai hannābî*‡		
Zech 1:1	*baḥodeš haššemînî . . . hāyâ debar-YHWH*		*ʾel-zekaryâ ben . . . hannābî*§		
Mal 1:1	*maśśāʾ debar-YHWH*		*ʾel-yiśrāʾēl*	*beyad malʾākî*	

* *šnatayîm lipnê hārāʿaš*
† *ʾăšer-ḥāzâ ʿal-šōmerôn wîrûšālēm*
‡ *ʾel-zerubbābel . . . weʾel yehôšuaʿ . . . lēʾmōr*
§ *lēʾmōr*

SUPERSCRIPTIONS IN ISAIAH, JEREMIAH, AND EZEKIEL

Isa 1:1	*ḥazôn yešaʿyāhû ben-ʾāmôṣ wîrûšālēm bîmê. . . .*	*ʾăšer ḥāzâ*	*ʿal-yehûdāh*
Jer 1:1	*dibrê yirmeyāhû ben-hilqiyyāhû* min-hakkōhanîm. . . .*		
Ezek 1:1	*wayehî bišlōšîm šānâ . . . waʾanî . . . waʾereh marʾôt ʾelōhîm*		

*Cf. Prov 30:1 *dibrê ʾagûr bin-yāqeh hammaśśāʾ*
Prov 31:1 *dibrê lemuʾēl melek maśśā ʾăšer-yisserattû ʾimmo*
Eccl 1:1 *dibrê qōhelet ben-dāwid melek bîrûšālēm*

COMMENT

The heading to the entire book reinforces the two oracular references, *neʾum YHWH* in 2:12 and *kî YHWH dibbēr* in 4:8 [3:8]. Joel does not ordinarily distinguish carefully between those statements represented as divine speech (only 2:12, 19–20, 24–30; 3:1–5 [2:28–32]; 4:1–8, 21 [3:1–8, 21]) and his own words to the Judeans, although pronominal subjects and suffixes assist readers in determining who purports to be speaking, e.g. *ʾarṣî* ("my land," 1:6), *rûḥî* ("my spirit," 3:1 [2:28]) and *ʿammî wenaḥalātî yiśrāʾēl* ("my people and Israel, my possession," 4:2 [3:2]). The manner by which YHWH communicated to the prophet—whether audition or vision—is not reported, whereas Amos 1:1 combines visionary and auditory reception in the same way the book of Amos intermingles oracles and visions. The heading of Micah also includes references to oracle and vision, whereas Nah 1:1 and Hab 1:1 combine visionary communication with verbal, though using the foreboding word *maśśāʾ* (*hammaśśāʾ*, Hab 1:1) and Ob 1 restricts itself to vision. The superscription to Joel emphasizes the divine source of the prophet's interpretation of vexing events and the means by which the Judeans may claim YHWH's promises.

The meager information about Joel is limited to his name and patronym, both of which bear religious affirmations. Like the name Elijah, Joel probably means "YHWH is God"; this confession attests to belief in YHWH's sovereignty rather than equating the Canaanite God El with YHWH. The names of Samuel's two sons are probably symbolic affirmations (1 Sam 8:2): Joel ("YHWH is El") and Abiyah ("YHWH is my Father"). The equation of Israel's deity with the head of the Canaanite pantheon was highly polemic. If the form is verbal rather than nominative, it might mean "(YHWH) is willing." Pethuel, Joel's father's name, means "seduced (persuaded) by God," probably without any pejorative sense, or "youth of God" (cf. Peniel). This reference to Pethuel is unique in the Bible, which may explain the Greek substitution of a more familiar name, Bethuel. The heading lacks any data about the historical period during which Joel addressed the Judeans, perhaps because his activity did not correspond with the reigns of any Israelite or Judean kings. Joel is not even called a prophet, but this reticence is not unusual; only Hab 1:1 and Zech 1:1 explicitly designate the recipient of the divine oracle a *nābîʾ*.

Divine Judgment Against Judah and Its Response (1:2–2:17)

A Summons to Lament and Return to YHWH (1:2–20)

1:2 Take heed to this, old timers,
listen, every local resident.
Has anything comparable happened in your time
or in that of your parents?

1:3 Tell it to your children;
and they to theirs,
and their children to the next generation.

1:4 What the chewer left the swarming locust consumed;
and what the swarming locust left the jumper ate;
what the jumper left the finisher devoured.

1:5 Wake up, imbibers, and weep;
sob, all who drink wine,
because of the sweet wine denied you.

1:6 For a nation has attacked my land,
one powerful and innumerable,
with leonine teeth and fangs.

1:7 It made my vineyard into a desolation,
and my fig trees into splinters,
stripping off the bark and hurling it aside,
leaving whitened cuttings.

1:8 Cry aloud like a young woman clothed in sackcloth,
over the husband of her youth.

1:9 Cereal offering and libation are withheld
from YHWH's house;
the priests mourn—
YHWH's officials.

1:10 The fields are devastated,
the ground groans;
indeed, the grain is destroyed,
the wine dried up, the oil depleted.

1:11 Be ashamed, farmers;
sob, vintners,
on account of wheat and barley;
for the harvest is ruined.

1:12 The vine has withered,
the fig is scorched,
pomegranate, date, and apple—
every tree in the orchard has wilted;
indeed, joy has utterly vanished
from the populace.

1:13 Don mourning garments and lament, priests;
sob, presiders over the altar;
come, spend the night in sackcloth,
ministers of my God;
for withheld from your God's house
are cereal offering and libation.

1:14 Arrange a sacred fast,
announce a religious assembly;
gather the elderly,
every resident of the area,
to the house of YHWH your God;
and cry out to YHWH.

1:15 That day! Horrors!
For YHWH's day is imminent,
dawning like destruction from the Destroyer.

1:16 Is food not being cut off
before our very eyes,
joy and gladness,
from the house of our God?

1:17 Seeds have shriveled under their shovels;
storage bins are desolate,
granaries ruined;
for the grain has dried out.

1:18 How the beasts moan,
the herds weep,
for lack of fodder;
even flocks of sheep are hurting.

1:19 To you, YHWH, I cry out;
for fire has consumed the pasture land,
a flame has licked all the trees in the field.

1:20 Even the beasts in the field
complain to you;
for the water sources have dried up,
and fire has devoured the pasture land.

NOTES

1:2 *Take heed.* The initial strophe (1:2–4) launches the prophet's rhetorical strategy—balanced imperatives and vocatives, with a lone direct object suspended in air and left unspecified. Joel's invitation to pay attention is a widespread phenomenon, occurring within biblical parenesis as diverse as Deuteronomic teachings, proverbial maxims, and prophetic oracles. Wolff's claim that the call to attention derives from sapiential instruction (1977:25–26) lacks credibility in light of its applicability to virtually any situation. One need not read long in ancient Near Eastern literature outside the Bible to come across examples of the appeal for an attentive audience.

Come here, Enmerkar,
let me instruct you,
and may you take my advice,
let me say a word to you,
and may you listen!

Jacobsen 1987:284

Sapsu calls out to Mot:
Hear, O you *mt bn il!*
How can you contend with *ʿAliyan baʿlu?*

IAB col. VI

An exact formal parallel to Joel's use occurs in Hos 5:1 where imperatives and vocatives balance each other and where an unspecified demonstrative pronoun conceals the topic the people are being called to hear.

šimʿû zōʾt hakkōhanîm
wehaqšîbû bêt yiśrāʾēl
Take heed to this, priests,
and pay attention, house of Israel.

Hos 5:1

One may also compare Mic 3:9.

šimʿû-nāʾ zōʾt raʾšê bêt yaʿăqob
ûqeṣînê bêt yiśrāʾēl
Take heed to this, leaders of the house of Jacob,
and decision-makers of the house of Israel.

In the first line, which alone resembles Hos 5:1, the particle of entreaty, *nāʾ*, provides ballast (cf. Mic 3:1, *šimʿû-nāʾ raʾšé yāʿaqōb ûqeṣînê bêt yiśrāʾēl*).

The rich vocabulary for hearing prevented the expressions from becoming fixed, as the data in a concordance quickly demonstrate. The imperative *šimʿû* is found in parallelism with several verbs (*ʾzn, qšb, rʾh, qbṣ, ydʿ*, etc.), and the practice extends from earliest times to postexilic literature. Nevertheless, one finds *šimʿû* paired with *haʾazînû* in archaic poetry and in eighth-century prophecy.

šimʿû melākîm
haʾazînû rōzenîm
Take heed, kings,
listen rulers.

Judg 5:3 (cf. Gen 4:23)

šimʿû šāmayîm
wehaʾazinî ʾereṣ
Take heed, heavens,
and pay attention, earth.

Isa 1:2 (cf. Jer 13:15)

With a single vocative, YHWH, the imperatives often occur in psalms of lament (e.g. Pss 17:1, where three verbs appear, *šmᶜ*, *qšb*, *ʾzn*; 55:2–3; 61:2 [1]).

this. The precise object of attention is veiled for the moment, like curses in ancient oaths, which became more dreadful for lack of specificity. One cannot prepare for an unknown threat, hence failure to name the punishment increased its psychological impact. Not until v 4 will Joel unravel the mystery behind the demonstrative *zōʾt*, which he uses twice in v 2 and which remains hidden in a pronominal suffix in v 3. The first *zōʾt* refers to the prophet's statements about a unique calamity; the second *zōʾt* signifies an event, or a series of events, that resembles nothing else in the people's history.

old timers. The designation *hazzeqēnîm* here and in v 14 has a general meaning rather than its restrictive one, elders, who joined the chief priest in presiding over the official life of the Judean community from the time of Ezra onward (cf. Ezra 10:8). Although mature adults may have enjoyed considerable authority from premonarchic and even from monarchic times, especially in rural communities, the office of elder achieved unprecedented political recognition in the Ptolemaic era. Joel's interest lies in accumulated years, not in special rank and privilege. He appeals to those individuals in society who had the longest memory. The parallel term encompasses the entire countryside, that is citizens of the small Judean community rather than every inhabitant on earth. The first vocative addresses the issue of collective memory, the second makes it all encompassing within the Jewish settlement.

anything comparable. Appeal to the unprecedented seems to have been a literary topos in the ancient world. From early Sumerian texts one reads:

Since time of yore,
who ever saw
a sister revealing
the hiding place
of her brother?

Dumuzi's Dream (Jacobsen 1987:38)

Who ever saw a man find safety for his life
in a house not his own?

Inanna's Descent (Jacobsen 1987:230)

For all of seven years
Naram-Suen (Naram-sin) persevered,
—who ever saw a king
holding (his) head
in (his) hands for all of seven years?

Jacobsen 1987:365

The national plague tradition in Israel emphasizes its uniqueness (Exod 10:6, 14, which reports that locusts filled the houses to an unprecedented extent, one not witnessed before by "your parents or their parents" and one that will never be repeated). Similarly, the devastation associated with the Babylonian conquest of Judah in 586 B.C.E. evoked a poetic query as to the uniqueness of the resulting sorrow (Lam 1:12). The religious polemic in Deutero-Isaiah depends on the concept of YHWH's incomparability (C. J. Labuschagne 1966), and legend relies on common belief that some individuals achieve singular status, for example, the tradition that Solomon's wisdom and its accompanying rewards surpassed anything in the entire ancient Near East (1 Kings 5:10 [4:30]). Joel's use of a rhetorical question after imperatives for paying attention resembles Isa 1:10–11 and 28:23–24.

or. In disjunctive questions the usual form is *ʾim*, but exceptions occur. GKC 150g lists Job 21:4 and Joel 1:2, where *weʾim* occurs.

1:3 *Tell it* (lit., "tell about it"). The memory of events associated with the escape from Egypt and revelation of the law at Sinai was kept alive through conversation between parents and their children, a practice that did not always produce the desired result. For example, enthusiastic recounting of YHWH's remarkable activity on Israel's behalf *in the past* threw into greater relief those epochs devoid of special divine assistance. This principle was at work in the story about Gideon's sharp retort to a divine envoy: "But sir, if YHWH is with us, why then has all this happened to us? And where are all his wonderful deeds that *our ancestors recounted* to us . . . ?" (Judg 6:13). Moreover, exclusive concentration in parental instruction and in liturgical settings (cf. Pss 44:2 [1]; 78:3–4) on YHWH's saving acts offered a convenient vehicle for parody, one which the prophet Amos used with considerable effect (Amos 4:6–12; cf. J. L. Crenshaw 1971:27–37). Given the paucity of mighty acts of YHWH on Israel's behalf, the survival of anticipated deliverance *in extremis* within a book such as Sirach (36:6, 8) testifies to the foresight of the Deuteronomist, who called on all Israel to transmit the tradition from generation to generation (Deut 4:9; 6:6–7, 20–23; cf. Exod 12:26–27). Nevertheless, the capacity for doubt always lurked in the background (Hab 1:5, "For a deed is being wrought in your time you would not believe if told").

The verb *sappērû*, which also occurs in Judg 6:13, along with an unspecified *kol-zōʾt* made more explicit in the Septuagint *(ta kaka tauta)*, and in Pss 44:2 [1]; 78:6, is not the verb of choice in the above texts from Exodus or Deuteronomy. Like its object *ʿaleyhâ*, this verb is emphatic, demonstrating Joel's communicative skill through reversing normal word order and through his selection of vocabulary. What does he want his hearers to relate? The next verse will divulge this information. Perhaps he intends for the story to include both disaster and deliverance; in that case, 1:2–3 introduces the first two chapters of the book (W. Rudolph 1971:42). The shift in 2:18–20 to classic narrative style depicts the prophet Joel in the role of transmitter of YHWH's saving deed in the same way 1:4 hands down a less welcome account of YHWH's action.

Your children. I take the noun to be inclusive, for the family setting dictates a broader interpretation of *libnêkem* than sons.

the next generation. The customary scope of two generations opens out to include a third, as if in an unbroken chain of tradition. The proposal in *BHS* to accommodate the text to the usual sequence overlooks the resulting infelicity (*ledor ʾaḥēr* after a single transmission of information from parents to their children). Ps 78:3–4, 5–6 conjoin "our ancestors, their children, and the next generation"; the use of *ledor ʾaḥarôn* corresponds to Joel's expression. The story of the locust plague in Exodus 10, which Joel undoubtedly draws on, mentions three generations (Exod 10:6).

1:4 *the chewer.* The suspense created by Joel's lack of specificity in the twice-repeated *zōʾt* and the pronominal suffix eases with the identification of the unprecedented incident. A devastating invasion of locusts consumed every green leaf in its path, leaving destruction in its wake and depleting the potential foodstuffs of a struggling Judean community. Joel uses four words to describe the agents of destruction, all with a definite article—*haggāzām, hāʾarbeh, hayyeleq,* and *heḥāsîl*—from a total of nine within the Hebrew Bible. Etymological identification of these names for locusts is not very helpful. The verb *gzm* refers to a biting activity (cf. Amos 4:9), hence my translation of the noun as "chewer." The second term, *haʾarbeh,* probably derives from *rbh,* with addition of a prosthetic *ʾaleph,* and signifies the great number of insects associated with a crop infestation. I translate this word "locust" and understand it as the general term for mature locusts. The term *hayyeleq* may relate to Akkadian *ilqitu* (O. R. Sellers 1935–36:83) or Arabic *walaqa* with the sense of "jumping" or "quickness" (cf. Nah 3:16; Jer 51:27). Hence my translation "jumper." The noun *heḥāsîl* seems to mean "finisher," at least in the verbal use at Deut 28:38, where the locusts thoroughly consume the harvest (*yaḥselennû hāʾarbeh,* cf. 1 Kings 8:37; 2 Chr 6:28; Isa 33:4; Ps 78:46). In all likelihood, the four terms have lost their original meaning and are used here to indicate a complete destruction (cf. Ezek 7:2), the number four being chosen because the wind which swept the locusts into Judah may have come from any one of four directions. Such use of four items for completeness is as old as the text of Jer 15:2–3, which refers to four agents of destruction (pestilence, sword, famine, and captivity) and Ezek 14:21, which has wild animals instead of captivity.

Some interpreters think the four terms designate different developmental stages of infestation, only three of which are recognizable to ordinary observers. The youngest locust, *hayyeleq,* is the larva that has just hatched but still lacks visible wings. The second stage *heḥāsîl,* is one in which the wings become noticeable, although still folded together in a sack. The next term, *haggāzām,* yields itself least well to this understanding; it is taken by some to be the penultimate stage of locust, while others see it as another term alongside *haʾarbeh* designating the mature locust. H. W. Wolff thinks they may represent mature locusts of two species, the gregarious locust and the solitary one (1977:27–28). Joel's use of the four terms in a different sequence in 2:25, where one finds *haʾarbeh, hayyeleq, wehehāsîl, wehaggāzām*, does not rule out this interpretation, although weakening it somewhat. One can explain the sequence in 2:25 as follows: he first names the mature locust as the genus, then pauses to name various stages of insects that combine to make up the mature locust swarm. The last three names are therefore in proper order, having been introduced by the more familiar term. Such an explanation does not apply, however, to 1:4, making this interpretation highly dubious. Such reference to distinct stages of locusts would also be unique to Joel.

D. N. Freedman explains the sequence of the four terms as purely literary, a classic example of chiasm or inclusio. In his view, part one, *haggāzām*, equals A, whereas part two, the combination *haʾarbeh, hayyeleq*, and *heḥāsîl* equals B. In 1:4 we have A + B and the sequence in 2:25 is the reverse, B + A. The subtle reversal in sequence matches the reversal of calamity contained in the divine promises of 2:18–27 (written communication).

In Lev 11:22 three other terms occur in association with *haʾarbeh*, but the meaning of *hassāleʿam, haḥargōl*, and *hehāgāb* is unclear (see J. Milgrom:665–67). The general flexibility of terms for locust is obvious from their use in parallelism.

ḥāsîl // ʾarbeh	Ps 78:46
ʾarbeh // yeleq	Ps 105:34; Nah 3:15
ʾarbeh // gōbay	Nah 3:17 (cf. Amos 7:1)
ḥāsîl // gēbîm	Isa 33:4

Only Nah 3:16 implies a developmental stage, one in which the *yeleq* sheds (its skin) and flies away *(yeleq pāšaṭ wayyāʿōp)*, unless *pāšaṭ* is elliptical for stripping leaves from their host plant. In 1 Kings 8:37 the term *ḥāsîl* refers to a distinct plague alongside the locust *(haʾarbeh)*; as a matter of fact, two of the other three terms linked with *ʾarbeh* in Joel 1:4 have been viewed as insects other than locusts: *gāzām*, caterpillar, *ḥāsîl*, cockroach; so Koehler (*KBL*, 319). By the middle of the third century, Ephraem the Syrian understood Joel 1:4 symbolically. He recognized Tiglath-pileser III in *haggāzām*, Shalmaneser V in *haʾarbeh*, Sennacherib in *hayyeleq*, and Nebuchadnezzar in *heḥāsîl* (Wolff 1977:28). Later interpreters developed this symbolic reading of Joel 1:4 and 2:25 further, viewing the four terms as ciphers for Assyria, Babylonia, Greece, and Rome (R. F. Horton, n.d.:88).

left. The word *yeter*, in emphatic position, echoes Exod 10:5 (*weʾākal ʾet-*

yeter happeleṭâ, "and it will consume the surviving leftovers"). Joel's threefold repetition of *yeter*, which is followed by a similar threefold use of the verb *ʾākal*, focuses attention on the tender shoots that escaped the initial onslaught of locusts. Even this surviving greenery becomes food for a second wave of insects.

According to one scenario, mature locusts arrived and left their eggs behind, which hatched after three weeks into young jumpers. These insects quickly reached the next prewing stage, and then that of the winged stage before achieving maturity and migrating, a process that lasts about two months. Each successive invasion consumed what had been left by the previous one.

In another scenario, successive devastations of adult locusts, designated by four terms to indicate the totality of destruction, occurred over a span of at least two years (cf. Joel 2:25, *ʾet-haššanîm*). The full extent of destruction is emphasized in Taanith 3:66d, which plays on the sense of *ḥāsîl* ("Why is the locust called *ḥāsîl*? Because it brings everything to an end.")

Ronald Simkins's recent investigation into the life cycle of locusts (1991:101–20) provides considerable information about the two species of desert locust, solitaria and gregaria, with an intermediate stage. Among his observations, the following are helpful in understanding Joel's use of the infestation. Young gregarious locusts are pink, turning brown and then bright yellow at maturity, whereas solitary locusts are mostly brown. With their ovipositor, females deposit one to six egg pods, each containing from twenty to one hundred eggs, into the ground. At this time water is essential, although too much moisture will drown the potential hatchlings. Lacking water or moderate temperature, eggs enter a dispause stage, hatching when both factors are favorable. Female gregarious locusts mature faster than solitary ones and become sexually active earlier, but their life span is also shorter. The normal adult life of a mature locust is about seventy-five days. Locusts move by a sort of rolling motion with distinct chain reactions; they require fluctuations in temperature, ordinarily settling down in the evening. Locust plagues and droughts can coincide, mild stress on plants (1) increasing their nutrients, (2) making the plants warmer and thus assisting in the feeding process, and (3) turning them into more attractive food. Severe droughts, however, can bring locust plagues to an end. Preferring patchy vegetation over uniform growth, locusts have no fondness for leaves and twigs from date and olive trees, although eating them as a last resort. Locusts have actually been known to devour other locusts.

Wolff adds that modern entomologists recognize five larva stages; that Joel's multiple designations may apply to various regions where mature locusts were known by different names; that their metamorphosis is less obvious than that of butterflies, bees, and flies; and that locusts eat the same way in all stages, by a cutting motion rather than licking (1977:27–28).

A. Taylor reports on a riddle—a term he uses quite loosely—for a locust.

> A curious Algerian tale relates how Satan looked at the world God had created and said he could have done better. God heard him and gave him the power to endow with life whatever he might create. As Satan wandered about, he saw a noble animal proudly lifting its graceful head in a meadow. "I shall take this horse's head," said he, and ordered a servant to carry it to hell. Farther on, the gentle eye of an elephant caught his fancy. He admired the long, curving horns of a herd of antelopes as they were running in a ravine. When he saw a bull fighting a lion, he chose the bull's neck and the lion's breast. "What more do I need?" he said to himself, and, meeting a camel, he took its strong thighs, and then, the splendid legs of an ostrich. "What do I need now?" he said, and sought out the scorpion in the hot stones of the desert. From it he took its stomach. "Shall the creature of my making be damned to crawl on the earth? No! I wish it to have the wings of an eagle." And he shot an arrow at the king of birds and took its wings. "Now to work," said Satan. He spent a long time fitting these bits of animals together. Some were too clumsy, others were too small. He filed and sawed, cut and patched so diligently that at the end of the hundred years granted him only a tiny creature lay in his hands. He blew on it and gave it life. "Well, what have you?" said God. "There is the result of my skill," said Satan. "Is that then your handiwork? O Satan! As a sign of your weakness may this creature multiply on earth and teach men that there is no God but God." Satan departed in confusion, and since then locusts have flourished in Arabian lands.
>
> (1951:429)

EXCURSUS: References to Locusts in Ancient Near Eastern Texts

Not surprisingly, ancient Near Eastern texts from Egypt, Canaan, and Mesopotamia refer to locusts because of their vast number and destructive nature (J. A. Thompson 1955:52–55). The circumstances in which these references occur vary from royal inscriptions and prayers to astronomical diaries and magical incantations. They appear in letters written to kings, legendary accounts of royal exploits, and curses. In general, Egyptian allusions to locusts emphasize the great number of soldiers who fell to Pharaohs Rameses II and Merneptah, whereas Mesopotamian references stress the destructiveness of locusts.

Four Egyptian texts suffice to indicate their character.

> They covered the mountains and the valleys; they were like grasshoppers with their multitudes.

> Good God, valiant son of Amon, lord of the sword, protector of his army in

battle . . . piercing through the allies, crushing the rebellious upon the mountains; they enter into their valleys like grasshoppers.

Libya is like a petitioner brought as a captive. Thou hast made them to be like grasshoppers, for every road is strewed with their bodies.

. . . he sees the thick of the multitude like grasshoppers, smitten, ground down, crushed like [ ] (R. Simkins 1991:126–27).

A Ugaritic text (*CTA* 14:103–11) emphasizes the size of Keret's army.

Like the locusts that dwell on the steppe,
Like grasshoppers on the borders of the desert—
March a day and a second;
A third, a fourth day;
A fifth, a sixth day—
Lo! at the sun on the seventh;
Thou arrivest at Udum the Great,
Even at Udum the Grand.
Now do thou *attack* the villages,
Harass the towns.

A Sumerian curse of Agade from the end of the third millennium depicts Gutian troops of King Naram-Sim as numerous like locusts.

In vast numbers, like locusts, they covered the earth,
their "arm" stretched out for him in the steppe like an *animal-trap*,
Nothing escaped their "arm,"
No one eluded their "arm."

Assyrian documents from the time of Sennacherib and Sargon II emphasize the vast hordes of locusts that invaded the land in the spring.

. . . one and all they were risen against me
to offer battle, like a spring invasion of countless locusts.

. . . my warriors swarmed like locusts out of the ships (and)
on to the bank and brought about their defeat.

. . . I had the vast armies of Assur cover their cities like locusts.
. . . with the mass of my troops, as with locusts, I covered the city.

The first two citations come from Sennacherib, the last two from a boastful Sargon II.

A single locust, perched on a palm tree, is depicted prominently on a relief of Asshurbanipal and his queen feasting after defeating the Elamites, and an enameled orthostat from Assur in Sargon's time pictures an official with a locust over his head in the presence of Shamash.

Victor Avigdor Hurowitz has recently examined the Hymn to Nanaya by Sargon II, particularly the prayer for relief from locusts (1993:597–603). It reads

The evil locust which destroys the crop/grain,
the wicked dwarf/locust which dries up the orchards,
which cuts off the regular offerings of the gods and goddesses—
(Verily) Enlil listens to you, and Tutu is before you—
May by your command it be turned into nothing.

Hurowitz calls attention to exact parallels with the language of Joel: (1) the use of merismus to embrace all sizes and species of locusts; (2) the description of the locusts as "destroyer of the grain," and (3) the reference to locusts cutting off the daily offerings of the gods and goddesses. Because the Akkadian text uses lexical equivalents of Joel's vocabulary for destroying the harvest of the field, drying up all the trees of the field, and cutting off the daily offerings, Hurowitz argues that such precise parallels cannot be accidental, particularly in light of the absence of these features in the story about the plague of locusts in Egypt. He thinks Joel may have used a traditional liturgical composition that would have been recited in ancient temples during an infestation of locusts. Such a radical conclusion on the basis of the evidence hardly seems justified, given the two texts. Moreover, the vast distances in time and geography separating parallels are easily explained on the principle of polygenesis—a similar phenomenon producing similar results naturally evoked descriptions with many features in common. What could be more natural than to depict the effect of locusts as destroying, drying up, and rendering the cereal crops unworthy of offerings?

Other texts from Mesopotamia refer to an infestation of locusts over a three-year period.

> For three years because of the affliction of the locust, the district has not produced crops. (Andiñach 1992)

A later Babylonian astronomical diary also refers to an infestation of this duration.

> If Libra is dark: for three years locusts will attack and devour the harvest of the land. . . . (source unknown)

Pablo R. Andiñach has reached quite a different conclusion on the basis of these references to locusts (1992:433–41). He thinks such allusions to locusts are metaphors for soldiers and that Joel's references to locusts function in the same way despite his "innovative" use of the preposition "like." Andiñach's interpretation of Joel 1:1–4 as a prologue to the book and 4:18–21 [3:18–21; Andiñach mistakenly has 2:18–21] as the epilogue conveniently removes the introductory reference to locusts and allows him to focus on the military imagery in chapter two. His hypothesis falls apart, however, in light of the comparison of the locusts with soldiers. If locusts are a metaphor for soldiers, how can they be compared with an army?

1:5 *Imbibers.* Either the contentment resulting from drinking sweet wine under one's fig tree and vine or lethargy induced by constant consumption of intoxicating drink (cf. Hos 4:11) furnishes an effective symbol for the national oblivion to divine action concealed in the locust hordes. Unlike most interpreters, I understand the vocative *šikkôrîm* (which lacks the definite article here and in 1:11; contrast 1:2, 9, 13) in a positive, or to say the least, neutral, sense. I do so partly because of its parallel, *kol šōtê yāyin* ("all who drink wine"), which included virtually everybody in the ancient culture, the only known exceptions being the followers of Jonadab ben Rechab (Jer 35:1–14) and Nazirites (Num 6:1–4). An enthusiastic endorsement of wine's contribution to the quality of life, the other reason for my understanding of *šikkôrîm*, is found within the Bible itself (Ps 104:15; Judg 9:13; Eccl 10:19; Cant 8:2; cf. Sir 9:10, which compares friendship with wine, specifically its improvement with age, and 31:27, which stresses moderate drinking and asks, "What is life to a person from whom wine is withheld?"). In Jotham's fable the vine boasts that its product makes the gods and mortals glad (*hamśammēaḥ ʾelōhîm waʾanāšîm*, Judg 9:13); the praise of wine's power in 1 Esd 3:18–24 does not go quite this far, although effectively describing the manner in which wine overcomes human essence, rationality, making them behave in foolish and dangerous ways (J. L. Crenshaw 1981:74–88, 119–20). In the New Testament, John the Baptist did not touch wine, in sharp contrast with Jesus who came "eating and drinking" (Matt 11:18–19).

Wake up . . . and weep. Joel places the emphasis on the imperatives rather than on the vocatives; the people must first become alert to the peril threatening them, and once they have done so, weeping will naturally follow (cf. Gen 9:24). Joel definitely does not anticipate the response mocked in Prov 23:35 ("When shall I awake? I shall seek still another drink"). A. S. Kapelrud's cultic interpretation of this verse on the basis of Canaanite ritual weeping over the death of Baal (1948:17–30) is not necessary, even if the terminology in 1:5 echoes the vocabulary connected with such worship. He lists the verbs "weep," "sob," and "denied" (which he renders literally, "cut off"), and the noun "sweet wine." The profound experiences associated with death naturally elicited common vocabulary among ancient Semites, so such affinities need occasion little surprise.

The initial imperative, *hāqîṣû*, does double duty, introducing the second and third imperatives: "wake up and weep; wake up and sob." The prophet envisions demonstrative action in definite contrast to the contentment resulting from drinking in moderation or the stupor produced by drinking to excess. Ancient Israelites, like their neighbors in the Near East, released their emotions by means of dramatic display, although sometimes in combination with quiet remorse (cf. Job 2:12 for the visible demonstration of grief and 2:13 for its sequel, a subdued silence). It has been plausibly argued that "the movement is from behavior to feeling rather than the other way around" (G. A. Anderson 1991:95). The Septuagint takes *ʿal-ʿāsîs* with *kol-šōtê yāyin*, rendering *hoi pinontes oinon eis methēn* ("the ones who drink wine unto drunkenness"). This leaves the verb *nikrat* without a subject, which is therefore supplied from 1:16 ("joy and gladness," *śimḥâ wāgîl*, omitting the primary cause, food, snatched from before their eyes). Neither this *euphrosyne kai chara* ("joy and gladness") nor *ex oinou auton* ("from their wine"), the gloss attached to the vocative, *šikkôrîm*, commends itself for adoption.

The usual structure in these verses—first an imperative, then a vocative, and finally a *kî* clause—is broken momentarily by *ʿal-ʿāsîs*, but a *kî* follows. The reference to sweet wine also points to a nonpejorative understanding of the vocatives, for its association with idyllic existence under one's fig tree and vine hardly provokes censure (Amos 9:13; implicitly in 2 Kings 18:32; Mic 4:4; Zech 3:10). Such sweet wine was allowed to ferment only five to seven days instead of the usual nine, but according to Isa 49:26 it still possessed the quality to bring on drunkenness. The noun *ʿāsîs* derives from the verb *ʿss*, "to tread on, trample" (cf. Mal 3:21 [4:3]), and refers to juice pressed from the vintage.

denied. The verb *nikrat* evokes the image of a powerful sword flashing inches from one's mouth and depriving the individual of anticipated pleasure. Its appropriateness derives from the cutting action of locusts that consumed the vintage in full view of the people. Something more than economic loss is envisioned; life itself stands in jeopardy, as 1:16 will make clear. Paucity of food will bring an end to religious functions, thus imperiling the people from another source.

1:6 *a nation.* This verse elaborates on the previous *kî* clause of 1:5, offering a military explanation already implicit in the expression "cut off from their mouth," which I translate "denied them." The locust swarm is described in the language of an invasion by a hostile nation whose soldiers are too numerous, hence powerful, to count. Reference to insects as a nation *(gôy)* has an analogy in Prov 30:25–26, where *ʿam* designates ants and badgers (cf. Joel 2:2, with *ʿam* instead of *gôy*). The following verse, 30:27, associates locusts with military "precision marching," in the absence of a leader *(melek)*. Comparison of insects with a nation is also found in the Iliad (II 87, bees; II 459, birds; II 469, flies; Rudolph 1971:44, n. 8).

my land. The pronominal suffix in this verse and in the next ("my vine, my fig") is strange in a unit which otherwise takes the form of a prophetic address with YHWH in the third person (1:9, 14–16), second person (1:19–20), or with a possessive suffix (1:13). Prophetic inconsistency in regard to the actual speaker, whether YHWH or the messenger, is not at all extraordinary. While Joel could refer to his own property that the locusts have stripped of greenery, he more likely slips momentarily into the divine persona, perhaps to telegraph the deity's involvement in the repercussion of the siege. After all, the old tradition that YHWH gave the land to Israelites implies divine ownership. Wolff's interpretation of the first person suffix as a literary motif associated with invasion by a hostile power (Ezek 38:16) accords with his hypothesis that Joel uses proto-apocalyptic language (1977:29).

innumerable. The locusts in Exod 10:4–6, 12–15 were so numerous that they obscured the sky and covered the surface of the land. The author of Ps 105:34 draws the logical conclusion that none could count them *(we'ên mispār)*. Joel does likewise, adding the notion of power (*ʿaṣûm*, cf. 2:2, 5, 11). This association of vast numbers with the idea of strength occurs also in Amos 5:12a, "For I am aware of your many transgressions and your weighty *(waʿaṣumîm)* errors" (cf. Mic 4:3 —the parallel in Isa 2:4 lacks *ʿaṣûm*—; Jer 5:6, and the textually varied Deut 26:5).

Comparison of invading armies with locusts became a literary motif in early times. An early Sumerian text reads:

Numerous like locusts
they came striding,
stretched out their arms in the desert for him
like gazelle and wild ass snares,
nothing escaped their arms,
nobody did their arms leave.

Jacobsen 1987:379, cf. 483

Simkins (1991:126–27, cf. J. A. Thompson 1955:52–55) cites texts using this simile from Egypt, Canaan, and Mesopotamia. Biblical examples occur in Judg 6:5; 7:12; Jer 51:14; Nah 3:15–17.

leonine teeth (lit., "its teeth are the teeth of a lion, and the fangs of a lion belong to it"). The choice of a lion in this comparison derives from the indispensability and savagery of its teeth (cf. Job 4:10–11, where five words for lions occur), perhaps also from the similarity in sound *(ʾarbeh/ʾaryēh)*. The rare word *metalleʿôt* occurs exclusively in parallelism with *šēn* (Ps 58:7 [6]; Job 29:17; Prov 30:14) and means jawbones or teeth. I translate "fangs" to convey a sense of dread. The second word for lion, *lābîʾ*, is limited to poetic texts (Gen 49:9;

Num 23:24; 24:9; Deut 33:20; Isa 5:29; 30:6; 56:11; Hos 13:8; Job 4:11; 38:39; Nah 2:13 [12]).

1:7 *It made my vineyard into a desolation*. The alliteration in 1:6b (*šinnāyw šinnê)* continues in *śām . . . lešammâ* (1:7a) and in *ḥaśōp ḥaśāpâ* (1:7b, the last word echoing *liqṣāpâ* in 1:7a). These two objects of locusts' destructive appetite, vine and fig, symbolized life's fullness (1 Kings 5:5; [4:25]; 2 Kings 18:31; Mic 4:4; Zech 3:10). Their ancient association with an era of peace is reversed here; locusts have denuded the vines and trees, even cutting off small twigs and bark, leaving them to be blanched by the hot sun. The singular suffix on *śārîgeyhā* ("its cuttings") refers to the fig trees and grape vines, the two being so closely connected in popular thought that a singular suffix suffices.

1:8 This brief verse presents two major difficulties: who is the addressee and what does the simile imply? The feminine form of the imperative *ʾelî* is suggested by the simile itself, for only a woman would qualify as one who grieves the loss of a husband. Nevertheless, the whole population could cry out *like* a woman in mourning. Beyond that, it is possible to argue that Joel has in mind the traditional personification of Jerusalem as a woman (cf. 2 Esd 9:38–10:28 where Zion mourns the loss of her son on his wedding night). The Targum makes this understanding explicit by adding "Israel," the result of *pars pro toto* reasoning (cf. Zeph 3:14). The Septuagint confirms the unique *ʾelî*, although misunderstanding the form (*pros me: ʾēlay)* and thus necessitating a verb, which it supplies (*thrēnēson*, "lament") from the much-used *hyll* (1:5, 11, 13). The widespread personification of Jerusalem, Judah, and YHWH's people in Jeremiah, Lamentations, and Deutero-Isaiah indicates that Joel's silence with respect to the addressee would have occasioned little if any misunderstanding among his audience.

Wolff's tentative reconstruction of an original Hebrew text in the sequence 9b, 8, 9a, and 10 (1977:18, n.i.) lacks cogency for the following reasons: (1) a unique occurrence in Joel should be retained if it makes sense, and *ʾelî* certainly can be explained from the root *ʾlh*; (2) Joel omits the vocatives in several instances where their identity is clear from what precedes (1:3, 13b, 14); (3) the longer Greek text has resulted from corruption of *ʾelî* or *ʾelû*; (4) The Septuagint's *pentheîte* ("mourn") is a possible reading of an unpointed *ʾblw*, and the use of *thusiastēriō* ("altar") may derive from 1:13; and (5) the factive verbs in 1:9b accord with others in 1:10.

like a young woman. The second difficulty in this verse concerns the meaning of *kibetûlâ*, virgin or young woman. The first of these possibilities seems out of place in light of the further identification of the cause for her grief—a dead young husband. A legal explanation is possible (F. Zimmerman 1954:98–99), for Deut 22:24 calls a betrothed woman a wife (*ʾešet rēʿēhû)* even though the marriage has not yet been consummated and she is still a virgin (*betûlâ*). Joel would then refer to the death of a young man between the time his family had paid the bridal price *(mōhar)* and his actual taking her (Deut 20:7). The image thus resembles that in 1:5, a denial at the moment of intense anticipation. The pathos connected with such profound loss could easily have become proverbial.

G. Wenham has argued that *betûlâ* alone never means virgin but refers to a young woman without specifying whether or not she has had any sexual experience (1972:326–48). If correct, this explanation of *betûlâ* fits nicely with the strange expression, *baʿal neʿûreyhâ* in 1:8, for which we possess a parallel in *ʾešet neʿûrîm* (Prov 5:18; Isa 54:6; Mal 2:14–15). The wife of one's youth could also refer to the period between betrothal and wedding, but it more naturally recalls the early years of a marriage.

Another interpretation of this verse rests on Canaanite myth and a conjectured ritual in which Baal's sister Anat annually mourns the death of her husband. The epithet Virgin was applied to her as perpetual virgin/wife, and the name Baal is reflected in the expression *baʿal neʿûreyhā* (F. F. Hvidberg 1962:140–42). Kapelrud strengthens this hypothesis by interpreting *betûlâ*, *ʾelî*, and *baʿal neʿûreyhā* in the light of such ritual enactment (1948:32–34). Ahlström's endorsement of this theory, with modifications, rests on the survival of religious syncretism as late as the book of Malachi. G. Jeshurun's interpretation of Job's initial oath in 31:1 (1928:153) assumes the same religious background: Job launches his daring oath of innocence by denying allegiance to the Virgin Anat, i.e., apostasy. Although such an interpretation of Joel's language is possible, the necessity for this understanding is greatly reduced by evidence that *betûlâ* means young woman of a marriageable age (*baʿal neʿûreyhā*, therefore, indicates "husband" rather than "bridegroom").

The text does not state that the husband is dead, although that conclusion seems natural in light of the allusion to sackcloth and the verbal reminiscence of 5b *(ʿal-ʿāsîs kî nikrat mippîkem)* in *ʿal-baʿal neʿûreyhā*. The donning of garments made from loosely woven goat's hair was not exclusively associated with mourning, for these signs of mortification were also worn as tokens of repentance and fasting. Still, the reference to "wife of his youth" (*ʾešet neʿûreykā)* in Mal 2:15 raises the possibility that a rejected wife would have put on sackcloth to depict her utter misery (but contrast Tamar's reaction to her brother's crime, which the text calls *hannebālâ*, translated "folly" in the KJV, 2 Sam 13:12, 19).

1:9 *withheld.* The unique Hophal perfect verb *hokrat* links this verse with 1:5, which uses the same verb in Niphal perfect. There the sweet wine was cut off from those accustomed to drinking it. Here the daily offerings that accompanied the burnt offering of a lamb—flour (mixed with salt and olive oil) and wine—are cut off from the temple. In the postexilic community such offerings were made at the temple after its restoration and dedication in 516 B.C.E. twice daily, morning and evening. We do not know precisely when the *tāmîd* sacrifices became regulatory; Neh 10:33–34 [32–33] reports that the governor and leading citizens assumed responsibility for seeing that the required offerings were made at the appropriate time. This specification of *tāmîd* sacrifices does not include the drink offering. The combination of grain and drink offering occurs in late texts only (Exod 29:38–42; Lev 23:13, 18; Num 6:15; 15:24; 28:3–9; 29:11, 16–39). Joel singles out these two sacrifices because they were most affected by the locust invasion.

The cessation of daily sacrifices dealt a severe blow to those who ministered before YHWH in the temple, for the priest normally ate a portion of the offerings (Lev 2:3, 10). Joel describes these officials as already mourning. Their reason was more than personal loss; in their eyes the failure of the cult was a serious event, one that affected the way YHWH related to the people of Judah. The terminology for these supervisors of the altar varies considerably in Joel's usage; three nouns occur in construct with *mešārETê*: YHWH in 1:9 and 2:17; *mizbēaḥ* in 1:13a (and the Greek of 1:9); and *ʾelohay* in 1:13a. Wolff contrasts Ezek 44:15, where the priestly servant is perceived as YHWH's personal attendant, with Joel's understanding, which Wolff thinks is restricted to a caretaking role at the altar (1977:31). This point is undercut by 2:14b, which boldly states that the cereal and drink offerings are provided for YHWH your God *(laYHWH ʾelōhêkem)*.

Some scholars follow the Septuagint's *pentheîte* in reading *ʾibelû*, Qal imperative, for *ʾābelû* and understand *hakkōhanîm* as a vocative. The first major section of this literary unit, 1:2–14, does have a structural feature consisting of imperative and vocative in 1:2, 5, 8 (without the vocative, which has either fallen out or is implicit), 11, 13. This emendation is both unnecessary and misguided for two reasons: (1) v 13 addresses priests (2) with stylistic consistency found in 1:2, 5, 8(?), 11. Verses 2, 5, and 8 seem to address the entire population, whereas vv 11 and 13 specify particular classes within society, namely farmers and vintners, on the one hand, and priests, on the other hand. In all these instances, imperatives *initiate* the strophe, which is not the case here in 1:9. Joel is certainly capable of stylistic variety, but reading *ʾābelû* as Qal perfect lends quiet force to the description of ruin.

1:10 *devastated.* Alliteration and concatenation of five succinct descriptive word pairs are concentrated in this verse, as are traditional terms in usual sequence for the essentials of livelihood. The alliteration in *šuddad śādeh*, *ʾābelâ ʾadāmâ*, and vocalic inversion in *hôbîš tîrôš* cannot be reproduced in English. Joel's dirge-like language imitates the heavy blows being reported, falling with hammer-like force. In the Septuagint, *hoti* introduces the first colon, but this addition mars the effect of the terse Hebrew. Cultivated fields are devastated (Pual of *šdd*), the ground groans (returning to the verb *ʾbl* applied to priests in 1:9b), for the grain is destroyed (the same verb used with reference to fields in 1:10a), the wine dried up (Hiphil internal transitive of *ybš*), and the olive oil depleted (Pulal of *ʾml*). The daily staples—grain, wine, and oil (cf. Hos 2:8)—were equally essential in the temple.

Joel uses the verb *ybš* in 1:12 (three times) and 20. On the basis of graphic identity, some interpreters (K. Marti 1904:121) take *hôbîš* from *bôš* ("be ashamed") and understand the reference as personification (cf. 1:11 where farmers are urged to experience shame and Ps 65:13 [12] for the response of personified valleys in happier times); this interpretation is normally reinforced by reading *ʾābelâ* as "mourn" rather than "dry up," despite Hos 4:3 (*ʿal-ken teʾebal hāʾāreṣ weʾumlal kol-yôšeb bâ*) and Amos 1:2 (*weʾabelû neʾôt haroʿîm weyābeš rōʾš hakkarmel*). Perhaps Joel uses the verbs *ʾbl* (Kapelrud 1948:38) and *ybš/bōš* (Rudolph 1971:39) because of their rich possibilities through ambiguity.

dried up. The language of drying up and wilting poses the possibility that a locust infestation was not the only source of anguish among the people. One could stretch the imagery sufficiently to accommodate a single calamity, the locusts, in one of two ways: (1) by insisting that the loss of leaves to locusts brought such stress to plants during the dry season that they could not survive the heat until sufficient moisture came (J. D. W. Watts 1975:19–20), or (2) by understanding "grain, wine, and oil" as metonymns for the grain crop, the grape vine, and the olive tree, so that *ʾumlal* and *hôbîš* can bear the senses of withering and drying out (R. Simkins 1991:137). In any event, 1:20 removes all doubt, for here Joel explicitly mentions the effect of a drought that has left depleted water sources and an appearance of fire's ravages.

1:11 *Be ashamed*. The third strophe of the call to lamentation begins by playing on the ambiguity of *hôbîš* in 1:10b, but the application to peasant farmers is restricted to its sense of shame. Verse 11 addresses the two classes of workers responsible for growing the three products so essential to the economic viability of the nation—those who grow grain and those who tend the grape vines and fruit trees. Thérése Frankfort argues that these farmers and "vintners" are culpable in that they allowed the locust invasion to interfere with their performance of duties, specifically keeping the irrigation ditches flowing with enough water to enable fruit trees to flourish (1960:445–48). The argument is undercut by 1:7, which attributes the destruction of vine and fig to locusts rather than to dereliction of responsibility on the part of vine growers.

The structure of v 11 resembles v 5 in all essentials: initial imperative followed by a vocative, a parallel imperative (the same one, the only difference being the *waw* conjunctive on *hêlilû* in v 5), *ʿal* with the noun it governs (used twice and with different nouns in v 11), and a *kî* clause.

Farmers . . . vintners. Joel uses the rare loan word *ʾikkārîm* (cf. Akkadian *ikkaru*), as did Amos (5:16b, *weqāreʾû ʾikkār ʾel ʾebel*, "and they will call the farmer to mourning," cf. Isa 61:5; 2 Chr 26:10). Joel seems to expand the usage of *kōremîm* to include orchard growers (cf. v 12). Anderson contends that external expression of remorse was not the result of grief but was calculated to generate appropriate internal response (1991:95–97).

on account of. The reason for Joel's urgent counsel to the farmers is introduced by *ʿal* rather than a *kî* clause, which then follows with general elaboration. They should be ashamed on account of a ruined grain crop, both the more desirable wheat and the staple of the poorer people, barley. The *kî* clause reverses normal expectations; the anticipation of joyous celebration at harvest time gives way to a heavy heart. The verb *ʾābad* establishes the mood: "ruined is the harvest." The ancient association of guilt with calamity seems to reside beneath the surface of Joel's urgent plea to the farmers; if so, he does not press the point. The *ʿal* of this verse does not govern the explanation for Joel's command to the vintners; for that, v 12 uses an entirely different form.

The verbs *hōbîšû* and *hêlîlû* can be read either as imperatives or as perfects, but the structure of vv 5, 8, and 13 favors the imperative. The Septuagint translates *hōbîšû* as perfect and *hêlîlû* as imperative.

1:12 *withered*. This translation of *hôbîšâ* loses the poetic force present in the implicit personification of the vine if one understands the verb as a form of *bôš* ("the vine is ashamed") rather than *ybš*. Parallelism with *ʾumlālâ* supports the more prosaic rendering ("Vine has withered // fig is scorched").

pomegranate, date, and apple. Besides grapes and figs, other fruits necessary to a thriving economy have succumbed to the ravages of the locust swarm. According to Num 13:23, the spies who were sent ahead by Moses to explore the land brought back grapes, figs, and pomegranates. The glowing description in Deut 8:8 of this land bestowed on YHWH's loyal subjects emphasizes its abundant springs, wheat and barley, vines, fig trees, and pomegranates, olive trees, and honey. Date palms grew in the Jordan valley near Jericho, the city of palm trees (Deut 34:3; Judg 1:16; 3:13; 2 Chr 28:15). The translation of *tappûaḥ* is disputed; N. H. and A. L. Moldenke opt for apricot from the several choices—apple, quince, citron, apricot (1952:184–88). The word *tappûaḥ* occurs only in late texts (Prov 25:11; Cant 2:3, 5; 7:9; 8:5)—perhaps an accident of occurrence, for an ancient city was named Tappuach (Josh 12:17). This enumeration of ruined vine and fruit trees uses the singular as a collective, the concatenation of words increasing in intensity until the specific identification of affected trees gives way to a comprehensive summary statement: "every tree in the orchard has wilted" (1:12bβ; cf. 1:5). In this linkage of fruit trees, *gam* functions as conjunctive *we* ("and") but perhaps with a bit of an emphatic push forward in the enumeration.

indeed. *kî* cannot convey a causative sense here, for it introduces the result of the failure of a fruit harvest, not the reason for that disaster. "Indeed, joy has vanished" states the natural outcome of a failed harvest; the normal accompaniment of gathering the crops, *śāśôn*, has given way to dejected countenance, perhaps the result of shame—if Joel continues the double entendre set up by the verb *hōbîš*. Kapelrud connects *śāśôn* with ancient Canaanite cultic festivals during which jubilant celebration expressed the people's appreciation for an abundant harvest betokening Baal's return from the underworld and nature's rejuvenation (1948:42–45). Kapelrud also notes the prophetic fondness for this word, especially by Jeremiah and Isaiah.

from the populace. Simkins recognizes the unusual nature of this expression, *min benê ʾādām*, and tries to relate it to foreigners (1991:139–41). His argument is based on the use of *hōbîš* followed by the unassimilated preposition *min*, which he takes to mean "be put to shame by." Because 2:23 uses *benê ṣiyyôn* in describing the reversal of the misfortune described in 1:2–20, Simkins thinks this text furnishes the decisive clue for understanding *benê ʾādām* in 1:12. The contrast lies in the reversal of the effects brought on by locusts and drought, however, and not in the people affected. The same Judeans suffer the loss of harvest and experience its bounty.

Simkins's other reason for reading "be put to shame by" relates to *hōbîš* as a verb from *bôš*, which is problematic here. This rejection of *bôš* as the operative verb renders his evidence useless. Not all of his translations of the pertinent clause are convincing; for example, Isa 1:29a can be rendered more naturally "For you will be ashamed of the oaks in which you took delight" (cf. Jer 12:13; Mic 7:16), although some of them are persuasive (e.g., Jer 2:36; 10:14).

Simkins's attempt to relate Judah's lack of joy to mockery by foreigners over YHWH's failure to overcome the disastrous effects of the locust invasion allows him to read *kî* in v 12c causally, but he relates the clause to v 11 and views it as further reason for farmers and vintners to be ashamed and weep. In seeing *kî* as causative, he agrees with Thérése Frankfort (1960:445–48), but her placing of blame on derelict workers of the fruit trees differs from his interpretation of v 12c.

The phrase *benê ʾādām* (lit., "children of humankind") concludes the third strophe of this lamentation by embracing all those persons who have been brought to shame and who weep over the calamity that has struck the community—those who drink wine (the first strophe), the personified city (the second strophe), the farmers and tenders of the vine and fruit trees (the third strophe), and even the priests whose misery has been reported and to whom a special summons will immediately follow in v 13. Hence my translation of the phrase here as "populace." The initial strophe (v 5) also has a comprehensive expression, *kol-šōtê yāyin* ("everyone who drinks wine"), one that is echoed in *kol-ʿaṣê haśśādeh* of v 12b ("every tree in the orchard"). The choice of *benê ʾādām* rather than *ʾîš haśśādeh* may have been occasioned by the distant echo of *ʾadāmâ*, thus bringing together in dismay those who are interrelated, the ground and human beings who, according to tradition, derive from it and depend on its gifts for survival.

1:13 *Don*. The absolute use of *ḥigrû* occurs elsewhere only in Isa 32:11

(*waḥagôrâ ʿal-ḥalaṣayim*, "gird [sackcloth] on your loins"); the ellipsis of a direct object presents no difficulty, particularly in view of *lînû baśśaqîm* that follows (cf. also *ḥagurat-śaq* in v 8). Ancient Israelites wore sackcloth as a sign of mourning and of fasting. Strips of coarse cloth were tied around the loins, and persons in extreme sorrow struck (or clawed) their naked chests.

priests. The initial imperative of this verse alluded to v 8 by omitting the object of *ḥigrû*; the next imperative recalls v 9, although applying a different verb to the priests' activity and using a variant of the appositional phrase, *mešārətê YHWH*. Joel urges the priests to lament *(wesipdû)* and sob *(hêlîlû)*, but this time he designates them "presiders over the altar" instead of "YHWH's officials" (v 9).

spend the night. The fifth imperative in this verse, *lînû*, is preceded by *bōʾû* ("come"), without any indication of the place to which the priests are expected to come (home? the temple?). On the basis of Amos 4:4 ("Come to Bethel. . . ."), where the prophet mocks priests who invite people to come to the sanctuary at Bethel, we may conclude that Joel urges priests to come to the temple. Examples of deep sorrow in which individuals are said to have worn sackcloth throughout the night are reported in biblical narrative. David's unconventional behavior on the occasion of the illness of his ill-fated child by Bathsheba included fasting during the night (*wayyāṣām dāwid ṣôm ûbāʾ welān wešākab ʾarṣâ*, "David fasted, went in, spent the night, and lay on the ground," 2 Sam 12:16). The incident involving King Ahab's response to another prophet's stinging denunciation, Elijah's, specifically mentions sackcloth, although remaining silent about nocturnal conduct (*wayyāśem-śaq ʿal-bešārô wayyāṣôm wayyiškab baśśaq wayehallēk ʾaṭ*, "and he put sackcloth against his skin, fasted, lay around in sackcloth, and walked about dejectedly," 1 Kings 21:27). The natural implication of such conduct is that the king wore sackcloth night and day. Because Joel already has received a divine oracle, he does not suggest that the priests practice incubation (cf. Amos 2:8 and 1 Samuel 3 for possible instances of this religious rite).

my God. The Septuagint has *theō*, "God," which has been understood as original, the Masoretic Text being corrupted as a result of the *yod* ending on the word that precedes *ʾelōhîm* and the one that follows it (R. Simkins 1991:144, n. 80) or because a later scribe did not recognize the abbreviated form *ʾelōh* or *ʾelōhî* and corrected it to *ʾelōhāy* (K. Marti 1904:122, J. A. Bewer 1911:86). The personal pronouns in this verse are striking: *ʾelōhāy* and *ʾelōhêkem*. No subtle contrast seems to be intended. At most, Joel uses "my God" to reinforce the authority by which he summons the priests to lamentation. The pronouns emphasize the solidarity of prophet and priests, for a common threat has placed both Joel and the leaders of the cult in the same jeopardy.

withheld. The similarity between v 13b and v 9a has led some scholars to consider only v 9a original (J. A. Bewer 1911:85), but the variation of vocabulary typical of Joel's style points to the authenticity of both. In v 9 the verb *hokrat* governs "cereal offering and libation," whereas v 13 uses *nimnaʿ*, "withheld." Both verbs are appropriate to their context; locusts cut off the sacrifices from the temple and the people consequently withheld their gifts. Simkins discerns a volitional aspect in the verb *nimnaʿ*, which implies that the distraught citizens of the Judean state kept back the ingredients for daily offerings as a hedge against starvation (1991:145). Amos' use of this verb in a liturgy of wasted opportunity (*wegam ʾanōkî mānaʿtî mikkem ʾet-haggešem*, "I also withheld rain from you," Amos 4:7) corresponds to Joel's ominous nuance.

from your God's house. The position of *mibbêt ʾelōhêkem* in this colon shifts the emphasis to the temple, whereas v 9a stressed the offerings.

1:14. *Arrange*. The imperative *qaddešû* ("sanctify") seems redundant when applied to a fast, which is inherently religious (cf. 2:15–16). In 4:9 [3:9] Joel uses this verb even more startlingly, at least from a modern viewpoint (*qaddešû milḥāmâ*, "sanctify a battle"), although preparation for warfare in the ancient world included religious ritual from early times, particularly the consulting of a divine oracle or seeking prophetic advice. *qirʾû*, the imperative that stands in parallelism with *qaddešû*, governs the noun *ʿaṣārâ*, "religious assembly." The word *ʿaṣārâ* originally referred to a cessation from work for a specified period (E. Kutsch 1952:57–69); its use in connection with religious events gradually colored its connotation, yielding "solemn assembly." That sense already occurs in Amos 5:21 (*śanēʾtî māʾastî ḥaggêkem welōʾ ʾāriaḥ beaṣṣerōtêkem*, "I despise, I reject your festivals, and I will not be appeased by your solemn assemblies") and Isa 1:13b (*ḥodeš wešabbāt qerōʾ miqraʾ loʾ-ʾûkal ʾāwen waʿaṣārâ*, "new moon, sabbath, and calling a convocation—I cannot put up with the iniquitous solemn assembly." The latter phrase is an instance of hendiadys, the two terms combining to form a single idea.

gather the elderly. The exact meaning of *zeqēnîm*, even its syntax, is much debated. The noun appears to be a direct object, not a vocative, denoting "old people" rather than an official class of leaders within society, the elders, as argued earlier at 1:2. In addition, the asyndetic phrase, *kol yōšebê hāʾāreṣ*, further elaborates the persons to be convoked, namely everyone living in the vicinity, and hence does not stand in opposition to *zeqēnîm*. The laconic style of this verse lends a staccato feature to the whole series of imperatives. Indeed, the two imperatives in v 14aα are balanced by single imperatives in 14aβ and 14b.

The old people may be singled out here because they functioned in v 2 as the community's collective memory; on the other hand, their role alongside nobles in proclaiming a fast at Jezebel's behest (1 Kings 21:8–9, 12) suggests that the term in Joel 1:14 may be technical. The gathering is to take place in the temple, *bêt YHWH ʾelōhêkem*. The absence of a preposition in *bêt* is the result of a common contraction, thus is not an example of a scribal abbreviation (haplography), although it may have originated in the tendency to elide the second *bêt* (D. N. Freedman, written communication). The expression, "YHWH your God," is frequent in Deuteronomy. It occurs seven times in Joel (1:14; 2:13, 14, 23, 25, 27; 4:17 [3:17]).

cry out. The context of this verb is one of distress (cf. 1 Sam 28:12); its object is YHWH, whom the assembled people will endeavor to move to repentance like their own so that the misfortune will be removed from the land (cf. Hos 7:14, *welōʾ zaʿaqû ʾelay belibbam*, "they do not cry out to me with their hearts" and 8:2, *lî yizʿaqû ʾelohay yedaʿnûkā yiśrāʾēl*, "they cry to me, 'my God, We, Israel, know you.' ") W. S. Prinsloo (1985:38) observes that this entire strophe is markedly theocentric; it is difficult to escape that conclusion if explicit references to God (three times) and YHWH (two times) are used as criteria for such a judgment. Nevertheless, Wolff senses in this strophe no awareness on Joel's part of the hollowness often accompanying religious ritual that led to censure in such texts as Jer 14:12; Isa 58:1–14; and Zech 7:5–7 (1977:33).

1:15. *That day*. Unforgettable events in Israel's history, such as the day of Midian (Isa 9:3 [4]), reinforced by divine promises of extraordinary assistance to a faithful covenantal partner, generated intense expectation in some circles. Amos crushed such hope because it lacked a firm grounding in moral responsibility (5:18–20). Presumably, he turned popular expectations of YHWH's punishment of foreign nations on a special day into a terrible threat against Israel itself. Joel 1:15 follows Amos in this respect, although 4:14 [3:14] applies the day to foreign nations also.

The precise origin of this special day remains unclear. Several explanations have been advanced: (1) an apocalyptic notion associated with cataclysmic events; (2) a concept connected with a cultic festival and divine manifestation; (3) an idea developed in connection with holy war; and (4) the execution of treaty curses. Its meaning must have been obvious to Joel's audience, for he introduces the term by using a pregnant dative *(layyôm)*; only in the second colon of the verse does he add the governing noun YHWH. The subjective genitive implies divine activity against someone or a nation, rather than action directed against the deity.

The similarity between v 15 and other literary texts within the prophetic canon raises the problem of relationship, whether literary borrowing or dependence on a common tradition. In Ezek 30:2b–3a the following imperative appears—along with its rationale:

hêlîlû hāh layyôm
kî-qārôb yôm weqārôb yôm laYHWH
Wail, "That day! Horrors."
For the day is imminent; yes, YHWH's day is imminent.

Joel's failure to use *hêlîlû* is noteworthy, for such imperatives, noticeably absent in 1:15–20, structure the entire unit thus far. Ezekiel's choice of exclamation and his rhetorically effective withholding of the name YHWH until the repeated use of the ominous announcement concerning the nearness of the day resemble Joel's strategy, although Joel uses a longer form of exclamation and a shorter delay tactic. The Septuagint expands the exclamation to three times; the Peshitta uses it twice. Such numinous expressions of deep feelings often take monosyllabic form (cf. *hôy*, *ʾaḥ*, *hāh*).

The affinities between Joel 1:15 and Isa 13:6 are even more striking.

> *hêlîlû kî qārôb yôm yhwh*
> *kešōd miššadday yābôʾ*
> Wail, for YHWH's day is imminent,
> Dawning like devastation from the Devastater.
>
> Isa 13:6

The pun on the divine name El Shaddai, the Priestly Writer's preference for the deity's identity during the patriarchal period (Exod 6:3), does not solve the controversial issue of its etymology. This proverbial manner of speaking echoes Amos 4:11, *kemahpēkat ʾelōhîm ʾet-sedōm weʾet-gamōrâ* ("like God's overthrowing Sodom and Gomorrah").

Both Isaiah and Ezekiel address their oracles concerning the day's nearness to foreign nations (cf. Ob 15, *kî-qārôb yôm-YHWH ʿal-kol-haggôyîm*, "for YHWH's day is imminent against all nations"), but Joel turns the awful threat against Judah. The context suggests that he understands the locust invasion as a sign of the nearness of an even more destructive force.

The nearness of YHWH's day is also proclaimed in Zeph 1:7.

> *has mippenê ʾadōnay YHWH*
> *kî qārôb yôm YHWH*
> Be silent in Lord YHWH's presence,
> for YHWH's day is imminent.

As in Joel 1:15, Judah stands under YHWH's threat in Zeph 1:7. The same is true of Zech 14:1–3, but that text corresponds to Joel's usage in placing both Judah and foreign nations, as we shall see, under the dark cloud of divine judgment, the *yôm YHWH*.

1:16 *Is not*. The rhetorical question in emphatic position emphasizes the helplessness of the people to withstand either the locust invasion or the greater catastrophe for which the insects provided a visible sign. The actual speakers are not identified, but the context suggests that the people describe their unfortunate situation that has evoked the cry of fright in v 15. Alternatively, the priests addressed in 1:13–14 may be characterized as giving expression to their own and others' dismay over the destruction of grain and its dire consequences—the cessation of the sacrificial cult and thus of the means for achieving YHWH's favor.

before our very eyes. The calamity did not steal upon the people like a thief but accomplished its deed in full view of everyone. This sense of *neged ᶜênênû* occurs frequently, even though the actual form is unique (cf. Exod 10:10, *neged penêkem*; Hos 7:2, *neged pānay*; Ps 31:20 [19], *neged benê ʾādām*; Ps 18:25 [24], *leneged ᶜenāyw*). The same idea is conveyed differently, for example, by *leᶜênêkem* (1 Sam 12:16), *leᶜênênû* (Deut 6:22).

The language echoes ancient futility curses (cf. Deut 28:31, "Your ox will be slaughtered in your very presence [*leᶜêneykā*] and you will not get to eat any of it; your donkey will be seized before your eyes [*millepāne kā*] and you will not recover it") and the horrors of war in general (Isa 13:16, "Their little ones will be splattered before their very eyes" [*leᶜênêhem*]). This mode of expression conveys a feeling of utter helplessness, a sense of being victimized by a power none can resist. The emphatic position of the phrase *neged ᶜênênû* within Joel's rhetorical question shifts the focus momentarily to the persons undergoing loss and away from the actual thing being taken away.

food. Joel's concern here is restricted to the food offerings required for the routine operation of the temple cult, although the lone word *ʾōkel* naturally includes the people's daily rations, now seriously depleted. The prophet's verb for the deed that occurred as the people looked on, *nikrat*, derives from the same root that describes the ratification of a covenant. Economic hard times have fallen on the Judean community, and the loss of agricultural productivity, with its inevitable consequences for livestock, has threatened the survival of the cult. Daily offerings are cut off, being withheld to ensure personal survival in difficult times.

joy and gladness. Cessation of the sacrificial system carried with it considerable repercussion. Life lost its luster. According to Deut 12:7, normal operation of the daily cult brought rejoicing, which Joel expresses in hendiadys (*śimḥâ wāgîl*). A sharper contrast with Joel 1:16 can scarcely be found than Deut 12:5–7, which enjoins all Israel to go to the place YHWH chooses (i.e., Jerusalem in later times, perhaps Shechem originally), bearing their offerings, and to eat in YHWH's presence, together with their family, rejoicing over all YHWH's blessings. Both Isaiah and Jeremiah refer to the loss of joy and gladness; the jubilation associated with treading a vintage is missing (Isa 16:10 and Jer 48:33, *śimḥâ wāgîl*) or desperately simulated (Isa 22:13, *śāśôn weśimḥâ*).

In the ancient world emotional experiences such as joy and grief included a performative element, their behavioral components being more than mere epiphenomena. Thus external forms of religion generated the inner experience of religious people. A sexual connotation accompanies joy in biblical (Prov 5:18; Cant 1:4) and rabbinic texts (cf. b. Sukkah 25b), as well as in ancient Near Eastern texts more generally (G. A. Anderson 1991:27–37).

1:17 The long-anticipated publication of the Qumran manuscript on the Minor Prophets has failed to resolve the ambiguities of this notoriously difficult verse (R. E. Fuller 1988). Three of the first four words occur but once in the Masoretic Text, leaving *taḥat* as the only familiar term in v 17a. The versions provide little assistance toward clarifying the obscure verse, prompting several emendations, none of which inspires confidence. Perhaps the wisest course is to leave the first four words untranslated (cf. R. Simkins 1991:146–47). On the other hand, the rest of the verse is reasonably clear, and Joel's tendency to balance ideas within a single verse suggests that the first four words have something to do with the state of the grain.

Seeds. The noun *perudôt* has traditionally been rendered "seeds" on analogy with Syriac *prdʾ* ("grain, seed, berry") and Aramaic *perîdaʾ* ("pebble, sand, berry"), although *KBL* lists "dried figs" under this entry. The expected meaning of this form, Qal passive participle of *prd*, "to separate, divide," is "pieces," although the separation of seeds from their pods might be conveyed by it. More common words for seeds certainly exist in Hebrew. Several manuscripts seem to have read a word for domestic animals, either "she-mules" (Vulgate) or "cows" (Septuagint, Syriac, 4QXII[c]). The latter interpretation represents a different word, *pôrôt*; the former view is based on reading *perudôt* as a form of *peridâ*, "mule."

shriveled. *Abisa*, the Arabic cognate of the verb *ʿābešû*, refers to an activity affecting the face ("to draw up the face, to frown"). From this use, the sense of shriveling has been extracted. Quite a different verb, *ʿāpešû* ("they rot"), is reflected in 4QXII[c], Vulgate, and Symmachus. Confusion of labials has obviously taken place, as well as loss of the initial guttural (cf. the Septuagint, which may translate *pāšû*, "they paw the ground," and Theodotion, which seems to read *bōšû*, "they were ashamed").

their shovels. The antecedent of the personal pronoun is missing, although it could imply impersonal ownership ("anyone's"). Rabbinic exegetes (Ezra, Kimchi) explained *megrepōtêhem* as a form of *grp*, "to sweep away," hence clods of dirt to be swept aside. Postbiblical Hebrew *(megrāpâ)* and Aramaic *(megrôpîtāʾ)* designate a tool, either a shovel or a trowel. It has been conjectured that an implement was regularly used to lift clods of dirt in order to inspect for germination, the implication being that in this instance such inspection revealed seeds in a sorry state.

The state of the Masoretic Text has naturally led to proposed emendations (cf. *BHS*, *ḥattû gornōtêhem*, "their threshing floors are dismayed"; K. S. Nash (1989:47), *hôbîšû pōredôt ḥattû megrepotêhem*, "the women who separate [into piles] are confounded; their brooms are appalled"). The latter reading assumes a hearing error, *ʿābešû* for *hôbîšû*, but why would any scribe make such a mistake in a context weighted with this familiar *hôbîšû?*

storage bins. The importance of storehouses for oil, wine, and grain made it imperative to obtain loyal supervisors (cf. 1 Chr 27:25–28; Neh 13:12–13). That policy failed in Joel's day, if it actually obtained, and the treasuries (*ʾoṣārôt*) were deserted (*nāšammû*, Niphal perfect of *šmm*). Likewise, the granaries had fallen into disrepair (reading *megurôt* for the hapax legomenon, *mammegurôt*), possibly by violent action (cf. the promise in Jer 31:40 that the area adjacent to Jerusalem will never again be overthrown, *welōʾ yēhārēs ʿôd leʿôlām*). Rudolph understands the *mem* on *megurôt* as partitive, thus yielding "some of the granaries" (1971:40).

dried out. Having begun in total obscurity—for modern readers—, v 17 concludes with a familiar phrase ("for the grain has dried out"). The verb, *hōbîš*, has already appeared in vv 10 (with *tîrôš*) and 12 (with *haggepen* and again with *śāśôn*): a similar form, *hōbîšû* ("be ashamed"), also occurs in v 11 with reference to farmers. If the *kî* functions causatively, it suggests that the failure of the harvest discouraged those responsible for the care of the storage bins from carrying out their task. Because the locusts were so thorough, and the ensuing drought precluded any recovery in time for crops to ripen, there was nothing to store in the houses, which deteriorated from neglect.

1:18 Domestic animals suffer just like their owners, for locusts have consumed the green blades of grass, preventing the growth of stalks of grain. Joel's personification of the cattle emphasizes their unity with the people and implies that a threat to animals endangers the very cult itself. The solidarity of owners and cattle is pushed to an extreme in Jonah 3, the cattle actually being described as joining in acts of repentance. Without healthy sheep and oxen for the burnt offerings, and lacking cereal and wine, the priests have nothing tangible to present to YHWH on behalf of the Judean community.

how. The Septuagint translates *ti apothēsomen en autois*, "what shall we store in them?" The antecedents of the pronominal suffix are "storehouses and granaries," but that makes no sense, for these storage bins have deteriorated so that even if something could be found to replace the lost grain they would not be suitable repositories. The emphatic position of *māh*, "how," focuses attention on the extraordinary behavior of the cattle. They, too, groan under the heavy weight of the event that Joel interprets as divine activity. The *behēmâ*, a word used collectively for domesticated cattle, as opposed to the untamed beasts that roam the steppe (cf. *bahamôt śādeh* in v 20), wander about and low, *neʾenḥâ* (Niphal perfect of *ʾnḥ*). Joel's personification of cows and oxen justifies the unique application of this verb to animals. Extreme suffering from hunger evokes in them a desperate sigh.

weep. The verb *nābōkû* (Niphal perfect of *bkh*) balances *neʾenḥâ* and indicates that inner sighings express themselves in visible signs of distress. The herds weep outwardly. The symmetry is complete: the domestic animals sigh; the herds weep. The unusual rhyme in the initial section *mah neʾenḥâ behēmâ* and assonance in *nābōkû . . . bāqār* increase the verse's dramatic effect. The allusion may recall the experience of the Israelites in the wilderness (cf. Exod 14:3, *nebukîm hēm bāʾāreṣ*, "they are wandering about in the land") and derive from a different verb, *bôk* (cf. *KBL*).

lack. Joel's fondness for *kî* clauses is evident here, although the cause of the animals' dismay should be obvious from what has preceded. Nevertheless, he gives the reason: *kî ʾên mirʿeh lāhem*, "for they had no food."

sheep. Even small animals accustomed to foraging in drier areas fare no better than cows and oxen. These sheep are also deprived of food *(neʾšāmû)*. This unique use of *ʾšm* in Niphal perfect can mean "they bear guilt," hence suffer hunger understood as punishment for sin (cf. Hos 4:15, *ʾal-yeʾšam yehûdâ*, "let not Judah incur guilt," and 13:1, *wayyeʾšam babbaʿal wayyāmôt*, "but he [Ephraim] became guilty by means of Baal and died"). Joel's choice of this verb may derive from its echoing the name of the guilt offering. The Septuagint reads *ephanisthēsan*, "they have been demolished," which presupposes a form of *šmm* (cf. v 17b). This omission of an *ʾaleph (nāšammû* for *neʾšāmû)* corresponds to its reading of *ʾnḥ (nannîḥâ* for *neʾenḥâ)*.

1:19 The prophet lifts up a prayer of intercession, restricting himself to three words (cf. Pss 28:1; 30:9; 86:3). Then he offers a rationale for the brief petition. The parallel to this *kî* clause in v 20 supports this understanding of the prayer as only the first three words in v 19. The two verses are interconnected nicely, each opening with a cry to YHWH and then giving a rationale for this prayer, which functions as a refrain. In v 19 the refrain, "for fire has consumed the pasture lands," is followed by a parallel clause, whereas the parallel clause in v 20 precedes the refrain. The only differences are the introductory *kî* and conjunctive *waw*, as well as a definite article attached to the second *midbār*.

to you. The syntax of this prayer directs all eyes to the one who can ease the situation into which both humans and animals have fallen. The apposition, YHWH, identifies that source of hope as the same one who brought the calamity in the first place, even though through indirect means. The singular subject "I" implies that Joel provides an example for the people, particularly for the priests whom he has urged to cry out *(zʿq)* to YHWH (v 14). Comparison with Jonah 3:7–8 does not necessarily require one to read, "to you, YHWH, they cry" (i.e., the suffering domestic animals), which is then filled out in v 20 by the addition of a prayer by untamed beasts. The prophet Jonah is also described as praying in 2:3, *qārāʾtî miṣṣārâ lî ʾel YHWH wayyaʿanēnî* ("I cried out to YHWH in my distress and he answered me").

fire has consumed. Although the image of fire is not altogether foreign to descriptions of locusts, their destruction giving the appearance of fire-blackened areas, the reference in v 20 to dried water sources suggests that the prophet introduces a new threat, drought, which will come to prominence in the next chapter. The centrality of fire within descriptions of theophany, a possible context for the concept of YHWH's day, may have encouraged Joel to expand his imagery in this fashion.

the pasture land. neʾôt midbār (cf. Jer 9:9 [10]; 23:10; Ps 65:13 [12]) is uncultivated grazing land to which small animals were led, not the bare desert (cf. Amos 1:2, *neʾôt hārōʿîm*). The parallel in v 19b, *kol-ʿaṣê haśśādeh,* contrasts with cultivated fruit trees. The emphasis of the verse falls on the region beyond normal cultivation, thus suggesting that the usual area to which one might go to supplement a bad harvest can offer no relief on this occasion. The licking flame has destroyed every tree just as fire has devoured the grasses of the pasture land. The expression, *welehābâ lihaṭâ,* is chosen for more than its assonance; the graphic image of a flame licking the trees like a giant lollipop continues the personification used so effectively in the section.

1:20 *Even the beasts in the field.* Joel indicates how all-encompassing the threat to survival has become; his own desperate cry for help is matched by wild animals' begging for food. Extraordinary lexical affinities exist between this verse and Ps 42:2 [1]; these include the rare verb *taʿarôg* and the expression *ʾapîqê-māyîm.* In the psalm, a worshipper's longing for God resembles that of a deer for a water source. The idea that wild creatures, in this instance ravens, call to El for sustenance is also found in Job 38:41 (*kî-yelādāw ʾēl-ʾēl yesawwēʿû,* "when its young cry out to El"). A similar concept pervades Ps 104:21, where a lion's roar is understood as prayer for food. Joel prefers *bahamôt śādeh* or *bahamôt śāday* (2:22) to the usual term for wild beasts, *hayyat haśśadeh.* The use of the plural with a singular verb is acceptable (cf. GKC145k), particularly with animals.

taʿarôg. The LXX translates this verb with *aneblepsan* in Joel 1:20 and *epipothei* in its other two uses, Ps 42:2 [1] (41:2), and the Peshitta seems to render it by "cry out." The LXX's different interpretations of the verb are merely an extension of the implicit sense in *aneblepsan,* "to look up *with longing,* hence to pine for" *(epipotheî).* Perhaps that inner longing is thought to have been made articulate, as in "complain" or "cry aloud." In this verse the emphasis falls on *gam,* which has the sense of "even" rather than merely "also." The reversal of position for *ʾēleykā* ("to you") forms a kind of inclusio with v 19, which the refrain then undercuts: "*to you,* YHWH, I cry out . . . even the beasts in the field complain *to you.*"

water courses. This reference to dry water beds proves that Joel thinks of the disaster facing the community as more than a locust invasion (cf. 4:18 [3:18]). This additional threat can only be drought, which intensifies locust ravages. The *ʾapîqê māyim* are the streams that dry up in prolonged summer rather than artesian springs (cf. Isa 8:7 where *kol-ʾapîqāyw* stands in parallelism with *kol-gedôtāyw*). Evidence from Ugaritic literature has led some scholars to understand the term as "fountains" or "gushing springs." El dwells on a mountain at the source of the two rivers *qrb apq thmtm*, "in the midst of the fountains of the deep." Simkins argues that biblical towns bearing the name Apheq always had a water source nearby, but he acknowledges that the *ʾapîqîm* sometimes ran dry, depending "on the subterranean water table and the presence of certain rock formations" (1991:151). The use of *ʾapîqê maginnîm* in Job 41:7 for furrows in a crocodile's hide accords better with "water channels" as the translation of *ʾapîqê māyim* than with "springs." Joel's use of *yābešû* in this verse recalls the earlier puns on *hôbîš* and its variants (1:10, 11, 12, 17).

fire. A refrain taken from v 19 concludes this first major section: "and fire has devoured the pasture land." The imagery of fire to designate a severe drought occurs also in Amos 7:4 in conjunction with an attack of locusts (7:1), where his quick intercession halted both threats. Like Amos, Joel uses repetition for dramatic effect (see C. Kuhl 1952:1–11).

COMMENT

The initial literary unit within the book, following the superscription in 1:1, consists of seven strophes, the first five of which are dominated by imperatives signaling the urgency of acting in an appropriate manner, by vocatives indicating the prophet's targeted audience, and by descriptive narrative introduced by causal markers. The sixth strophe opens with a shriek of terror, which gives way to an explanation of the cause for fright, introduced by *ki*; then a rhetorical question opens up into expansive description employing verbs in the perfect. Imperfect verbs initiate both verses in the seventh strophe, thereby announcing a decisive shift from reflecting on the recent disasters to the hopeful response on Joel's part, one replicated in the realm of wild animals.

The first strophe, 1:2–4, makes a general appeal for an attentive audience; in a way this brief section introduces the call to lamentation in 1:5–14. The initial colon is balanced—imperative and vocative // imperative and vocative—with the lone direct object, "this," occurring in the first half. The longer form of the second vocative accords with an enlarging of the audience to include everyone, not just old people. A rhetorical question with a verb in the perfect announces the finished nature of the unprecedented, and to this point unspecified, event. The same individuals who have been summoned to attention are now enjoined by another imperative to spread the news among their children, even instructing future generations to do likewise. The strophe ends by identifying this extraordinary *traditum*, the data that will become part of the core curriculum for the religious instruction of children. Joel's sparse vocabulary in describing the action—a single verb, *ʾākal*, used three times—contrasts with his lavish choice of four words for the actors. Balancing the verbs is a thrice-used direct object, *yeter*. His fourfold use of "children" in v 3 and twofold use of *zōʾt* in v 2 demonstrate a fondness for repetition. Two bicola are followed by two tricola (v 2; vv 3–4).

Strophe two commands the general audience to give expression to lamentation, at the same time providing a reason for doing so (1:5–7). The initial colon resembles that in v 2, except that the first half-colon substitutes another imperative for the direct object ("wake up . . . weep"). Typical of a call to lamentation, this verse offers a rationale for doing so, here introduced by *ʿal* and followed by description of a past event *(nikrat)* with *kî*. The reference to "your mouth" echoes the oral emphasis in vv 3–4 (each in a distinct manner), which has succeeded the audial aspects of v 2.

Verses 6–7 continue the descriptive narration begun in v 5b, this time introduced by *kî*. At first the enemy is described in human terms ("a nation"), as if to connote a vast invading army, but the language quickly turns to imagery from the dreaded realm of lions (cf. Amos 3:4, 8; 5:19; 1 Kings 13; 2 Kings 17:24–28). The mention of teeth and fangs in v 6 continues the concentration on the mouth already evident in the three previous verses. The mere hint in v 6 *(ʾarṣî)* is developed more fully in v 7, where YHWH's grape vines and fig trees are said to have suffered badly during the enemy's march on YHWH's land. Denuded vines and fig trees provide a stark background for cuttings of twigs and bark discarded on the ground to be blanched in the sun; all this is sufficient basis for people to rise from their lethargy and to weep mightily.

A tricolon opens this strophe, and four bicola complete it. Alliteration adorns vv 6b and 7b *(šinnāyw šinnê* and *ḥaśōp ḥāśāpāh)*. The vocabulary is remarkably varied, with repetition of nothing except "teeth" and conjunctive *kî* and *ʿal*. The neat parallelism of vv 2 and 5 is missing from vv 6 and 7, except for 6b.

The third strophe, 1:8–10, exhorts an unidentified female to grieve over her loss like a young woman bereaved of a husband; reports on mourning already in progress among the officials of the cult; and explains the reason for such unhappiness—the destruction of cereal crops, wine, and olive oil. An opening bicolon is balanced by a short and a long bicolon in v 10, with two compact bicola in between.

The usual imperative in this unit lacks a vocative, although one seems implicit, probably Zion. Two fundamental institutions, family and temple cult, feel the brunt of the locust attack. Personal distress is accompanied by ritual expression as clothing communicates the depth of sorrow. The deity's identity, partially hidden in pronominal suffixes in vv 6–7, first bursts into full view with the mention of the temple and its personnel. The daily offerings of cereal and wine are withheld from YHWH, causing distress to the local priests. Even the land, here personified, participates in the general sorrow over a total crop failure.

The powerful simile in v 8 ("like a young woman clothed in sackcloth, over the husband of her youth"), the personification in v 10 ("the ground groans"), and the stylistic niceties, including alliteration and vocalic inversion (*šuddad śādeh* and *hôbîš tîrôš*), partly compensate for the otherwise artless sentences (Wolff 1977:24) characterizing this literary unit.

The descriptive prose typical of strophes two and three, as well as the final verse in the first strophe, continues to dominate the fourth, 1:11–12. Imperatives in synonymous parallelism and comparable vocatives are followed by *ʿal*, this time repeated and governing complementary nouns (wheat and barley), and by *kî*. Attention rests on the cultivated land, its workers, and its products.

The *hêlîlû* of v 5 and *hôbîš* of v 10 recur in the fourth strophe, with multiple uses of the latter and with a play on a similar root, *bôš* ("to be ashamed"). The consequence of a dried-up harvest is a similarly emaciated joy, which has disappeared from one and all (the *benê* *ʾādām* possibly echoing the ancient tradition that human beings were fashioned from dust and eventually will return to the ground, *ʾadāmā*). Two bicola are followed by three, as if expressing expansive speech born in desperation.

The emphasis in strophe five shifts from a description of what has already transpired to urgent insistence on a course of action to be undertaken immediately by religious leaders (1:13–14). Imperatives mount up like the tears flowing freely in a stricken community ("don," "lament," "sob," "come," "spend the night," "arrange," "announce," "gather," and "cry out"). Three vocatives, a third as many as imperatives, identify the priests as those ministers upon whom the responsibility for action falls. A single *kî* justifies all nine imperatives: "for withheld from your God's house are cereal offering and libation."

Religious terminology colors the language of this strophe from first to last: "priests," "ministers of the altar," "ministers of my God," "cereal offering and libation," "sacred fast," "religious assembly," "the house of YHWH your God," "cry out to YHWH," i.e., "pray." Indeed, even the imperatives urging the priests to carry out specific ritual practices fall into this category as well. The exceptional length of both verses (three bicola each) signals the urgency of the moment and the necessity that proper ritual be followed to the letter.

The sixth strophe, 1:15–18, opens with a fragmentary cry of terror, one that derives from recognizing in the locust attack a sign of an even more dreadful occasion, the dawning of YHWH's day of judgment against Judah. Citing traditional belief about the imminence and destructive nature of this day, the prophet proceeds to link the sign with that which it portends and to extend its destructive swath beyond human circles to the animals they have brought under their control. The three names for deity (YHWH, *šadday*, *ʾelōhênû* ["our God"]) provide transition from the heavily sacral fifth strophe.

No imperative occurs in vv 15–18, which utilize exclamatory utterances (*ʾahah; mah*) and a rhetorical question with graphic imagery ("Is food not being cut off before our very eyes?"). The familiar *hôbîš* returns, and a pun (*nābōkû* and *bāqār*). A single colon and a bicolon make up v 15, whereas the next three verses have two bicola each.

The seventh strophe, 1:19–20, extends the suffering further still; even wild animals feel the effects of the locust attack and a severe drought. In such dire circumstances, the prophetic response employs traditional language from cultic laments; it stops short, uttering only the cry of distress to YHWH, and omits the customary petition, vow, and confession of trust. The emphasis falls on YHWH, to whom the prophet Joel prays and the beasts of the field raise a complaint (or look up).

Like v 15, the initial colon of this strophe is fragmentary; two bicola follow. Verse 20 has three bicola. A refrain serves as a sort of inclusio in v 19b and 20c. Personification of fire and flame reverts to the oral imagery so dominant in the first two strophes; the prevalent image denoting a voracious appetite (*ʾākal*) is linked up with one connoting licking (*lhṭ*). A flaming tongue has lapped up the green leaves, and fire has consumed every blade of grass. The thirsty tongue has reached the deepest water channels, leaving them completely empty (the verb *ybš* occurs once more). Imperatives have been completely silenced; action has begun, however limited and partial.

YHWH's Efficient Army (2:1–11)

2:1 Sound the alarm in Zion,
the warning shout on my sacred mountain;
every citizen will tremble
because YHWH's day is coming—
indeed, near.

2:2 A time of darkness and murkiness,
a day of cloud and haze
like dawn engulfing mountains;
a numerous, mighty people
the like of which has never appeared,
nor will do so again
into the remote future.

2:3 Before it—fire consumed,
behind it—a flame licked;
like a garden of Eden—the land ahead of it,
like a desolate wilderness—that behind it;
nothing escapes.

2:4 Its appearance resembles horses;
it gallops like steeds;

2:5 It hurtles on mountain tops
like the rumble of chariots;

like the popping of fire
devouring stubble;
like a formidable army
organized for battle.

2:6 In its path people writhe,
every visage gathers sorrow.

2:7 They attack like soldiers;
like warriors they scale a wall,
each going in its own trail;
it does not encroach on others' paths.

2:8 One does not shove another,
each treads its own way;
they descend into a tunnel,
not breaking away.

2:9 In the city they rush about,
running on the wall,
entering houses,
going through windows
like thieves.

2:10 In its vanguard earth trembles,
sky quakes,
sun and moon are darkened,
stars gather their splendor.

2:11 Then YHWH spoke
in his army's presence;
for his encampment is particularly numerous,
mighty the one who carries out his decree;
for YHWH's day is great,
exceedingly fearful;
who can stand it?

NOTES

2:1 *Sound the alarm.* The event described in chapter one has already taken place; what purpose, therefore, would an alarm serve now? Furthermore, the description in chapter two refers to an imminent threat, one poised to strike at any moment. The relationship of the two accounts is thus unclear, leading to three basic theories: (1) the past event refers to a locust infestation, and the imminent threat is the day of YHWH for which the locusts acted as precursors;

(2) the locust invasion inspired a semi-apocalyptic description of YHWH's day in terms of these insects; and (3) the entire book consists of symbolic descriptions of military attacks (G. S. Ogden 1983:97–106).

The clear reference to YHWH's day in 2:1b and 2:11b focuses the description, which fuses earlier imagery of locusts with military language. Swarm after swarm of locusts had effectively consumed everything in their path; YHWH's army will be even more efficient, wave after wave of soldiers destroying everyone in their way. The prophet graphically depicts the army's initial appearance on the distant mountains; its destructive march toward Jerusalem, instilling terror; its deliberate approach; its mounting of the city walls; its penetration into the homes, with accompanying cosmic shudder; and the active involvement of YHWH in leading the mighty army. The final rhetorical question, "who can stand it?" carries its own response: none can endure such efficiency in YHWH's cause.

The speaker, YHWH, can only be inferred from the personal pronominal suffix attached to the adjective *(qodšî)*. The deity actually assumes responsibility for warning the citizens residing in Zion (cf. Ezek 33:2–4 for the serious task of watching out for danger and alerting the city in time to take action). From this point (2:12), the prophet speaks in his own persona, referring to YHWH in the third person. Because the expression, *yôm-YHWH*, is fixed, the entire description through v 10 could be attributed to the divine persona, with only v 11 being a prophetic response.

Guard towers on the walls of ancient cities provided a view of the surrounding horizon; those persons assigned to the important job of scanning distant hills for signs of approaching soldiers were equipped with a *šôpār*, a curved horn from a ram, which, when blown, emitted a sound equivalent to a modern siren. The verb, *tiqʿû*, refers to the act of blowing into the small end of the horn. The imperative form echoes the prominence of this rhetorical device in chapter one. The addressee is not stated, although the prophet Joel functions in the capacity of sentry. A similar ambiguity surrounds the same imperative in 2:15, for if priests sound the alarm (so W. Rudolph 1971:54–55), in this instance a call to solemn ritual, the allusion to their weeping and making intercession in 2:17 seems strange. One expects second person address there if they are actually the addressee of the command to alert the populace to danger.

in Zion. For the first time thus far, the identity of the endangered city is made known, although it may be implicit in 1:8, and the references to YHWH's house already point to Jerusalem, YHWH's sacred dwelling place. Various features eventually contributed to a concept of Zion's inviolability, chiefly the belief that YHWH chose the city and watched over it, preserving it from all harm (cf. Jeremiah 7), but also its survival in the wake of Assyrian might. Even the destruction of Jerusalem by Babylonian forces in 586 B.C.E. was not understood as refuting the notion of Zion's inviolability, inasmuch as YHWH was thought to have commandeered this foreign army to punish Judah for its rebellion. Yet even Zion cannot withstand YHWH's army, now poised to strike.

the warning shout. This colon stands in synonymous parallelism with 2:1a (*tiqʿû // wehārîʿû; beṣîyyôn // behar qodšî*), except for conjunctive *waw*. The parallelism between *tqʿw* + *šwpr* in the first colon and *hryʿw* in the second colon is then matched by the parallelism of *bṣywn* in the first colon and the two words *bhr qdšy* in the second colon. This neat balance produces the overall symmetry 2 + 1 // 1 + 2. The extra *waw* is a feature of classic poetry, as compared with archaic poetry. The syllable counts reflect this balanced structure: 2 + 2 + 3 = 7 // (1) + 3 + 2 + 2, with (1) being initial *waw*. Although the order of the words is exactly parallel, the internal arrangement is chiastic as shown by the 2 + 1 // 1 + 2 pattern and the 2 + 2 + 3 // 3 + 2 + 2 syllable count (D. N. Freedman, written communication). *terûʿâ*, a noun related to the verb *rûaʿ*, signals alarm as well as joy, just as the *šôpār* functioned to alert citizens to danger and to call them for festive occasions, depending on the sound made by the sentry. The *terûʿâ*'s association with divine battle in some biblical accounts makes the verb in this verse especially appropriate (see Paul Humbert 1946).

The concept of divine residence on a mountain had a long prehistory when Greeks spoke of Mount Olympus. Ugaritic literature, for example, already refers to Mount Saphon in this way.

btk ǵry ʾil ṣpn
bqdš bgr nḥlty
bnʿm bgbʿ tlʾiyt

In the midst of my mountain, divine Saphan,
In the "sanctuary," the mountain of my possession,
In the sublime place, the height of my conquest.

CTA 3 (=UT ʿnt) 3.26–28 (Wolff 1977:43)

tremble. The verb *yirgezû* may be simple Qal imperfect or jussive; in the latter case, emphasis would fall on the weakened command to let the inhabitants reel in terror. Otherwise, the verb describes an already existent state, the peoples' shaking in fright. The subject, *kol yōšebê hāʾāreṣ*, identifies the endangered subjects in universal terms ("every inhabitant of the earth"), although the scope of this description extends no farther than Judean hills.

because. The *kî* functions causatively here, giving the basis for fear. The verb form, *bāʾ*, may be either a Qal perfect or a participle; in context it must mean "is coming," hence a participial use. The qualifying statement, *kî qārôb* (cf. 1:15b), contradicts a rendering of *bāʾ* as a finite verb: "for YHWH's day has come, yea, is near."

The association of these two concepts, arrival and nearness, in Ezek 7:7b (*bāʾ hāʿēt qārôb hayyôm*, "the time is coming, the day is near") calls attention to some common expressions in the larger context of this verse and in the book of Joel, e.g., divine judgment, the formula of recognition of the deity, a day of tumult, the "pouring out" of divine wrath, buyers and sellers, blowing the horn, field and city, survivors, putting on sackcloth, and shame. Such similarities suggest that both prophets employed traditional ideas dealing with divine judgment. Wolff enlarges this traditional language to include an alarm (Hos 5:8; Jer 4:5–6) in connection with YHWH's punitive campaign and the theophanic imagery from Sinai linked with the concept of YHWH's day (1977:43–44; cf. Zeph 1:14–16).

2:2 A *time*. The Hebrew text repeats *yôm* from v 1; grammatically and semantically v 2a belongs with v 1, the new thought beginning with *kešaḥar*, possibly even *pāruś*. Amos' remarks have influenced the description of YHWH's day as darkness rather than light (*ḥōšek, ʾapēlâ*), danger to YHWH's people instead of comfort (cf. Amos 5:18–20, with *ʾāpēl*). An echo can be heard of the ancient account of the locust plague that struck Egypt on Moses' initiative (Exod 10:15, *watteḥešak hāʾāreṣ*, "so that the land was dark," cf. 10:22, *ḥošek- ʾapēlā*, which describes the following plague, darkness). The exact phrase occurs in Zeph 1:15b (*yôm ḥōšek waʾapēlâ yōm ʿānān waʿarāpel*) and is followed by *yôm šôpār ûterûʿâ*. In the initial verse of this chapter Joel uses *šôpār* and the root *rwʿ*. The singular form *ʿānān* ("cloud") is used here collectively, clouds forming a mass and shielding the deity from human view; the same idea attaches to the word *ʿarāpel*, "thick cloud." YHWH's day will be dark and cloudy.

Theophanic imagery also infuses these expressions for utter darkness, particularly Deut 4:11 (*ḥōšek ʿānān waʿarāpel*) and 5:22–23 (*hāʾeš heʿānān wehāʿarāpel . . . haḥōšek*). In the Deuteronomist's view, YHWH's self-manifestation at Sinai was veiled in order to protect divine freedom and to prevent harm befalling those who looked upon deity.

The threefold reference to *yôm*, beginning in v 1 and continuing with the twofold use in v 2, reinforces the negative tradition about YHWH's day, one characterized by four frightening adjectives. The repetition of *dôr* at the end of v 2 forms a fitting climax to this emphasis on *yôm*, a word that will not occur again until the final verse of this description (v 11).

engulfing. Either *yôm* or *ʿam* can serve as subject of the Qal passive participle, *pāruś*. The Masoretic pointing indicates that the early scribes opted for *yôm*, thus yielding the sense: "an ominous day spread out on the hills like dawn," or "like blackness" if one vocalizes *šḥr* differently, (*kiš[e]ḥōr*). Alternatively, and ignoring the athnach, one can read: "a . . . people dispersed on the hills" or "a . . . people dispersed like dawn on the hills."

a numerous, mighty people. The word choice in 1:6 with reference to a *gôy* combines *ʿāṣûm* and *weʾēn mispār*, with emphasis on the sheer number of locusts. Now the language changes, perhaps to stress the vast strength of the attacking army (*ʿam rab weʿāṣûm*, cf. Isa 13:4, *demût ʿam-rāb*). Nothing to this point has identified this invading force with the locusts of chapter one, although their effect resembles a darkened earth and sky, the rays of the sun reflecting on their wings approximating dawn's appearance. The next assertion in 2:2b echoes the language about the unprecedented and inimitable nature of the locust plague in Egypt: nothing like it has ever occurred before or will ever do so again (cf. Exod 10:6, 14). The *terminus à quo* mentions the remote past as far as memory recalls (*min-hāʿôlām*); its opposite employs the expression, *ʿad-šenê dôr wādôr*. Like 2:1a, these concluding two bicola are parallel (*kāmōhû // weʾaḥar-āyw; loʾ nihyâ // loʾ yôsēp; min-hāʿôlām // ʿad-šenê dôr wadôr*). A similar sentiment in 1:2–3 uses both *dôr* and *ʾaḥēr*.

2:3 *Before it*. Verses 3, 6, and 10 begin similarly by focusing on what precedes the army. Already in 1:19 flame and fire appear together in describing the thorough devastation wrought by locusts. The same verbs also occur, except that 2:3 uses the Piel imperfect of *lhṭ* instead of the Piel perfect form. The intensive verb matches the intensity of heat generated by the marching force. The notions "before" and "after" link this verse with the previous one, although there the emphasis was temporal and here it falls on the spatial dimension. The constancy of language in Hebrew does not carry over into English, *weʾaḥarāyw* being rendered differently in the two verses. The *lepānāyw* in vv 3 and 10, as well as *mippānāyw* in v 6, stand in the emphatic position.

Ancient theophanic imagery animates this account of YHWH's army being preceded by fire (cf. Pss 50:3; 97:3). The second of these royal psalms associates divine judgment with images derived from the Sinaitic theophany (darkness and clouds, cf. Deut 4:11–12; 5:22–26; Exod 19:16–18).

The spatial use of *lepānāyw* and *weʾaḥarāyw* continues in 2:3αβ, which contrasts the paradisaic countryside prior to the army's march with the desert conditions after it has passed through the land (cf. Jer 12:10). According to 1:7, locusts devastated the grape vines (*lešammâ*, noun), and the vital storage bins became unusable (*nāšammû* cf. 1:17). The noun *šemāmâ* returns in 4:19 [3:19], where it twice designates foreign countries, Egypt and Edom, that have become desolate through YHWH's punitive action.

The tradition about a delightful garden, *gan ʿēden*, plays a limited role in the Hebrew Bible. It occurs in Genesis (2:8, 10, 15; 3:23, 4:16), which also mentions a garden of YHWH (13:10), resembling the well-watered Egypt. A garden also features prominently in Song of Songs, where it provides a setting for the lovers. The mythological notion of paradise gains momentum in Ezekiel's fertile imagination (28:13; 31:9, 16, 18). The obvious contrast with a desolate area occurs in Ezek 36:35 and Isa 51:3, both with emphasis on YHWH's transforming power. Joel uses this natural comparison to convey the stark change in the state of nature brought about by YHWH's *ʿam*.

The emphatic *wegam* shifts the attention from nature's ravaged verdure to the human population of the transformed land—"Also no living person survived." In military parlance the noun *pelēṭâ* indicates a survivor (cf. 3:5b [2:32b]; Gen 45:7; 2 Sam 15:14; Jer 25:35; 50:29; Ob 17; 2 Chr 12:7; 20:24).

The perspective from which action is viewed determines the tenses in this verse: fire preceded the army (*ʾākelâ*, Qal perfect), a flame follows (*telahēṭ*, Piel imperfect), none survived (*hāyetâ*, Qal perfect). The same phenomenon occurs in 2:1b, where the terror-filled shaking of the citizens is viewed as an event that will follow the sounding of the alarm, hence the Qal imperfect form, *yirgezû*.

2:4 *Its appearance.* This verse makes two comparisons, one dealing with looks, the other with movement. The remarkable resemblance of a locust and a horse's head has long been noted, as the Arab story above demonstrates. That perception carries over into two modern languages, the German *Heupferd* (hay-horse) and Italian *cavaletta* (little horse) indicating locusts. The New Testament apocalypse, Revelation, states that "In appearance the locusts were like horses equipped for battle" (9:7). The author of the book of Job turns the comparison around, likening horses' leaping ability to that of locusts (39:20).

Although this style of expression emphasizing likeness achieves prominence in Ezekiel (1:13; 8:2, 4; 10:1, 10; cf. Isa 5:28–29 and Judg 13:6), Rudolph observes that Joel did not need to learn it from that prophet (1971:56). The comparison applies in Joel's case to the total army of locusts, and not as much to an individual locust. The mere mention of horses evoked fear, for their primary use was military, and in Judean historiography King Solomon's acquisition of horses and chariots gave rise to ambiguous response (cf. Deut 17:16). Brought to Judah by foreign armies, horses symbolized atrocities associated with military aggression (Hab 1:8; Isa 30:15–16; 31:1; Jer 4:13; 6:23; Hag 2:22).

it gallops. The Qal imperfect verb *yerûṣûn* contains the archaic energic *nun* ending, as do many of the other verbs in 2:4–9 (*yeraqqēdûn*, v. 5; *yerûṣûn*, *yēlēkûn*, and *yeʿabbeṭûn*, v 7; *yidḥaqûn* and *yēlēkûn*, v 8; *yeruṣûn*, v 9). These ancient forms increased the gravity of the description by evoking an unnatural mood conveyed by traditional language, particularly words expressing movement and velocity (W. S. Prinsloo 1985:42). The technical term for war horses, *pārāšîm*, conveyed the same terror (cf. the graphic poetry in Nah 3:2–3 where *sûs* and *pārāš* occur together).

In such a terse statement the unnecessary *kēn* ("thus," "so") seems strange, although it may stress the exactness of the comparison. Repetition of the word for appearance, *marʾēhû*, in this brief verse also stands out. Because of the prefixed preposition *ke* on both uses of this word and the initial consonant in *kēn*, the threefold *k* sound is noteworthy.

2:5 Visual imagery gives way to audial expressions as the prophet expands the description of the "war horses" to include chariotry. The emphatic position of *keqôl* in 5aα and 5aγ invites one to cup a hand beside the ear so as to catch the rumble of chariots on distant mountains, a noise that increases in decibel as minutes pass. Joel uses this effective image of an approaching army to convey the awesome sound caused by millions of locusts chewing away at green leaves, their wings whirring ceaselessly. To this sound of approaching cavalry he adds that of a rapidly advancing brush fire, the flames leaping uncontrollably and the intense heat generating loud cracking explosions (cf. Isa 5:24 and Nah 1:10). Joel's third comparison, that of a formidable army arrayed for battle, lacks the *keqôl* applied to chariots and fire. The operative word with respect to this vast horde is the Qal passive participle *ʿerûk*, "battle-drawn." This army is laid out in such a manner that it can obtain maximum fighting capability.

Naturally, the symbolic language excludes people as the point of reference; the only meaningful sense of the comparison is that locusts are being described as if they were a foreign army. This means that a locust plague described in chapter one has been intensified with emotion-laden rhetoric in chapter two. The reference in 2:25 to "the *years* that locusts consumed" suggests that the infestation lasted longer than a single season, an occurrence that has often been documented.

2:6 *In its path.* The singular pronominal suffix corresponds to the suffixes throughout this unit, despite the plural verbal endings in vv 4–5, 7–8. The locusts are still the subject, but the language of military conquest continues. Nevertheless, the vocabulary of royal "enthronement" psalms also comes into play, specifically YHWH's theophany. That influence affects the choice of subject and verb, *ʿammîm* and *yāḥîlû* (cf. Pss 96:9–10; 97:4–6). Moreover, affinities with Isa 13:8 include (1) the notion of writhing like a woman experiencing labor pains and (2) the reference to an observable change in the pallor of faces. Wolff connects this language with Jeremiah's observations about the dreaded enemy from the north in 4:31 and 5:3, 22 (*ʾim mippānay lōʾ tāḥîlû*, "Do you not writhe in my presence?" [1977:47]).

The noun "peoples" may indicate Judeans in their individual communities, although it more naturally refers to broader ethnic entities such as Moabites, Ammonites, and Edomites—peoples who also would have suffered because of the locust invasion. Joel's immediate concern, however, is limited to the small territory of Judah. Perhaps the powerful influence of theophanic language explains the choice of *ʿammîm* in this verse.

gathers sorrow. The idiom *qibbeṣû pāʾrûr*, which occurs elsewhere only in Nah 2:11 [10], has been understood as a flushed face or as one from which all color has fled. The Septuagint translates *pān prosōpon hōs proskauma chutras* ("every face like a scorched pot"); Vulgate renders the phrase similarly (*omnes vultus rediguntur in ollam*, "every face will be made like a pot"). Both versions have identified *pāʾrûr* with *pārûr*, "cooking pot," and perhaps they read *keqes* for *qibbeṣû*. Etymological explanations of *pāʾrûr* from *pʾr*, "to glorify," and of *pārûr* from *pwr*, "to boil," are less than satisfactory, but M. Görg's (1978:12–14) hypothesis of both *pāʾrûr* and *pārûr* as Egyptian loan words related to *ḥrr* is equally problematic. Simkins leaves the word *pāʾrûr* untranslated (1991:156).

Even if *pāʾrûr* is somehow related to a cooking pot, what does the verb "to gather" imply? One possibility is that faces become bright red with the rushing of blood to this area under extreme excitement. Another possibility, the one chosen in this commentary, that the red glow of fear is gathered up, implies the loss of all color, resulting in a look of anguish; "every visage gathers sorrow" (cf. NRSV, "all faces grow pale"). Either meaning suits the context, which suggests utter fright brought on by impending doom. Such hyperbolic rhetoric accords well with the ancient literary convention associated with receiving bad news from messengers (cf. Hillers 1965:86–90).

2:7 *attack*. On the basis of Ps 18:30 [29], *kî-bekāʾ āruṣ gedûd* ("for by your help I can attack a troop"), one can translate *yeruṣûn* adversatively like *yārûṣ ʾēlāyw* in Job 15:26. The implication of soldiers' running is that they are attacking the city, as the second colon makes clear—warriors scale the wall. Synonymous parallelism justifies this translation of *yeruṣûn*, for *kegibbôrîm* corresponds to *keʾanšê milḥāmâ* while *yeruṣûn* is parallel to *yaʿalû ḥômâ*. The brevity of the first colon contrasts with the longer expressions in the second, giving the impression of progress.

encroach. *yeʿabbeṭûn* makes no sense in this context, for it refers to the making of a pledge. The Septuagint has *ekklinōsin* ("they do not bend aside"), an appropriate reading in context. Two emendations, *yeʿawwetûn* (from *ʿwt*, "to bend aside") and *yaṭṭûn* (from *nṭh*, "to turn aside"), commend themselves to those who find parallels from other languages lacking. G. R. Driver associated *ʿbṯ* with an Arabic root *ʿbṯ* meaning "to spoil or disturb what is sound or intact" (1933:378), and S. E. Loewenstamm connected the Hebrew word with Akkadian *ebētu* ("to make crooked or bend" 1959–60:107–8). A. Guillaume suggested that *yeʿabbeṭûn* is related to Arabic *ḫbṯ* ("to go off the middle of the road," [1960:27]), a view that C. F. Whitley reinforced by associating Hebrew *ḥbṭ* ("to beat out") with Arabic *ḫbṭ* and by appealing to Aramaic cognates that mean "to shake, agitate," which allowed him to connect *ḥbṭ* and *ʿbṭ* (1984:101–2).

Neither Amos 2:7 (*wederek ʿanāwîm yaṭṭû*, "and they shove the poor out of the way") nor Mic 7:3 (*wayeʿabbetûhā*, "and they pervert it"), nor even Ps 146:9 (*wederek rešāʿîm yeʿawwēt*, "but he turns aside the way of the sinner"), solves the problem presented by *yeʿabbeṭûn*, although their fundamental meaning is the same. The remarkable ability of locusts to remain on a straight path despite the presence of so many insects became proverbial in ancient Israel (Prov 30:27, *melek ʾēn lāʾarbeh wayyēṣēʾ ḥōṣēṣ kullô*, "without a ruler, locusts proceed in an orderly manner").

2:8 The initial word in this verse is identical with that of the second colon in the previous verse, but the sequel differs in that v 8 uses a Hebrew idiom for "one . . . another" *(weʾîš ʾaḥîw)*. The Septuagint translates the verb *yidḥāqûn* by *aphexetai* ("it keeps apart from"), which could either support the Masoretic Text or it may reflect the verb *yirḥāqûn* resulting from confusing *dalet* with *reš* and yielding "none remains distant from another." The usual connotation of the verb *dḥq*, "to thrust, jostle, push aside," when negated as here, hardly applies to locusts, but the controlling imagery of a military conquest may explain its use. Simkins justifies its presence by appealing to "Aramaic and Arabic cognates which more accurately denote driving away or removing" (1991:157).

In translating the second colon of this line the Septuagint departs radically from the Masoretic Text (*katabarunomenoi en toîs hoplois autōn*, "weighed down by their weapons"), while accurately reflecting the final verb (*poreusontai*, "they move on"). The divergent readings in Aquila *(syntripsei)* and Theodotion *(thlipsei)* fail to clarify the actual texts lying behind their translations. The Masoretic Text does not pose insuperable difficulties, for *mesillâ* offers an adequate parallel to *derek* and *ʾōraḥ*.

they descend. The verb *npl* can indicate intentional descent (Gen 24:64), although it usually refers to involuntary falling. The destination of the descent in this colon, *haššelaḥ*, seems to be an aqueduct (cf. Neh 3:15, *berēkat haššelaḥ*, "pool of Shelah"), to which may be compared *mê haššelaḥ* in Isa 8:6. The "army" is represented as entering the Siloam tunnel, through which water from the Gihon spring flowed to supply the needs of Jerusalem's inhabitants. The word *šlh* occurs once in Ugaritic literature to designate a weapon, but its biblical use is limited to 2 Chr 23:10; 32:5; Neh 4:11 [17], 17 [23]; and Job 33:18 and 36:12.

The Septuagint interprets the expression *beʿad haššelah* as a weapon (*en toîs belesin autōn*, "through their spears"). A. Schoors uses a text from Ugarit (CTA 14.1.20–21, *bšlḥ ttpl* "they fell by the spear") to support the following translation of the Hebrew: "and with the spear they fell" (1972: 49). Wolff takes the Hebrew term to mean "spear, missiles" and translates "through the midst of missiles they attack" (1977:38). Loewenstamm connects *haššelaḥ* with Akkadian *šalḫu*, leading him to identify the Hebrew word with the city's outer wall (1962:62).

The final verb, *yibṣaʿû*, indicates the determination of this attacking force, which refuses to break away regardless of the opposition. The soldiers find an entrance to the city and pursue it relentlessly, or they cannot be deterred by a hail of missiles. Neither understanding of *haššelaḥ* is entirely a hidden access to the city, and defenders of a city against locusts do not hurl missiles at them. The imagery thus remains confusing, for the actual and the symbolic press in upon one another less obligingly than the invaders did. Both methods of attack were well known in the ancient world, as shown by the reliefs of Sennacherib's army capturing Lachish and the story in the Bible about David's men entering the city of Jerusalem by means of underground watercourses.

2:9 The short, staccato rhythm of this verse enhances the realistic description of locusts invading Jerusalem like foreign soldiers. The comparison of their mode of entering houses invokes yet another source of dread in the ancient world, thieves climbing through the windows essential for natural light.

they rush. The verb *yāšōqqû* (here a Qal imperfect) occurs elsewhere in Isa 33:4b (*kemaššaq gebîm šōqēq bô*, "as locusts leap, they leap on it"), Nah 2:5aβ [2:4:aβ] (*yištaqšeqûn barehōbôt*, "they rush around within the wide places"), and Prov 28:15a (*ʾarî-nōhēm wedōb šōqēq*, "a growling lion and a charging bear"). Its use is restricted to threatening movement, whether by voracious insects and animals or by vicious warriors riding on chariots.

enter. *yaʿalû* normally indicates upward movement, but here it refers to entering houses with no emphasis on ascending, although from the point of departure the movement has been uphill (cf. Aramaic *ʿll*, "to enter"). In 1:14 *bêt* was used without a preposition, but here one is supplied, *babāttîm*. The other occurrences of this noun in the book of Joel have the preposition *min* (1:9, 13, 16; 4:18 [3:18]), all of which, along with 1:14, refer to YHWH's temple. The plural form in 2:9 emphasizes ordinary residences. Amazingly, in this vivid narration of invading forces, Joel does not specifically mention the threat to the temple.

like thieves. The form is singular, a collective, to indicate a group of individuals who enter houses by stealth. In ancient mythology the most notorious individual to gain access to houses through windows was death (cf. Jer 9:20 [21]), which some interpreters have used to explain Baal's anxiety over constructing windows in his temple. The preposition *beʿad* echoes the initial word in v 8b (*ûbeʿad*), the only other time it occurs in the book of Joel. Reiteration of verbs (*yeruṣûn*, 4a, 7a, 9a; *yēlēkûn*, 7b, 8a; *yaʿalû*, 7a, 9a) and the choice of *beʿad* highlights the rapid motion being described in this section.

2:10 *In its vanguard.* What is the antecedent of *lepānāyw* ("before him")? On the one hand, Joel's easy shift from singular to plural in this unit (4a, 5b, 6 in the singular; 4b, 5a, 7–9 in the plural) suggests that the singular suffix may refer to the locusts envisioned as a mighty army. The interrelationship between vv 10a and 10b, achieved stylistically by reversing the order of verbs and subjects and forming a chiasmus between the two bicola, strengthens the identification of locusts as the antecedent of *lepānāyw*. Another stylistic feature, the reminiscence of the initial words in vv 3 and 6, points to locusts as subject.

On the other hand, the rough transition from v 10 to v 11 and the shift in the tenses of the verb make it probable that YHWH is envisioned as the antecedent concealed in the pronominal suffix (Wolff 1977:46–47). By connecting v 10a with 11a and b rather than with 10b, Kutsch reaches the same conclusion (1962:87–88). The argument calls attention to the clear movement in the direction of theophanic description, phenomena that locusts cannot generate even in one's wildest imagination. To be sure, locusts can temporarily obscure the sun for onlookers below, and the rolling motion of these insects on the ground simulates a mild tremor, but the extent of cosmic manifestation in vv 10–11 implies something far more terrifying than such phenomena as these. If locusts remain in Joel's thoughts at all here, they have been transformed into an apocalyptic army in the fullest sense. Their effect, felt quite personally although the emphasis is placed on its national dimension—the threat extending to the capital and its shrine—has finally reached cosmic proportions in vv 10–11. Perhaps the ambiguity of the suffix on *lepānāyw* points to this transformation from history to a realm beyond history.

These verses stand in a venerable tradition, one that informed the thinking of the author of such texts as Isaiah 13 and Ezekiel 32.

kî-kôkebê haššāmayim ûkesîlêhem lōʾ yāhēllû ʾorām
hāšak haššemeš beṣēʾtô weyārēaḥ lōʾ - yaggîah ʾôrô
For the stars of heaven and their constellations will not flash forth their light;
the sun will be dark when rising and the moon will not cause its light to shine.

Isa 13:10

ʿal-kēn šāmayim ʾarggîz wetirʿaš hāʾāreṣ mimmeqômāh
Therefore I will cause heaven to tremble, and earth will shake from its foundation.

Isa 13:13a

The differences between Joel's formulation of theophanic occurrences and this description from Isaiah 13 are noteworthy: (1) the application of the verb *rʿš* to earth and *rgz* to heaven, whereas the opposite is true in Joel 2:10; (2) the verbal use of *ngh* in Isa 13:10 and its nominal form in Joel 2:10; (3) the absolute use of "stars" in Joel, but "stars of heaven" in Isa 13:10, with "their constellations"; (4) the use of negations in Isa 13:10 with regard to stars and constellations and to moon, whereas Joel employs the idiom, "gather their light," to mean "withdraw" with respect to stars and the verb *qdr* to convey the idea that sun and moon became obscure; (5) the definite forms for "heaven," "sun," and "earth" in Isa 13:10, 13 (contrast "heaven" in 13:13 and "moon" in 13:10), and the consistently indefinite forms in Joel 2:10; (6) Isaiah 13 addresses Babylon; Joel refers to Zion. Such stylistic affinities as the chiasmus in the sequence of subject and verb in Joel 2:10 and Isa 13:13 do little to alter the impression that Joel's manner of expression owes nothing to these verses from Isaiah 13, although the two authors share a common vocabulary and tradition.

Another text resembling this verse, Joel 2:10, in its use of *qdr* and indefinite nouns ("heaven," "sun," and "moon") is Ezek 32:7 (cf. also 32:8 for the use of the verb *qdr*).

wekissêtî bekabbôtkā šāmayim wehiqdartî ᵓet-kokebêhem
šemeš beᶜānān ᵓakassennû weyārēaḥ lōᵓ-yaᶜîr ᵓôrô
When I extinguish you, I will cover the heavens and darken their stars;
I will engulf sun in a cloud, and the moon will not shine.

The ideas themselves—earth's quaking at YHWH's coming, darkened luminaries, and YHWH's thunderous shout—are associated with YHWH's day in the thought of Amos, Jeremiah, Nahum, Zephaniah, and Habakkuk, in varying degrees (cf. Amos 1:1; 8:8–9; 9:1; Jer 10:10; Nah 1:5–6; and Hab 3:6, 10 for earth's trembling; Amos 5:18–20; Zeph 1:15–16 for emphasis on darkness. But see Hab 3:4, for the opposite notion, the dazzling light accompanying a victorious YHWH). Certain theophanic psalms also emphasize these ideas (e.g., Pss 18:8–10, 13, 16 [7–9, 12, 15] and 77:17, 19 [18, 20], where both verbs, *rgz* and *rᶜš* occur).

stars gather their splendor. The idiom, *wekôkābîm ᵓāsepû noghām*, reverses the usual meaning of the verb, which would suggest that the stellar display increased in brilliance. Instead, this idiom implies a diminution in their brightness, as its parallel stich demonstrates ("sun and moon became dark"). This use of *ᵓsp* to mean "gather in, withdraw" occurs elsewhere (e.g., in 1 Sam 14:19, *ᵓesōp yadekā*, "withdraw your hand"; Job 34:14b, *rûḥô wenišmātô ᵓelāyw yeᵓesōp*, "his breath and his vital spirit he withdraws to himself," and Ps 85:4a[3], *ᵓāsaptā kol-ᶜebrātekā*, "you withdrew all your anger").

The staccato rhythm of v 9 continues in its sequel, despite the new images and, in all likelihood, a change in actor. Like v 9, too, v 10 begins with utmost brevity, becoming a little more expansive in the second line (v 9a conveys three ideas in six words; v 10a starts with the thematic *lepànāyw* [cf. vv 3 and 6] and subsequently communicates two ideas with four words; v 9b then uses four words to express the idea intended, and v 10b supplies two subjects for the verb *qādārû* and provides a direct object for the verb *ᵓāsepû*).

2:11 This verse returns to the explicit reference to the day of YHWH in vv 1–2 of the unit, at the same time identifying the invading army with YHWH's irresistible soldiers before whom none can endure. The relationship of the three clauses beginning with *kî* to the preceding ideas constitutes the chief problem of the verse. Do these *kî* clauses provide grounds for something that goes before? They do not offer the reason for YHWH's thunder while leading the troops, but they may continue the thought of v 10, interrupted by 11a—YHWH's thunderous shout at the head of his army caused the tumult in heaven and earth. The three *kî* clauses are coordinate, not consecutive (K. Marti 1904:129). Alternatively, the third *kî* clause gives the reason for earth's shaking and heaven's quaking, together with the awesome darkness—"for YHWH's day is great, exceedingly fearful; who can stand it?"

The final question appears elsewhere in Mal 3:2aα (*ûmî mekalkēl ᵓet-yôm bôᵓô*, "and who can endure [Pilpel active participle] the day of his arrival?"), and Mal 3:23 describes that day as *haggādôl wehannôrāʾ* ("great and awesome"). The denial that nations can stand YHWH's anger occurs in Jer 10:10b *miqqiṣpô tirʿaš hāʾāreṣ welō-yākilû gôyim zaʿmô*, "the earth shakes from his anger and nations cannot stand [Hiphil imperfect] his fury"). B. S. Childs's restriction of the preexilic uses of the verb *rʿš* to cosmic reverberation and to the motif of returning to chaos (1959:187–88) stretches the evidence too far (cf. W. Rudolph 1971:57, n. 15).

The expression, *nātan qôlô* ("utters his voice"), when applied to YHWH has the meaning, "he thunders." The expression, commonly employed with regard to deities responsible for the weather, Ba'al, for instance, came to describe YHWH's commands to an army (Pss 18:14a [13a], *weʿelyôn yittēn qôlô*, "and Elyon thundered," parallel to "YHWH shook [*rʿm*] the heavens"; 46:7b [6b], *nātan beqôlô tāmûg ʾāreṣ*, "he thunders; earth melts"; Amos 1:2a, *ûmîrûšālaim yittēn qôlô*, "and thunders from Jerusalem").

The two adjectives from 2:2bα, *rab weʿaṣûm* ("numerous and invincible"), occur in each half of 2:11aγδ. The army, *ḥêlô*, under divine leadership is no longer a locust horde, but the dreadful force inaugurating YHWH's day, one that Zeph 1:14 labeled "great," *haggādôl*, and "near," *qārôb*, and Mal 3:23 [4:5] described as both "great" and "awesome," *haggādôl wehannôrāʾ*. Parallelism in Joel 2:11 aγδ indicates that the subject of the participle *ʿōśê* is YHWH's army rather than its commander-in-chief.

COMMENT

The literary unit, 2:1–11, elaborates on the idea of YHWH's day, first mentioned by Joel in 1:15. The initial verse launches this theme and the closing verse reiterates it, thus forming an inclusio. Enclosed within this framework is a vivid account of YHWH's formidable army portrayed as attacking locusts, a description that strains to the breaking point in v 10, where apocalyptic terminology grounded in divine warrior ideology bursts through the imagery. Both form and content indicate that 2:1–11 belong together. These verses differ greatly from the previous unit, 1:15–20, with its fragmentary lament and prayer. The same is true of the relationship between 2:1–11 and what immediately follows, for *wegam-ʿattâ* ("But even now") introduces a call to repentance that becomes the dominant feature of the subsequent literary unit, 2:12–17. In addition, 2:1 presents a new tradition, Zion, that will assume greater prominence as the book progresses and even will have the last word (2:1, 15, 23; 3:5 [2:32]; 4:16, 17, 21 [3:16, 17, 21]). Moreover, a thematic word, *lepānāyw*, and the variant, *mippānāyw*, introduces three of its four segments (v 3, where it occurs twice, v 6, and v 10)—or two of three, if one takes vv 4–9 as a coherent description.

The preceding observation indicates that the distinct segments within 2:1–11 are less clear than one could wish. Although the thematic word suggests the following four units, 1–2, 3–5, 6–9, 10–11, a case can be made for only three, 1–2, 3–9, 10–11. The first one constitutes YHWH's command to sound an alarm over the imminent "day" which will witness an unprecedented divine army poised to strike vulnerable Judah. Segment two describes that invading force in images largely derived from locust attacks, while the third unit stresses the cosmic dimension of that army and its divine commander. The entire unit is a warning to sound an alarm and a description of the invading enemy at work.

Its precise setting cannot be ascertained. If YHWH acts as sentry, who receives the order to take up the ram's horn and blow shrill notes as a timely alert? The addressee remains anonymous, although either the prophet or priests may be the implied vocatives. The diverse traditions within the unit—the *yôm YHWH*, Zion, the Sinai theophany, the description of a foreign enemy, the exodus plague of locusts—fail to identify any particular group who might be responsible for alerting the populace to danger.

Like Hosea 1 and 3, chapters one and two of the book of Joel present a monumental problem because of apparent duplication of the story line punctuated by very real differences. In short, chapter one reports that a locust infestation wiped out every green leaf throughout Judah, whereas chapter two mentions an imminent threat and describes its approach in images appropriate for a locust invasion (2:4–9, perhaps also 2:3). When one takes into consideration the statement in 2:25 that the locusts devoured more than one year's growth of food stuffs, coupled with the information that locusts deposit their eggs and then depart in search of fresh green leaves and grass, it is plausible that the infestation lasted longer than one season. Does chapter two relate a second locust plague, *one decidely more severe* than that recorded in chapter one? That understanding of things is not likely, since the first invasion destroyed everything in its path, according to 1:4.

That the two accounts cannot refer to a single locust attack is obvious from the tenses of the verbs, completed actions in chapter one and future events in the second chapter. Corresponding to the tenses, chapter one invites the people to lament their awful plight, whereas chapter two insists that timely and genuine repentance may actually avert imminent disaster. Even the language of the unprecedented nature of the attack in chapter one does not match the claim in chapter two that the invasion has no equal in the past or future, hence is unique. The intensification of images for destruction in chapter two results from the additional traditions brought into play, particularly the divine warrior. Wolff emphasizes the apocalyptic features of YHWH's army (1977:42), but these momentary images lack the pervasive force of locust imagery in vv 3–9.

Why preserve such a description of impending doom? One legitimate reason for recording this account, and indeed chapter one as well, is liturgical. Like the well-known Solomonic prayer in 1 Kings 8, which specifies various vexing circumstances in which YHWH's people are directed to call on their deity for help, these two versions of accomplished and imminent disaster provide distinct circumstances for penitential action. Kapelrud's interpretation of the cultic use of the book of Joel applies nicely to the present literary unit, its claim to uniqueness notwithstanding (1948). After all, individuals under duress often understand their situation as absolutely different from anyone else's plight, a sentiment that easily becomes apt for the entire community perceived collectively.

Although 2:1–11 possesses its own integrity, it still shares some expressions with what goes before.

1:2a and 2:1b	*kōl yôšebê hāʾāreṣ*
1:3b and 2:2d	*ledôr* and *dôr wādôr*
1:6a and 2:2b, 5b, 11a	*ʿāṣûm* and *weʿāṣûm*
1:15b and 2:1b	*kî qārôb yôm* YHWH and *kî[bāʾ] yôm-YHWH kî qārôb*
1:19b, 20b and 2:3a	*ʾēš ʾākelâ* and *ʾākelâ ʾēš*

Particularly noticeable is the heavy use of the verbs *ʾkl* in 1:4 [three times], 19, 20; 2:3, 5 and *bwʾ* in 1:13, 15; 2:1, 9, the nouns *ʾereṣ* (1:2, 6, 14; 2:1, 3, 10) and *yôm* (1:2 [two times], 15 [two times], 2:1, 2 [two times], 11).

The first strophe reverts to the use of imperatives, a stylistic device that dominated much of the earlier chapter. The opening imperative stands in parallelism with the second, and both verbs govern a noun specifying the location of the alarm—"Zion" // "my sacred mountain." Only the first imperative has an object. An imperfect verb follows, and two participles in 2:1. No more imperatives will be used in the larger unit under discussion. The second verse is in apposition with *yôm YHWH*; this elaborative clause, marked by a twofold use of *yôm* and two descriptive terms each time, encloses a Niphal perfect verb between two participial clauses.

A single verse comprises the second strophe, which characterizes the impact of this invincible army on everything in its path. The operative words, "before" and "after" *(lepānāyw "weʾaḥarāyw")*, occur twice in this verse. Following the initial *lepānāyw*, the sequence is verb and subject; the same sequence is used after *weʾaḥarāyw*. This normal word order marks v 10, where *lepānāyw* introduces the sentence, whereas a different sequence sets off v 6. Here the opening *mippānāyw* is followed by a verb and then its subject, but the next verb comes after the subject and before its object, resulting in a chiasmus (verb-subject/subject-verb + object). A descriptive nominal sentence appears in the center of this strophe in the manner of strophe 1. A chiasmus occurs here ("like the garden of Eden-before-after-a desolate wilderness"). The dominant imagery is that of a raging fire turning paradise into a ruin, leaving no survivors. The latter term, *pelēṭâ*, mixes military language with natural symbolism.

Using the analogy of locusts, the third strophe provides a vivid description of an invading army. Five lines begin with the preposition *ke*, "like." The first one emphasizes the symbolic character of the description even further by adding *marʾê*, a noun that functions like the preposition *ke* ("like the appearance of") and repeating the fundamental idea (*marʾēhû*, "its appearance"). The final position of the verb and its archaic ending focuses attention on the simile itself. Sight precedes sound in the account, although sound receives double billing in v 5a. Once again comparisons are followed by participles (cf. 2:2aγ) in 2:5aγb. Because the imagery pertains to general devastation resulting from enemy soldiers, the victims are described in equally broad categories, *ʿammîm* ("peoples") rather than focusing specifically on Judeans for whom this literary record was intended. To be sure, incorporation of Zion theology in 2:1aαβ leads one to expect harsh condemnation of Judah's enemies such as Edomites, Ammonites, Philistines, and the like. The threat in chapters one and two is directed against Judeans, however, and nothing is said about danger reaching beyond the sacred precincts to enemy territory.

Verses 4 and 5 use more than a single comparison to describe the invaders. Two images mark v 4, appearance and manner of running, while three likenesses are highlighted in v 5, all associated with sound *(keqôl)*. In each instance the image is developed more fully than a mere allusion: like the rumble of chariots *on the peaks of the hills*, like the crackling of fire *as it devours stubble*, like a formidable army *in battle formation*. The account is written from the perspective of the victims facing annihilation, a point of view that occupies center stage in v 6 (peoples recoil in terror and turn white with fright). The next verse sustains the military vocabulary, at least in the first bicolon, which stresses the soldiers' advance and ascent of fortifications. This imagery recedes in vv 8–9, where innocuous terms such as *ʾîš*, *ʾaḥ*, and *geber* occur, allowing one to recover the dominant idea of invading locusts once more. Nevertheless, the fighting words remain faintly discernible, for insects have little need for roads, paths, or highways (*derek*, *ʾoraḥ*, *mesillâ*), and *geber* readily offers a hint of *gibbôr*, "warrior." The same can be said for *haššelaḥ*, if it refers to some kind of missile. The comparison in v 9 of the invaders with a thief best applies to locusts, for soldiers in this army have no fear of resistance.

The fourth strophe, consisting of two verses, 10–11, begins with a reference to the universal reaction to YHWH's army, one in which earth and sky, sun, moon, and stars are visibly affected. The generalizing description of human response in v 6 pales in comparison. The emphatic position of the divine name in v 11 shifts the point of view to that of the invading army, which is thereupon described with adjectives instead of by means of images in action: the army is numerically strong, capable of effecting any command. The section concludes with an observation about the day of YHWH that occasions the military onslaught; that day is momentous and awesome, beyond human coping.

Strophe three opens with a bicolon, lengthens into three bicola, then reverts to a single bicolon. The following three verses have two bicola each. The fourth strophe has two bicola followed by three. The second half of v 10 recurs in 4:15 [3:15] and 4:16 [3:16] gives a variant of v 11aα (*waYHWH nātan qôlô* and *waYHWH yittēn qôlô*).

The movement from a divine sentry warning a city's inhabitants of imminent danger to a deity's battlecry at the head of an invading army comes by way of images from nature. Such symbolism does not hide the essential message underlying the vivid account. YHWH's judgment is transparent in the locusts (E. Kutsch 1962:94), which "represent the enemy in a grotesque enlargement" (G. Hölscher 1914:432). That judgment and the accompanying punishment affect Judah directly, but the whole universe also feels its impact.

A Call to Return to YHWH and to Lament (2:12–17)

2:12 But even now—a divine oracle—
return to me with your whole mind,
with fasting, weeping, and mourning.

2:13 Rend your inner disposition
and not just your clothes,
then return to YHWH your God;
for merciful and compassionate is he,
patient and abundantly loyal,
repenting about harm.

2:14 Perhaps he will turn and relent,
leaving a blessing in his wake;
a cereal offering and libation
for YHWH your God.

2:15 Blow the ram's horn in Zion,
inaugurate a holy fast,
announce a religious gathering.

2:16 Assemble the people,
sanctify a congregation,
bring the elderly together,
gather the infants
and those feeding on breasts;
let the bridegroom leave his room,
and the bride her chamber.

2:17 Between porch and altar
let the priests weep, YHWH's ministers;
let them say,
"Have pity, YHWH, on your people,
and do not surrender your property to reproach,
nations mocking them;
why should they say among the peoples,
'Where is their God?' "

NOTES

The invading locusts have already wreaked havoc, according to chapter one, and the unstoppable army of chapter two has gained access to the inner recesses of human dwellings. Calamity has already struck, so what purpose can a summons to repentance and lamentation serve other than enabling the people to sift through the ruins and begin life anew? The new departure in 2:10 suggests, nevertheless, that an even more dreadful catastrophe hovers over the city, one that prompt action may prevent. Joel invites the endangered populace to act immediately, and he does so under what he understands to constitute divine initiative. Furthermore, he bases the possibility of a stay of execution on the compassionate nature of the very one who, a moment before, is pictured at the head of an army intent on attacking Zion.

2:12 *But even now*. The adversative nature of the prefixed *waw* (E. Sellin 1922:161) acknowledges the late hour (A. S. Kapelrud 1948:81); such grammatical use (cf. H. A. Brongers 1965:289–99 and M. Weinfeld 1992:175 for the transitional "and now" in letters and orations, as at Lachish) to indicate sharp antithesis occurs also in Job 16:19a, *gam–ʿattâ hinnê–baššamāyim ʿēdî*, "even now my witness is in heaven." The divine oracular formula that follows, *neʾum YHWH*, emphasizes the lateness of the hour, while at the same time justifying the prophetic offer of hope. The rarity of this expression in the book—this is its only occurrence—suggests that the prophet did not wish to weaken its impact by indiscriminate use. Friedrich Baumgärtel's derivation of *neʾum YHWH* from priestly circles who interpreted it to connote a divine whisper (1961: 277–90) does not necessarily link Joel with the priesthood, for in 4:8b [3:8b] he also employs an alternative oracular expression, *kî YHWH dibbēr*, that derives from a more general audience than priestly personnel.

Although Wolff views *wegam- ʿattā neʾum YHWH* as a nominative sentence "But even now the oracle of YHWH is valid" ([1977:39]), the prefixed *waw* copulative on the verb *šûb* in 2:13aγ militates against such a reading. According to Wolff (1977:48), Joel quotes a traditional invitation to repent (2:12aγ–13aβ) before personally reinforcing it. The reference to YHWH in the third person thus presents no problem; otherwise the shift from first to third person within the divine oracle requires an explanation. Such shifting from first to third person frequently takes place, however, in prophetic literature because of the close identification between messenger and sender.

return to me. Both Hosea and Amos used the expression, *šûb ʿad* (cf. Hos 14:2 [1], *šûbâ yiśrāʾēl ʿad YHWH ʾelōheykā*, "Return, O Israel, to your God YHWH;" Amos 4:6–11, where the refrain, *welōʾ-šabtem ʿaday neʾum* YHWH, "Yet you did not return to me, YHWH's oracle," occurs five times following an introductory *wegam*). This mode of expression points also to Deuteronomy, where the links with Joel can scarcely be denied. According to Deut 4:30 a period of extreme distress will prompt the people to return to YHWH, who is merciful *(baṣṣar lekā . . . wešabtā ʿad-YHWH . . . kî ʾel raḥûm YHWH ʾelōheykā)*. The addition of "with all your heart and soul" in Deut 30:2 (*wešabtā ʿad-YHWH ʾelōheykā . . . bekol-labābkā ûbekol napšekā*, "and you will return to YHWH your God . . . with all your heart and soul") resembles Joel's attempt to include both the cognitive and the affective dimensions of existence (cf. Jer 24:7; 29:13). The characterization of YHWH in Deut 30:3 as compassionate (*weriḥamekā*, "and he will have mercy on you"), despite the deity's active involvement in bringing the curses upon the heads of those who violate covenant relationship, accords with Joel's guarded optimism in perilous times (cf. 30:10). The use of the preposition *ʿad* distinguishes these texts from the weaker *šûb ʾel* in Deuteronomistic parlance (cf. 1 Sam 7:3; 1 Kings 8:33, 48; 2 Kings 23:25; cf. 2 Chr 30:9). Kapelrud has discerned an intensification in Jeremiah's absolute use of *šûb* (3:12, 14, 22) that reflects two realities, an old cultic one and a new emotional affect (1948:82). W. L. Holladay's rich documentation of this verb's utility throughout the Hebrew Bible (1958) only accentuates the unexplained absence of the noun *tešubâ* that assumed such prominence in post-biblical times.

The verb *šûb* occurs in connection with the coming of YHWH's messenger of judgment in Mal 3:1–3, 7 (*šûbû ʾelay weʾāšûbâ ʾalêkem . . . bammeh nāšûb*, "Return to me so that I can return to you . . . how can we return?"). An alternative to the resultative reading of the prefixed *waw* is possible: "Return to me and I will reciprocate." The former understanding of the verb *weʾāšûbâ* places more emphasis on divine pleading than on God's freedom to act regardless of human response to adversity, whereas the latter interpretation acknowledges the power inherent in repentance.

with your whole mind. Although G. Ahlström places the emphasis on *ʿaday* ("to me") and understands the divine wrath as response to idolatry (1971:26), the way Joel elaborates the nature of the turning weighs heavily against this interpretation. Of course, the people are instructed to turn to YHWH, but they must do so without reservation, wholeheartedly. Ancient Judeans believed that the heart constituted the center of thought processes, the kidneys being the usual locus of feelings. Joel urges the people to turn toward YHWH with all their thoughts, for a divided mind stood no better chance of achieving its goal than an army comprised of vacillating soldiers (cf. Deut 20:5–8).

The addition of *ûbeṣôm ubebekî ûbemispēd* ("and with fasting, weeping, and mourning") proves that Joel continues to value outward manifestations of the religious life even while calling for drastic inward change. He uses what appears to be a standard cultic expression, otherwise found only in Esth 4:3 (*weṣôm ûbekî ûmispēd*, "and fasting, weeping, and mourning") preceded by vigorous lamenting (*ʾēbel gādôl*) and followed by sackcloth and ashes (*śaq wāʾēper*). Joel's fourfold use of the preposition *be* contrasts markedly with the language in Esther. The verbs for "fasting" and "mourning" appear together in Zech 7:5b (*kî ṣamtem wesāpôd*, "when you fasted and mourned").

2:13 *Rend.* In their distress, individuals ripped their outer garments to signify emotional turmoil commensurate with putting on sackcloth, an outward manifestation. Joel uses the imperative *weqirʿû* in a symbolic way akin to the expression in Deut 10:16 and Jer 4:4 for circumcising the foreskin of the heart (cf. the symbol in Ezek 36:26, Jer 31:33, and negatively, Zech 7:12). This imperative continues the verbal form begun in v 13 by *šubû*; like 1:2–14, this section has a string of imperatives (v 13, *weqirʾû, wešûbû*; v 15, *tiqʿû, qaddešû, qirʾû*; v 16, *ʾispû, qaddešû, qibṣû, ʾispû*). The *waw* copulative links 2:13a closely with 2:12b; this connection is underscored in 2:13aγ by the repetition of the imperative *wešûbû* from 2:12aγ.

The object of the tearing action, *lebabkem*, echoes the emphasis on wholehearted resolve in 2:12aγ. The sense extends beyond the organ that pumps blood through the body's arteries and veins to include one's inmost disposition, which must undergo a complete transformation before moving YHWH to have pity on the people. The addition of the phrase *weʾal-bigedĕkem*, "and not just your clothes," proves that Joel stood in the tradition of other prophets who preceded him such as Amos, Isaiah, Jeremiah, and Micah. The relative negation ("not merely . . . but also") occurs often in these prophets' remarks about the ritual of sacrifice. Like his predecessors, Joel recognized the danger of empty ritual, its deadening capacity to lull the worshipper into a false sense of security, and consequently sought to combat external religion that did not penetrate into the depths of one's being. The type of fast he encourages is described in greater detail elsewhere in Isa 58:6–14, with the contrasting empty ritual in vv 1–5.

then return to YHWH your God. The choice of the weaker expression, *šûb ʾel* rather than *šûb ʿad*, also marks a shift in person, from first to third. With that transition from divine speech to prophetic talk about YHWH in the third person that addresses the people and reminds them of their God (*ʾelōhêkem*, in apposition with YHWH, and with a second person plural pronominal suffix), Joel launches into a doxological characterization of the one to whom the people turn for deliverance. The mother lode of this priceless liturgical gem is embedded in Exod 34:6–7, where proclamation of the deity's attributes is placed in YHWH's mouth so that no one would be tempted to doubt them (cf. Exod 33:19b *weḥannôtî ᵓet ᵓašer ᵓaḥōn weriḥamtî ᵓet ᵓašer ᵓaraḥēm*).

for merciful and compassionate is he. Causative *kî* establishes the grounds for confidence that YHWH might be moved to compassion through genuine repentance, locating it in YHWH's essential nature rather than in extraordinary deliverances within the historical arena. Given the infrequency of these "mighty acts" *(ṣidqôt)*, and the temptation to draw unwarranted conclusions in their absence, Joel's strategy makes sense. Had he based the possibility of rescue from imminent threat on YHWH's much-heralded deliverances, Joel would have opened the door for anxiety over divine fickleness. Instead, he focused on YHWH's unchanging attributes. The five predicate adjectives in a verbless sentence indicate a character formed by regular practice; all of them stand in apposition to the preceding YHWH.

Together, they characterize YHWH as a superior who looks with favor on an inferior within a prescribed relationship *(ḥannûn)*, one who turns toward another with solicitous concern akin to that of parents *(weraḥûm)*, taking a long breath and counting to ten instead of having a short fuse when offended *(ᵓerek ᵓappayîm)* so as to demonstrate constant kindness *(werab-hesed)*, and even reconsidering intended punishment when circumstances warrant such action *(weniḥam ᶜal-hārāᶜâ)*. Naturally, Joel selects from the positive attributes in the ancient credal statement, for the judgmental attributes had already been experienced by the oppressed Judeans. Unexplainably, he drops *weᵓemet* ("and faithfulness") from the attribute of loyalty *(werab-ḥesed)*.

Joel's use of this doxological confession is but one of eight clear citations of it in one form or another within the Hebrew Bible.

Num 14:18	YHWH *ᵓerek ᵓappayīm werab-ḥesed . . .*
Ps 86:15	*weᵓattâ ᵓadonāy ᵓel-raḥûm weḥannûn ᵓerek ᵓappayîm werab-ḥesed weᵓemet*
Ps 103:8	*raḥûm weḥannûn* YHWH *ᵓerek ᵓappayîm werab-ḥased* (cf. 111:4b *ḥannûn weraḥûm* YHWH and 112:4b *ḥannûn weraḥûm weṣaddîq*)
Ps 145:8	*ḥannûn weraḥûm* YHWH *ᵓerek ᵓappayîm ûgedol-ḥāsed*
Nah 1:3	YHWH *ᵓerek ᵓappayîm ûgedol . . .* (*ḥesed?*)
Jonah 4:2	*kî ᵓattâ ᵓēl-ḥannûn weraḥûm ᵓerek ᵓappayîm werab-ḥesed weniḥām ᶜal-hārāᶜâ*
Neh 9:17, 31b	*weᵓattâ ᵓelôah selîḥot ḥannûn weraḥûm ᵓerek ᵓappayîm werab-ḥesed* (*ûḥesed*) *. . . kî ᵓēl-ḥannûn weraḥûm ᵓāttâ* (cf. 2 Chr 30:9b *kî ḥannûn weraḥûm* YHWH *ᵓelōhêkem*)

The striking similarities with the formulation in Jonah 4:2 have led to a hypothesis of literary dependency, especially when one also considers the parallel between Jonah 3:9a and Joel 2:14a *(mî yôdēaʿ yāšûb weniḥam hāʾelōhîm* and *mî yôdēaʿ yāšûb weniḥam)*, although it is not clear who borrowed from whom. The two texts do differ, chiefly in the mode of referring to YHWH (direct address in Jonah, third person with the unemphatic copula in Joel), but also by the addition of *ʾēl* after the second person pronoun in Jonah.

The basis for divine repentance in Jonah is pity for doomed people and cattle; that same emotion explains YHWH's decision to relent on hearing Amos' impassioned intercession for a doomed Israelite state (7:3, 6). A text in Exodus attributes YHWH's change of mind to remembrance of the covenant relationship with Israel (Exod 32:12–14). The prophet Jeremiah seems convinced that YHWH can be moved to repent regarding punishment for evil behavior (Jer 18:5–12; 26:3, 13, 19; 42:10), a point of view he shares with the Deuteronomist in 2 Sam 24:16, one that appears to have offended the later Chronicler. For Joel, however, YHWH's repentance forms a bridge between divine wrath and mercy (cf. Gen 6:6; 1 Sam 15:11).

The innerbiblical transformation to which the divine formulary was subjected testifies to the theological struggle over the application of justice and mercy in ancient Israel. Michael Fishbane has illuminated this controversy by demonstrating the way the *traditum* was controverted to produce a new *theologoumenon* (1985:335–50). By far the majority of reinterpretations exalted justice at the expense of mercy, the primary emphasis in Exod 34:6–7. The danger of such tipping of the scales as that exemplified by the divine speaker of Exod 34:6–7 can be seen in the popular viewpoint expressed to Ezekiel that YHWH acts without principle (18:25, 29; 33:17, 20). Both Jeremiah and Ezekiel rejected a proverbial saying, "The parents have eaten sour grapes and the children's teeth are sensitive" (Ezek 18:1, Jer 31:29) in favor of strict justice. They did so in a historical setting that had become paralyzed by belief that an unprincipled deity disregarded their virtues. These prophets shifted the emphasis to justice in order to overcome motivational indifference or presumption with respect to YHWH's favor and thus to inspire courage for repentance (Fishbane 1985:338).

A comparable shift in emphasis occurs in Deut 7:9–10, which actually has Moses revise the divine formulary and justify the change *by means of a presumptive misquote* (M. Fishbane 1985:343). On the other hand, Deut 5:9–10 endorses the principle of vicarious punishment at the expense of YHWH's compassion. This radical revision achieves its zenith in Nah 1:2–3; here the earlier *traditum* gives way to a new *traditio* proclaiming wrath completely devoid of divine mercy. How vastly different is Mic 7:18–20, a "catena of hope and thanksgiving" resulting from readapting the language of Exod 34:6–7 (M. Fishbane 1985:349). The emotive power of the ancient ascription of divine attributes occurs as an organizing principle in a host of psalms (cf. M. Fishbane

1985:347–48, where he lists 40:11–13, 18; 78:38; 79:5–6, 8–10, 12; 85:3–4, 6, 8, 11 [2–3, 5, 7, 10]; 86:2–3, 5–6, 11, 16; 99:8; 111:1, 4–5, 7; 145:7–10).

2:14 *Perhaps*. The unusual exact linguistic equivalent between Jonah 4:2b and Joel 2:13b continues in the expression, *mî yôdēaʿ* (cf. Jonah 3:9a, *mî-yôdēaʿ yāšûb weniḥam hāʾ elōhîm*, where the only difference is the divine appellative). The prophet Jonah's perplexity is located in YHWH's readiness to disregard human fault when compensated for by a repentant attitude, precisely the divine trait that offers a residue of hope to the inhabitants of Nineveh. Like these worshippers of a different *ʾelōhîm*, Joel grasps this fragile line and holds on for dear life. The rhetorical question, "who knows?" contains an implicit negative response: "nobody knows" (J. L. Crenshaw 1986:274–88). Its few uses within the Bible (2 Sam 12:22; Joel 2:14; Jonah 3:9; Ps 90:11; Eccl 2:19, 3:21; 8:1, Esth 4:14) approximate the sense of *ʾulay* in Amos 5:15b ("*It may be that* YHWH will have mercy") and in 2 Kings 19:4 ("*Perhaps* YHWH your God has heard all these remarks by the Rabshakeh"). Every presumption with regard to YHWH crumbles with the utterance of this tiny particle (cf. Zeph 2:3, Lam 3:29b, and Exod 32:30), for he acts in sovereign freedom. Every turning to YHWH in hope is grounded in a combination of divine patience and mercy (*ʾerek ʾappayîm werab-ḥesed*, v 13b). As 2 Sam 12:22 and Lam 3:29b indicate, the " 'perhaps' of hope" expressed in *mî yôdēaʿ* and *ʾulay*, respectively, "is appropriate to the humility of one who prays" (H. W. Wolff 1977:50).

turn and relent. The same verb, *šûb*, attributed to YHWH in a welcome invitation to the people and taken up by the prophet to issue a similar plea, is here applied to the deity's hoped-for response. The companion verb, *nḥm*, echoes one of the divine attributes in 2:13b, YHWH's potential for and willingness to relent with respect to planned evil. Both verbs may imply a turning away from wrath, hence may abbreviate the longer expression in Exod 32:12 (*šûb mēḥarôn ʾappekā wehinnaḥem ʿal-hārāʿâ leʿammekā*, "Turn from your intense fury and repent concerning the harm [planned] for your people"). The coordinated verb, *wehišʾîr*, proclaims the result of a change in YHWH's disposition toward Joel's contemporaries. Whereas rites of repentance, like their counterpart, sacrifice, do not automatically bring about the goal prompting them in the first place, such a reversal of divine intention carries desirable consequences, here summed up in a single word, *berākâ* ("blessing"). The earlier locative adverb (*weʾaḥarāyw*, v 3) carries special force in 2:14, providing a contrast between the scarred remains of the locust horde and what follows YHWH's repentance. The idea of something being left behind is already present in the verb *wehišʾîr* (cf. Ezr 9:8, *lehašʾîr lānû pelêṭâ*, "to preserve a remnant for us," where the author specifies that "escape" has survived by YHWH's kindness.

a cereal offering. The *minḥâ wanesek* recall 1:9, 13 where these daily offerings are said to have been withheld because of the shortage of ingredients resulting from the locust invasions. The blessing anticipated as a result of mutual repentance is obviously much broader in scope than these two offerings imply. It consists of a new harvest that replaces the one consumed by locusts; the *minḥâ wanesek* are *pars pro toto*, an extension of the result brought about by YHWH's wrath succumbing to mercy. The final phrase, *laYHWH ʾelōhêkem* ("for your God YHWH"), awkwardly acknowledges that both YHWH and Joel's contemporaries in Judah benefit from a healthy covenant relationship. This idea only faintly resembles bold arguments elsewhere that YHWH's well-being depends to some degree on devotees's praise, for which reason they should be preserved from harm.

2:15 As the Masoretic indication for a closed section after v 14 indicates, a new section begins here, although the language is old (cf. 1:14aαβ and 2:1aα). The settings are altogether different, however, for in 1:14 the cessation of cereal and drink offerings stirred the people to action, and in 2:15 the apparent genuine turning to YHWH encouraged Joel to urge his fellow Judeans to follow up their inner transformation with external ritual in the form of a national lament. This time the sound of the *šôpār* summons the inhabitants to a cultic seeking of YHWH; a running to YHWH has replaced an earlier fleeing from an imminent threat. The similarity rests in the parallelism of literary units, for in 1:13–14 Joel offers instruction after inviting the people to lament their misfortune, just as in 2:15–17 he offers counsel about specific procedures following the exhortation in 2:12–14 to turn to YHWH (H. W. Wolff 1977:50).

The absence of any clear statement about the people's receptiveness to the invitation to repent has troubled some scholars, who remove the lacuna by emending the verbs to narratives—they blew the *šôpār*, inaugurated a fast . . . (cf. J. A. Bewer 1911:107–8). The staccato speech is just as much at home among imperatives as imperfects, and the Versions provide no support for ignoring the Masoretic pointing.

2:16 *sanctify a congregation*. The instructions for assembling the people of Judah during the crisis brought on by the locusts are less specific (cf. 1:14, where the imperative *ʾispû* has two objects, *zeqēnîm* and *kol yōšebê hāʾāreṣ*). The new threat emanating from the *yôm YHWH* produces the same demand for religious fasting and cessation of normal activity, but the elaborate details indicate that the people are being requested to spare no effort in an attempt to move YHWH to repentance. The staccato imperatives, blunt and to the point, issue commands resembling orders barked out in haste by an army officer. These imperatives continue the three issued in the previous verse, in one instance repeating an earlier *qaddešû*. In late usage, the object of this imperative, *qāhāl*, indicates a large religious assembly, although Ezekiel frequently employed this noun in quite a different sense. A *qāhāl* represented for him an antagonistic camp or horde of belligerent people (cf. 16:40α, *weheʿelû ʿālayik qāhāl werāgemû ʾôtāk bāʾāben*, "they will bring up a mob against you and stone you"; 17:17, "*welōʾ beḥayil gādôl ûbeqāhāl rab yaʿaśeh ʾôtô parʿōh*, "and

Pharaoh will not accomplish it by means of a great army and a mighty host"). The author of Ps 107:32 uses *qāhāl* as a designation of YHWH's own people, *wîrōmemûhû biqehal ʿām ûbemôšab zeqēnîm yehaleluhû* ("and let them exalt him in the assembly of the people and praise him in the seat of elders"). A hint of recalcitrance may be detected in the ancient use of *qāhāl* in Gen 49:6, perhaps indirectly also in Lev 16:33, which characterizes the assembly as needing atonement. The multiple uses of this noun in 2 Chronicles 30 acknowledge the same necessity, although emphasizing the people's readiness to repent (vv 2, 4, 13, 17, 23–24).

gather the infants. Those summoned to observe religious duties in 1:14 are identified in the following sequence—the elders and all local citizens—whereas 2:16 specifies the total assembly first (*ʾispû-ʿam qaddešû qāhāl*, "gather the people; sanctify an assembly") before moving on to individual components of the larger body. The following groups are specifically mentioned: old people, infants and breast-feeding ones, bridegroom and bride. The Masoretic accentuation in v 16aαβγ suggests a different reading; the elders as an official religious body constituting the last of three general groups consisting of the people, an assembly, and the elders. This understanding of the verse does not seem likely, given the parallelism between *zeqēnîm* and *ʿôlālîm* ("old people" and "infants"). The contrast becomes even more stark by the elaborative phrase *weyōneqê šadāyîm*, "even those feeding on breasts." Neither the aged nor tiny children were immune from the hazards of war, and numerous references to their suffering are preserved in the Bible, the most interesting being Isa 13:16 because of this text's extraordinary relationship with Joel (Isa 13:6 and Joel 1:15).

let the bridegroom. The exclusionary provision in Deut 20:7 and 24:5 (in legislation) permitting an engaged man, or a newly married man, to postpone military service for a year is nullified under these special circumstances imperiling the Judean community. In this instance the imperative gives way to a milder verb form, the jussive, as if signaling the extraordinary measures abrogating ancient legal precedent. The later force of this exclusionary law actually resulted in a special cancellation of the religious obligation of newlyweds to recite the *šemaʿ (yiśrāʾēl)* on the sabbath until their marriage was consummated (Berakhoth 2.5).

leave his room. The noun *ḥeder* refers to an inner room whose remoteness permitted privacy essential for lovers (Cant 1:4) and whose darkness made it ideal for (clandestine) sexual activity (cf. Judg 15:1; 2 Sam 13:10) or for covert political action (2 Kings 9:2). The parallel term for the bride's chamber, *ḥuppâ*, occurs only in Joel 2:16 and in Ps 19:6a [5a], *wehûʾ keḥātān yōṣēʾ meḥuppātô* ("and he [the sun] leaves his chamber like a bridgeroom"). Neither the groom nor the bride (*ḥātān* and *kallâ*) would ordinarily be disposed toward fasting, working, or continence, the three areas covered by the imperative *qaddešû*. A person became "holy" by abstaining from food, work, and sex, and thus was prepared to meet YHWH. The plight of bride and groom in circumstances of enemy invasion struck Jeremiah as worthy of comment (7:34; 16:9; 25:10).

Such an assembling of a threatened community is described in great detail in Jdt 4:9–13.

> 9And every man of Israel cried out to God with great fervor and they humbled themselves with much fasting. 10They and their wives and their children and their cattle and every resident alien and hired laborer and purchased slave—they all girded themselves with sackcloth. 11And all the men and women of Israel, and their children, living at Jerusalem, prostrated themselves before the temple and put ashes on their heads and spread out their sackcloth before the Lord. 12They even surrounded the altar with sackcloth and cried out in unison, praying earnestly to the God of Israel not to give up their infants as prey and their wives as booty, and the cities they had inherited to be destroyed, and the sanctuary to be profaned and desecrated to the malicious joy of the Gentiles. 13So the Lord heard their prayers and looked upon their affliction; for the people fasted many days throughout Judea and in Jerusalem before the sanctuary of the Lord Almighty (RSV).

The obvious affinities between this text, particularly its reference to the cattle's fasting, and Jonah 3:6–10 invite comparison with the religious activities to which Joel summons his contemporaries at Jerusalem (cf. also 2 Chr 20:4, 13). The presence of tiny infants seems directed at arousing YHWH's pity rather than conjuring up a pre-Jeremianic and pre-Ezekielian concept of corporate solidarity in guilt (cf. Josh 7:24–25 for punishment extending to Achan's entire family and Exod 34:6–7 for a credal affirmation of such theological reasoning). The extreme measures endorsed in this *qāhāl* justify Artur Weiser's astute observation that the extensive participation matches the intensive petition to YHWH ("with the whole heart," 1959:116). Of course, the masculine nouns (*ʿam* and *qāhāl*) function generically, thus including women, infants of both sexes, and their mothers who would necessarily have to accompany their little ones (W. Rudolph 1971:59).

2:17 *Between porch and altar.* Joel gives precise instructions with regard to (1) the place for intercessors to offer up their petition (cf. 1 Macc 7:36), (2) the actual ones who should make the request, and (3) the exact prayer to be intoned. According to 1 Kings 6:3 the entrance hall to Solomon's temple measured ten by twenty cubits; the Herodian temple was two cubits longer (MisMid 5.1). Because of the sanctity of this vestibule, acts of blasphemy like the one Ezekiel witnessed when twenty-five priests turned away from YHWH to worship the sun (Ezek 8:16) and of sacrilege such as the murder of Zechariah (2 Chr 24:20–22; cf. Matt 23:35) were thought to be particularly heinous. The altar for burnt offerings stood in front of the temple (1 Kings 8:64). This inner court served as a buffer zone separating the people from the holy place, YHWH's dwelling; great care was taken to avoid harm from the effect of holiness on sinful mortals.

let the priests weep. The jussive verb may imply that YHWH's ministers were already inclined to shed tears and therefore needed no prophetic directive beyond a mild suggestion. The form could be indicative: "the priests will weep." The apposition, "YHWH's officials," recalls 1:9 (cf. also *mešārətê mizbēaḥ* and *mešārətê ʾelōhāy* in 1:13). Joel puts words in the priests' mouths—two short prayers and a basis for the petitions.

Have pity. The verb *ḥûsâ* (Qal cohortative) occurs in Neh 13:22 and Jonah 4:10–11 with YHWH as the one who is asked to shed tears on the peoples' behalf, i.e., to spare them.

> *wayyōʾmer YHWH ʾattâ ḥastâ ʿal - haqqîqāyôn. . . .*
> Then YHWH responded, "You had pity on the qiqayon (plant)." . . .
> *waʾanî lōʾ ʾaḥus ʿal -nînewê hāʿîr haggedôlâ. . . .*
> As for me, should I not have pity on Nineveh, that huge city? . . .
>
> Jonah 4:10aβ, 11a

> *gam-zōʾt zākerâ llî ʾelōhay weḥûsâ ʿalay kerōb ḥasdekā*
> Remember this also for my sake, O my God, and have pity on me according to your abundant steadfast love.
>
> Neh 13:22b

The Deuteronomic use of the verb *ḥûs* has *ʿayin* ("eye") as subject (Deut 7:16; 13:9 [8]; 19:13, 21; 25:12; cf. Gen 45:20; Isa 13:18; Ezek 16:5), but it recedes in favor of a person as subject in other texts, for example Ps 72:13 (*yāḥās ʿal-dal weʾebyôn wenapšôt ʾebyônîm yôšîaʿ*, "He has pity on poor and weak, and he rescues the lives of the powerless"), Jer 13:14; 21:7; Ezek 24:14. The piling up of synonyms in Jer 21:7 is striking: Nebuchadrezzar will not have pity on the survivors in Jerusalem *(lōʾ -yāḥûs ʿalêhem)*, spare them *(welōʾ yaḥmōl)*, or extend mercy *(welōʾ ʾaḥûs)*. Similarly, Ezek 24:14 has YHWH vow not to hold back *(lōʾ ʾepraʿ)*, have pity *(welōʾ ʾaḥûs)*, or repent *(welōʾ ʾennāḥēm)*.

your property. The stated object of divine pity was *ʿammekā* ("your people"); the companion term, *naḥalatekā* ("your property"), reflects the sense of a related word, *naḥalum*, from ancient Mari. The idea that Israel was YHWH's unique possession pervades the Old Testament (cf. Friedrich Horst's analysis of the nouns *naḥalâ* and *ʾaḥuzzâ*, 1961:135–56). One term, *segullâ* (Exod 19:5), refers to Israel as YHWH's private possession. The rest of the world is YHWH's public domain, but Israel is God's privy purse.

mocking. The infinitive *limšol* can be translated in two quite different ways: (1) to rule over and (2) to mock. The larger context favors the second reading, inasmuch as vv 19 and 27 identify the nation's "reproach" and Judah's "shame" as items that YHWH will remove. On the other hand, the defeat of YHWH's possession provided the circumstances enabling foreigners to mock the subject people. Consequently, *limšol-bām gôyîm* may have both senses. Marti's appeal to the use of the preposition *be* instead of *ʿal* in Ezek 18:3 (1904:130) does not remove the difficulty of the unique usage in Joel 2:17, for *beyiśrāʾēl* is locative, not adversative; his appeal to the conjoining of *leḥerpâ ûlemāšāl* ("reproach and a byword") in Jer 24:9 is nonetheless instructive.

"Where is their God?" This manner of arguing occurs in Exod 32:12 (with regard to the Egyptians and in a context highly reminiscent of Joel 2:13–14) and in Deut 9:26–28 (with mention of YHWH's "possession" and with express concern over YHWH's perceived powerlessness or disinterest). Although such mockery would only have been heard by foreigners, the very thought that they could legitimately talk in this manner irritated Joel and Judeans generally. Their own reputation—and YHWH's—suffered when their close neighbors bandied such loose talk about and listened to it with glee.

The decisive turning point in the book is reached with this impersonal questioning of YHWH's actions. Like so many troubling ruminations surrounding the fundamental issue of theodicy, the doubting thought is thus articulated safely by attributing it to persons outside the elect community. Undoubtedly, the same sentiment had pressed itself upon the thinking of a few Judeans who saw no conceivable manner of explaining the calamity that had struck their helpless community. Like the convenient "fool" to whom a psalmist attributes blasphemous views, Judah's neighbors serve them well as hypothetical broachers of bold thoughts.

COMMENT

The scope of this unit is reasonably clear, although a plausible case can be made for extending it through v 18. Because I have chosen to characterize this brief section as a prophetic admonition, I conclude it with v 17. The difficulty of including the following verse derives from the intricate relationship between vv 18–19, particularly the *waw* consecutive prefixed to the initial verb in v 19, *wayyaʿan* ("and he answered"). It seems better, therefore, to connect v 18 with what follows and to treat the preceding unit as Joel's urging of the people to repent and to lament for the purpose of moving YHWH to pity. That admonition begins in v 12, which is both linked with and set apart from the previous verse by the additive-intensive *wegam- ʿattâ* ("but even now").

The prophetic admonition consists of a summons to repentance (vv 12–14) and a call to communal lamentation (vv 15–17). The appeal to wholehearted return to YHWH requires a personal decision and the resulting action, both of which are encouraged by a provisional promise of salvation. Joel stands in a long tradition of leaders in Israel's past who confronted the people with a decision to return to YHWH with all their being in the hope that such conduct would elicit divine compassion. Like priestly instruction, Joel's conditional promise of deliverance is based on the character of God rather than on any heralded *ṣidqôt* ("mighty acts"). The sovereignty of the deity remains intact; in Joel's view both the crisis and the catastrophe represent YHWH's hand extended toward his people (A. Weiser 1959:116), and the initiative for rescue originated in that same one. It follows that YHWH does not appear here as fickle but as one who uses calamity to prepare the people for repentance, making them worthy of receiving divine favor. The events constitute a drama produced in the historical arena as a result of a personal relationship between a small group of Judeans and its deity.

Joel's tenuous promise is also grounded in prophetic imperatives such as Amos' well-known directive to seek YHWH, the good, indeed life itself (5:4, 6, 14). Like this text in Amos, which opens with divine speech and continues in prophetic address, Joel's invitation begins with YHWH taking the initiative and inaugurating the crucial turning point, but the prophet then speaks in his own name and refers to YHWH in third person. Whereas Amos used the oracular formula *kô ʾāmar YHWH*, which Joel never does, to introduce the direct quotation, *diršûnî wiḥyû* ("Seek me and live"), Joel chooses an alternative oracular formula, *neʾum YHWH*, to introduce YHWH's invitation, *šubû ʿaday* ("Return to me").

The concentration of cultic terms in this literary unit, Joel 2:12–17, gives it a kind of cohesion (*ṣôm, bekî, mispēd*, v 12b; *berākâ, minḥâ, nesek*, v 14; *šôpār, qaddešû-ṣôm, qirʾû ʿaṣārâ*, v 15; *qaddešû qāhāl*, v 16; *ʾûlām, mizbeaḥ, kōhanîm, mešāretê YHWH*, v 17). Similarly, the string of imperatives gives an impression of oneness (*šubû*, v 12b; *qirʾû, šubû*, v 13a; *tiqʿû, qaddešû, qirʾû*, v 15; *ʾispû, qaddešû, qibṣû, ʾispû*, v 16; *ḥûsâ*; cf. the jussives *yēṣē*, v 16; *yibkû, yoʾmerû*, v 17).

Several traditional motifs are juxtaposed in this unit, with special focus on the idea of a people, YHWH's own possession, who received promise of an inheritance of land. Because of this relationship, mockery of the chosen people by foreign nations was particularly galling, but the closeness between YHWH and nation also provided the possibility for wayward people to repent of their rebellious ways and turn to YHWH with full resolve to maintain covenant loyalty. Their repentance was actually invited, because YHWH had demonstrated patience and mercy as the very essence of his character. That divine nature was captured in a confessional formula, the positive side of which was frequently cited in moments of great distress. The skeptical rhetoric, "who knows?" kept the people honest, preventing them from presuming too much on the basis of divine election (cf. Amos 3:2).

The notable relationship between vv 15–17 and 1:13–2:1 is broken in three respects at least: (1) the blast on the *šôpār* in 2:15 invites people to run toward YHWH, whereas the earlier alarm in 2:1 warned them to flee from divine wrath; (2) the circle of those summoned becomes more specific in 2:15–17; and (3) the cry to YHWH has specific content in 2:17, one that transcends economic necessity, concentrating on YHWH's honor and its profanation through mockery by foreign peoples. In short, flight away from YHWH gives way to running toward him, and assembling for a cultic event leads directly into words about returning to YHWH. One contrast, the distinct senses of *ʾaḥărāyw* in 2:3 and 14, speaks volumes. Behind the destroyer is a blackened ruin; behind YHWH is a possible blessing, the sign of divine forgiveness.

The first strophe, vv 12–14, consists of three verses of irregular length. The initial verse (12) has a very short bicolon followed by one of ordinary length. The next verse (13) has three bicola, while v 14 has two bicola. The rare oracular formula in v 12, one of only two in the book, combines with the emphatic particle, "but even now," to form an effective introduction to divine speech. The athnach sets apart the appeal to turn to YHWH wholeheartedly, but in so doing it also concentrates attention on the brief description of correct demeanor that is expected to accompany such a return. The next verse continues this emphasis on the inner being without sacrificing the corresponding external manifestations such as torn clothes. Once again the verse is divided at the crucial point between describing human beings and the deity. The adjectives stand out in this moving confession, and the copula *hûʾ* recalls a numinous expression that comes to prominence in Deutero-Isaiah (cf. 43:25, *ʾānōkî ʾānōkî hûʾ*, "As for me, I am that one"). The same expression, except for the short form of the personal pronoun, and the particle *kî* occurs in Deut 32:39 *(kî ʾanî ʾanî hûʾ)*. If *hûʾ* is only the copula, the translation would be "that I am I," the equivalent of Greek *ego eimi*, a significant expression in the Septuagint and New Testament. The skeptical question in v 14 rules out absolute denial of hope, for nobody knows what YHWH will do in any given circumstance. The positive side of such ignorance is the open door. In Joel's opinion, it was worth a try.

The second strophe consists of two short bicola (v 15), three bicola (v 16), and four bicola (v 17). The initial command to sound the call for a religious gathering (vv 15, 16a) issues short bursts of syntactic energy comparable to commands. Imperatives give way to jussives in v 16b, as if to acknowledge the extraordinary circumstances necessitating the cancellation of a legal statute protecting the rights of newlyweds. The specificity becomes almost too much in v 17, suggesting that priestly intercession would succeed only if taking place in a special location. Joel implies that YHWH had already established the conditions for restoring broken relationships, and the priests must play their proper role in this unfolding drama. Their prayer consists of a positive cohortative and a negative request (*ḥûsâ YHWH ʿal ʿammekā weʾal tittēn . . .*). Like the previous one, this strophe concludes with a rhetorical question (v 17). The question in v 14 dealt with YHWH's unfathomable nature; that in v 17 concerns the equally hypothetical mockery of both YHWH and his people.

A curious silence is maintained from beginning to end in regard to the specific offenses that separated YHWH from his people and, according to ancient belief, brought the catastrophe on Zion. Joel's insistence that the people repent and return to YHWH may imply fault, but none is delineated. Modern interpreters can speculate about the transgressions the prophet presupposes—insincere cult (H. W. Wolff 1977:48–53), religious syncretism (G. W. Ahlström 1971:26), excessive ritual and cultic self-sufficiency (G. Wanke 1984:17), breach of covenant (L. C. Allen 1976:77–84), failed leadership (P. L. Redditt 1986:225–40), presumption arising from election (H. W. Wolff 1977:48–53), reluctance to be identified with a loser in battle, an impotent deity (R. Simkins 1911:181–90)—but we do not possess sufficient information to answer the question, "Of what, if anything, were the Judeans in Joel's time guilty?"

THE RESTORATION OF JUDAH AND DIVINE JUDGMENT ON FOREIGN NATIONS

Replacing What the Locusts Consumed (2:18–27)

2:18 Then YHWH became zealous about his land
and had compassion on his people.

2:19 YHWH answered them,
"Look, I am about to send you
grain, new wine, and oil;
you will be satisfied with them;
never again will I make you
a reproach among the nations.

2:20 The northerner
I will thrust from your midst,
driving it to a thirsty and desolate land,
his vanguard to the eastward sea,
his rearguard to the westward sea;
his stench will rise,
together with his foul odor,
for he has acted reprehensibly.

2:21 Do not fear, land,
be happy and rejoice,
for YHWH has acted mightily.

2:22 Fear not, beasts of the field,
for the pasture land has put forth lush growth;
the trees have produced their fruit,
fig and vine have yielded their produce.

2:23 Citizens of Zion, rejoice and be glad,
In YHWH your God,
for he has given you the early rain in its season,
and sent down showers for you,
both early and late, as previously.

2:24 The granaries are full of grain;
the vats spill over with new wine and oil.

2:25 I will make up for you the years
the swarming locusts consumed—
the jumper, finisher, and chewer—
my mighty force that I sent against you.

2:26 You will continually consume food and always be satisfied;
you will praise the name of YHWH your God
who has worked wonderfully among you,
and my people will never again be shamed.

2:27 Then you will know
that I am in the midst of Israel,
and I, YHWH, am your God—
there is no other—
and my people will never again be shamed."

NOTES

2:18 *Then YHWH became zealous.* The *waw* consecutive on *wayeqannēʾ* (Piel imperfect) links this verse with the preceding prayer for compassion and restored honor. The return to narrative verbs recalls 1:3, the necessity of proclaiming memorable events from generation to generation. In the former instance the content of that proclamation was negative, but here the subject is completely positive, at least for YHWH's people. The imperfect verbs can be understood as prophetic perfect or as promissory; the Masoretic Text vocalization opts for the former understanding. The zeal for YHWH's land has become an established fact, transforming divine intention from judgment to blessing. The synonymous colon asserts that YHWH's pity extends to his people also *(wayyaḥmōl ʿal ʿammô)*.

Curiously, Joel neglects to report that the people responded favorably to the summons to repent, although YHWH's response probably suggests that they did. Perhaps this missing information explains the readiness on the part of some interpreters to view the rest of the book as promises yet to be realized. As such, the grand prospects for the future motivate the repentance and lamentation. One could argue that YHWH's compassionate character as announced in 2:13b pertains regardless of human response, and numerous biblical texts celebrate YHWH's mercy heaped upon undeserving transgressors, but the ancient credal statement in Exod 34:6–7 balances mercy with strict justice. Moreover, the context of the second chapter in Joel argues against this emphasis on ignoring human conduct, for both the locusts and YHWH's formidable army are said to function at divine bidding.

YHWH's zeal appears prominently in Deut 5:9–10 as the reason for worshipping no deity except him. Although this demand for exclusive loyalty includes a threat to impose punishment on sinners over a span of four generations, it compensates by promising long-lasting favor to faithful devotees. Just as the opposite feelings of love and hate distinguish the contrasting relationships to YHWH in this text, so they mark extreme affections in Cant 8:6.

kî- ʿazzâ kammawet ʾahabâ qāšâ kišʾol qineʾâ
For strong as death is love,
mighty as Sheol is passion.

The extraordinary effect of jealousy on a cuckolded husband is described in a biblical proverbial saying that warns potential adulterers against incurring such unforgiving fury (Prov 6:34). The application of the verb *qānâ* to YHWH's zeal for his people occurs in Isa 9:6 [7] and 37:32 as a *theologoumenon* (*qineʾat YHWH ṣebāʾôt taʿaśeh-zōʾt*, "the zeal of YHWH of hosts will do this thing"). The larger context of Ezek 39:25 shares many ideas with Joel: (1) the so-called formula of recognition, 39:22, 28; (2) the promise of restoration, 39:25; (3) divine jealousy, 39:25; (4) the presence and removal (forgetting) of shame, 39:26; (5) secure living in the land without fear, 39:26; (6) the gathering and return of YHWH's exiled peoples, 39:27; and (7) the outpouring of the divine spirit, 39:29. The nations' insignificance in implementing YHWH's punishment of his people for transgression sets the tone of this divine promise.

Another text, Zech 1:14, takes the form of divine speech, mediated to the prophet through an angel.

kô ʾāmar YHWH ṣebāʾôt qinneʾtî lîrušalayim ûleṣiyyôn qineʾâ gedôlâ
YHWH of hosts said this, "I am exceedingly zealous for Jerusalem and Zion."

The language matches the intensity of YHWH's fury, employing a Piel perfect verb with the preposition *le* and elaborating further on divine jealousy by adding "a powerful zeal." The root *qnʾ* has both connotations, zeal and jealousy. The basic passion may express itself either negatively as jealousy or positively as zeal. Similarly, 8:2 opens with the same oracular formula, uses identical words except for omitting Jerusalem as a parallel to Zion, and adds a compensating repetition, *weḥēmâ gedôlâ qinnēʾtî lāh* ("and I am zealous for her with extreme anger"). The prophetic indictment of Nineveh in the book of Nahum begins by applying the old credal formula from Exod 34:6–7 to YHWH's enemies, who suffer at the hands of an angry God. The twin concepts of jealousy and fury occur in 1:2a (*ʾēl qannôʾ . . . ûbaʿal ḥēmâ*, "a jealous God . . . and furious"). The language of Zeph 1:18 differs markedly when applying this idea of divine wrath to the day of YHWH (*beyôm ʿebrat YHWH ûbeʾēš qinʾātô teʾākēl kol-hāʾāreṣ*, ". . . in the day of YHWH's anger; and the whole earth will be consumed by his fiery zeal," cf. Zeph 3:8).

This anthropopathic way of talking about YHWH is grounded in a concept of intimate relationship between the people and their deity. Like the jealous husband in Prov 6:34 who insists on revenge for such a personal offense as adultery, YHWH struck out violently against those who injured his honor. The other side of such passion is expressed in the notion of pity for YHWH's people (*wayyaḥmōl ʿal ʿammô*; Joel 2:18b). Such an emotion can move human beings to exceptional deeds.

wehinnê—naʿar bōkeh wattaḥmol ʿālāyw
. . . now the child was crying—and she pitied him.

Exod 2:6aβbα

Here the narrative tradition about Moses attributes this powerful affection to none other than a pharaoh's daughter. As a negative image for YHWH's lack of mercy, this verb occurs in Jer 13:14 and frequently in Ezekiel and Lamentations (cf. Ezek 5:11; 7:4, 9; 8:18; 9:5, 10; Lam 2:2, 17, 21; 3:43). The image in Lam 3:43 effectively communicates the horror of a potentially positive emotion that has gone awry (*sakkōtâ bāʾap wattirdepēnnû hāragtâ lōʾ ḥāmāltā*, "you enclosed yourself with anger and pursued us, slaughtering us mercilessly"). The verb retains its positive sense, however, in Ezek 36:21, although divine self-interest marks this text about the loss of YHWH's reputation, and in Mal 3:17, which compares YHWH's pity for Judah with parents' feelings for obedient children (*weḥāmaltî ʿalêhem kaʾăšer yaḥmōl ʾîš ʿal-benô hāʿōbēd ʾōtô*, "and I will take pity on them just as a man pities his son who serves him").

The parallel form of the two cola in Joel 2:18 raises the question whether or not divine solicitude is aimed at two distinct objects rather than just one. In all probability, "land" and "people" represent different recipients of YHWH's warm feelings. Significantly, zeal applies to land whereas pity is directed toward the people. Synonymity is additive in this instance, signaling YHWH's changed feelings for the ruined land of Judah and its inhabitants who are probably thought to have brought on the calamity in the first place. At the same time, people and land are inseparably connected, and that linkage stands out despite the parallelism of the two cola.

2:19 *YHWH answered them*. In typically redundant language (lit., "Then YHWH answered and said to his people"), this verse retains the spotlight on YHWH, whom the prayer in 2:17 invokes. The slim basis for hope resting behind the expression, *mî yôdēaᶜ*, has been shown to be reliable once more. The divine response takes the form of word and deed; the word declares the imminence of the deed, like the earlier announcement concerning YHWH's day. The verb *ᶜnh* normally introduces YHWH's answer to prayer and lament, perhaps ritualized in the cult through priestly and prophetic mediators. The scope of the divine oracle is unclear, for the first person language is broken at v 21 and returns in v 25. Furthermore, the tenses of the verbs are inconsistent. If the verbs in vv 21–23 are prophetic perfects, why does a change take place in v 24? Rudolph recognizes the difficulty and insists on viewing all the verbs in this divine oracle as true perfects (1971:63). The initial response is thus restricted to vv 19–20, and the answer to prayer takes up two concerns: (1) the loss of food stuffs and (2) the ridicule aimed at YHWH's people.

The focusing *hinenî*, when followed by a participle as here, directs attention to the actor, hence the divine subject of *šōlēaḥ*. The emphasis falls on the immediacy of the action, its actual incipient development. The promised event is on the verge of taking place; YHWH is poised to inaugurate a new era. In this instance, *hinenî* truly signals a shift in point of view, although one to which the previous prayer progressed. The depth of human need fades momentarily to highlight the one who rouses himself to alleviate such misery.

YHWH's answer is dictated by a lack of an excess. The loss of grain, new wine, and olive oil (cf. 1:10) is about to be corrected, and the stinging ridicule by foreigners (cf. 2:17) will soon be vanquished. The threefold use of the *nota accusativi*, *ᵓet*, corresponds to the three types of food that will soon bring satiety to a hungry people. The oracle stops short of mentioning a concern that has already been expressed twice, that the daily cereal and wine offerings had ceased (1:9, 13), but silence about religious obligation merely accentuates YHWH's sole concern for the moment—the well-being of his people. A single verb sums up everything YHWH intends to accomplish; they will be satisfied (*śbᶜ*, "to be full"). The full stomachs of the people will be matched by ample honor, now greatly depleted by vulnerability to mockery.

2:20 *The northerner*. The *waw* prefixed to the accusative particle indicates that this verse continues the divine promissory oracle. The emphatic position of the direct object calls attention to it, as does the strange form, *haṣṣepônî*. Context suggests that the noun designates a ravager of the stricken people, but the primary cause of misery, a locust swarm, would not ordinarily have been described as "the northerner." Locusts usually approached from the east or southeast, and although an exception might have occurred in this instance, it would hardly have provided adequate linguistic basis for what appears to be a fixed expression. In any event, Joel uses the word with no explanation, leading one to assume that he expected his audience to recognize the precise thing to which the reference alluded. The second possibility is YHWH's army, if indeed it differed from the locust invasion. The description of the attack in 2:1–11 merges the two images, insect infestation and military assault, so thoroughly that a plausible case can be made for only one enemy, locusts. At the very least, they pose such a horrendous threat to survival that one naturally expects YHWH to address the problem forthrightly. Therefore, the most likely reference of *haṣṣepônî* is the locust swarm.

Why is it called "the northerner"? Two reasons quickly come to mind: (1) Joel draws on imagery from the mythological concept of the enemy from the north, or (2) he alludes to the mythical mountain of the gods in the north. Perhaps the two quite different concepts had come together by the time Joel formulated this divine speech. Both Jeremiah (1:13–15; 4:6; 6:1, 22) and Ezekiel (38:6, 15; 39:2) envision a powerful threat from the north. Even if Scythian hordes were shown to have been a figment of scholarly imagination, like the mythical Gog of Magog, the symbol of all warrior conquerors who will be destroyed in the final day of YHWH, the frequent southward march of soldiers, whether Syrian, Assyrian, or Babylonian, easily set minds to thinking about foes from the north. Prophetic hyperbole may have contributed to the notion of a mythic foe (cf. Isa 5:26–30), just as Isaiah's rhetoric painted a detailed portrait of royal aggrandizement (Isa 14:4b–21). The mythical concept of Mount Saphon as the dwelling place of the gods (Isa 14:13) is applied to Zion in Ps 48:3 [2], despite the oddity of locating this citadel in the far north (*har-ṣiyyôn yarkətê ṣāpôn*, "Mount Zion, the peaks of the North"). "The northerner" thus functions as a play on a prophetic symbol for the ultimate adversary; in so doing, it provides a powerful image to describe YHWH's sinister harbingers of a final day of judgment. The imagery continues that of 2:11 ("his army"), reiterated in 2:25 ("my formidable army").

Of course, many interpreters have proposed emendations for *haṣṣepônî*, although its form, a noun with a gentilic ending, is perfectly acceptable. Besides, no versional support for a textual change exists. Among the many proposed readings, two stand out, Sellin's (1929:165), *hṣpṣpny* ("the chirper"), and Budde's (1919:1–5), *wʾt hṣpny ʾrh yrḥyq hylq mʿlykm* ("and I will cause the north wind to blow, driving out the locust from your midst"). Neither emendation is necessary.

thirsty and desolate land. The destination of the locusts furnishes the subject for the rest of the verse. YHWH promises to drive them into an arid desert incapable of sustaining their needs. The two adjectives, *ṣiyyâ ûšəmāmâ*, characterize the land to which the northerner will be driven as both devoid of water and lacking foliage. The obvious geographical reference is the desert to the east and south, from which direction the locusts would probably have come. The verb *wehiddaḥtiw* (Hiphil perfect from *ndḥ*) connotes a scattering of the foe, an apt military image for defeated troops fleeing for their lives (contrast their orderly march in 2:7–8). Similarly, *ʾarḥîq* (Hiphil imperfect from *rḥq*) indicates removal from the premises, an idea reinforced by the adversative sense of the preposition *ʿal* (*mēʿalêkem*, "from upon you").

his vanguard. The language plays on the earlier use of *lepānāyw* in 2:3 and 10, as well as *mippānāyw* in 2:6, just as *his rearguard* echoes the two uses of *weʾaḥarāyw* in 2:3. The image suggests the frontal assault force and the final troops assigned the task of consolidating a victory. Joel implies that the eradication of the enemy troops will be complete, extending all the way from the initial attack to the "mopping-up" exercises. The locusts will be driven into the Dead Sea *(ʾel-hayyām haqqadmōnî)* and the Mediterranean Sea *(ʾel-hayyām hāʾaḥarôn)*. Because ancient Israelites determined directions by standing with the face to the east, the adverbs "in front of" and "behind" indicate the two bodies of water (cf. Ezek 47:8; Zech 14:8 and Deut 11:24; 34:2; Zech 14:8, respectively). The word rendered "his rearguard" *(sōpô)* occurs only in late texts (Eccl 3:11; 7:2; 12:13; Dan 4:8 [11], 19 [22]; 6:27 [26]; 7:26, 28; and 2 Chr 20:16).

his foul odor. Exact parallelism between subjects and the repetition of the verb demand this translation of the hapax legomenon *ṣaḥanātô* (cf. Sir 11:12), despite the anomalous verb form (*wetaʿal* instead of an expected *wetaʿaleh* or *weʿalatâ*). In connection with afflictions sent by YHWH against his people, the prophet Amos mentions a stench *(beʾōš)* in the Israelites' nostrils (Amos 4:10b; cf. Isa 34:3). The idea naturally belongs to the after-effects of advancing armies, specifically the odor of decaying flesh, although the expression could also point to nauseous fumes generated by drowned locusts that have washed ashore. Kjeld Jensen's implausible identification of "the northerner" with Antiochus IV Epiphanes (1941:111, cited from H. W. Wolff 1977:62) rests on the similarity between this image and the description of the Syrian ruler's death (2 Macc 9:9).

for he has acted reprehensibly. A more suitable contrast could hardly be contemplated than the one presented here: the rotting stench of one who has previously behaved in a grandiose manner. The verb and accompanying infinitive *(higdîl laʿaśôt)* ordinarily indicate impressive achievements, a meaning they definitely have in the next verse with YHWH as stated subject. However, the context of 2:20 favors a pejorative nuance with the northerner as an implicit subject. This divine agent of punishment has exceeded his commission by acting arrogantly, just as both Assyria and Babylon are said to have gone beyond their assignment (Isa 10:5–19 and Hab 2:6–19). The little horn that magnified itself in Dan 7:8 and the boastful king of Babylon in Isaiah 14 belong to the same category of arrogant persons as the villain in Joel 2:20.

2:21 *Do not fear.* The opening words of an oracle of assurance (cf. the priestly oracle of salvation, J. Begrich 1934:81–92 and E. Conrad 1985) indicate the changed circumstances resulting from YHWH's favorable answer to the desperate plea for help. The three addressees in vv 21–23 mark an ascending order from land to animals to Zion's children. The admonition to the land recalls 1:10, which reports that it had lost the potential for productivity. Now, however, the land has reason for rejoicing; *YHWH has acted mightily.* The brevity of this initial oracle contrasts with the expansive description in the previous verse. The negative admonition is reinforced by two positive imperatives, *gîlî ûśemāḥî* ("be happy and rejoice"). The land's former mourning (1:10a) is replaced by rejoicing like that associated with harvest, happiness that had ceased to manifest itself in YHWH's temple (1:16b).

A few psalms of thanksgiving (e.g., Pss 117, 135) resemble this verse with its (1) command or exhortation; (2) vocative; (3) reason for the jubilation, introduced by *kî*; and (4) designation of the divine basis for such gratitude, whether resting in YHWH's nature or deriving from his activity. Whereas the people's appeal for mercy in 2:17b is predicated on the description of the divine character in 2:13b, Joel's oracle of assurance shifts the emphasis from YHWH's nature to his deeds. It does so by repeating the clause that concludes 2:20, albeit with a specific subject. The declaration that YHWH has acted mightily occurs elsewhere in Ps 126:2–3.

higdîl YHWH laʿaśôt ʿim-ʾēlleh
higdîl YHWH laʿaśôt ʿimmānû hāyînû śemēḥîm
YHWH has done remarkable things for them;
YHWH has acted mightily among us (and) we rejoice continually.

Inasmuch as the cause for the land's unhappiness in 1:10 was its barren state, the specific mention of its lush growth is delayed until 2:22, which concerns itself with animals whose survival depends on the land's bounty.

2:22 *Fear not.* This imperative, *ʾal tireʾû*, is masculine plural despite the feminine plural addressee, *bahamôt śāday.* Because domestic animals of all kinds were viewed collectively, one expects a feminine singular form comparable to that in the previous verse, although Amos 4:1 exhibits the same peculiarity (*šimʿû haddābar hazzeh pārôt habbāšān* . . . , "Hear this word, cows of Bashan"; cf. Ruth 1:8b). For Amos, the vocative *pārôt* functions metaphorically, whereas Joel actually means oxen, sheep, and cattle of all kinds.

lush growth. The verb *dāšeʾû* (Qal perfect) occurs elsewhere only in Gen 1:11 in the Hiphil (*wayyōʾmer ʾelōhîm tadšēʾ hāʾāreṣ*, "and God said, 'Let the earth put forth lush growth' "), in contrast to the more widely dispersed nominative form *deše*ʾ. The parched grazing land that brought such misery in 1:10, 18–20 has put forth new growth resembling that first burst of foliage in the myth of paradise. Eden has been restored (cf. 2:3), making the earlier devastation resulting from the locust swarm a past event.

their produce. In this context *ḥêlām*, the direct object of the Qal perfect verb *nātenû*, means "their strength," i.e., their maximum capacity (cf. 2:11, where *ḥêlô* indicates YHWH's army). In contrast with the situation described in 2:12, the fig trees and grape vines have produced an abundant crop, all they could yield without damaging their branches and tendrils. The same sort of contrast pertains with respect to fruit trees, which have borne generously instead of drying up or dropping immature fruit (1:19).

2:23 *Citizens of Zion.* The expression, *benê ṣiyyôn*, occurs elsewhere in only two places, Lam 4:2 and Ps 149:2. Emendation of the first of these to *ʾabnê ṣiyyôn*, "Zion's stones," accords well with the context, which would suggest that sacred stones from the temple are being treated with no more respect than broken pieces of ordinary pottery. The other use of *benê ṣiyyôn* provides a parallel to Joel's, for both texts urge the Zionites to rejoice and be glad. The order of the word pair is the reverse in Ps 149:2 (*yiśmaḥ yiśrāʾēl beʿōśāyw benê ṣiyyôn yagîlû bemalkām*, "Let Israel be glad about his deeds; Zionites, rejoice in their king"). The reference in both texts is probably inclusive, embracing all persons in Judah who worship YHWH at Zion (K. Marti 1904:33). The Korahite veneration of Zion in Psalm 87 gives fresh meaning to the expression "children of Zion," particularly the concept of a divine registry of births (cf. *ʾîš weʾiš yullad-bâ*, "this person and that person were born in her [Zion]," v 5a) and *zeh-yullad šām*, "this one was born there," v 6b).

for he has given you. The motivation clause introduced by the particle *kî* has a Qal perfect verb indicating completed action. YHWH's remarkable activity referred to in the phrase *kî-higdîl YHWH laʿaśôt* of v 21b includes benefits for all three addressees, the land, domestic animals, and residents of Jerusalem. Notably, the prophet Joel reserves the second person pronominal suffix *kem* for the latter group, using it three times in v 23 (*ʾelōhêkem, lākem* [twice]). Vocatives alone sufficed in the admonitions to the land and animals, even when the same verb occurs (*nātenû*, Qal perfect plural, v 22b; *nātan*, Qal perfect third person masculine singular).

the early rain in its season. Context alone dictates this translation of the notoriously difficult phrase *ʾet-hammôreh liṣdāqâ*. In one other text, Ps 84:7 [6], the word *môreh* seems to mean "early rain," although the usual form is *yôreh* (thirty-four Hebrew manuscripts actually have the latter reading, but they undoubtedly represent an attempt to smooth out the difficulty). This example from the Korahite collection of psalms reads: *gam-berākôt yaʿeṭeh môreh*, "the early rain also covers it with pools." If this rare usage permits one to translate Joel 2:23 in a similar manner, what does *liṣdāqâ* mean? It has been understood as a reference to the manner in which the rain would fall, "moderately," or to its result, "for your vindication." I understand the term in the light of the broad meaning of *ṣedāqâ* discerned by Schmid, who compares the concept underlying this word to the Egyptian notion of *maʿat* and the Mesopotamian idea of *ME*, the tablets of destiny. This philosophical meaning of *ṣedāqâ* and *ṣedeq* is best rendered by "order"; thus it pertains to the very structure of the universe. The sense of Joel 2:23 may be related to this general understanding of creation; if so, it would mean "in an orderly fashion-in its season." Still, the redundant use of the unspecific term for rain, *gešem*, in the following clause (*wayyôred lākem gešem*, "and he sent rain for you") creates difficulty even in a book that actually repeats whole clauses.

The evidence from ancient versions probably suggests that another word originally stood where *hammôreh* now does, for both the Septuagint *(ta bromata)* and the Peshitta *(mykwlty)* point to a Hebrew word for food, perhaps *maʾakōl* (H. W. Wolff 1977:55) or *hammāzôn* (K. Marti 1904:133–34; cf. Gen 45:23; 2 Chr 11:23; Dan 4:9 [12], 18 [21]). Such a reading accords well with the context and echoes the lack of food mentioned in 1:16 (along with "joy and gladness," the word pair occurring in 2:21 and 2:23 in reverse order). "Food according to righteousness" suggests a covenantal relationship in which appropriate nurture is provided.

The Vulgate points in yet another direction, one also attested in the Qumran manuscripts. It reads *doctorem iustitiae*, "teacher of righteousness," the usual meaning of the two Hebrew words, *hammôreh* and *ṣedāqâ* (cf. Symmachus' reading, *ton hypodeiknonta*). This idea is also found in Hos 10:12b (*weʿet lidrôš ʾet YHWH ʿad yābôʾ weyôreh ṣedeq lākem*, "for it is time to seek YHWH until he comes and instructs you in righteousness"). The difference between the expression at Qumran, *mwrh hṣdq*, and *hammôreh liṣdaqâ* may rule out any attempt to derive the one from the other, especially since Qumran exegesis never appeals to Hos 10:12 or Joel 2:23 in regard to the teacher of righteousness (W. Rudolph 1971:66–67). The sign would be the coming of rain at the optimum time, as Joel goes on to say. Perhaps a reading of this verse along these lines led to the Targumic paraphrase and the rendering in the Vulgate. According to 1 Kings 8:36 and Isa 30:20, 23, rain accompanies correct teaching about cultic matters; on the basis of these texts, Ahlström claims that Joel offers a veiled promise of a new Davidic leader (1971:98–110). Both these texts, however, clearly state the YHWH gives *rain* at the conclusion of the lesson from the teacher (i.e., YHWH), and the move to a political leader is wholly unanticipated in the text. Moreover, such a novel idea would surely call for further elaboration in Joel, which does not take place.

and sent down showers for you. The customary word for a downpour, *gešem*, implies that YHWH's gift of rain will be sufficient to return the parched land to its productive state. The absence of an accusative particle contrasts with the repeated indirect object, *lākem* ("for you"), and the Hiphil imperfect with *waw* consecutive *(wayyôred)* differs from the simple Qal perfect *nātan* of the previous colon. Nevertheless, the sense of the second half of v 23 corresponds closely to that of this colon. Thus, the two phrases of the verse correspond, word for word; "he has given to you the early rain in its season" parallels "he has sent down for you showers, both early and late," as follows:

he has given	//	he has sent down
to you	//	for you
the early rain in its season	//	showers, both early and late

The apposition is one of specification (showers, specifically those in autumn and spring). Outside this exact correspondence stand the introductory *kî* and final adverb, "as previously." The Hebrew *bāriʾšôn* ordinarily refers to the first month, which is counted from Nisan and the time of Passover. That calculation accords quite well with the situation described by Joel. The early rain usually begins to fall in November (or late October) and the late rain comes in March or April. Perhaps one should adopt the reading presupposed by the Septuagint *(kathos emprosthen)*, Peshitta, and Vulgate, namely *karišôn* ("as previously"), and the meaning may even be more literal than this translation, referring to the restoration of things to their original condition ("as in the beginning"). The terms *yōreh ûmalqôš* appear together in connection with *gešem* in Jer 5:24 (*hannōtēn gešem weyōreh ûmalqôš beʿittô*, "who sends rain—the early rain and the late rain in its season"; cf. Deut 11:14 with *meṭar-ʾarṣekem*).

2:24 *The granaries.* This verse does not contain the slightest allusion to the erotic excesses sometimes associated with threshing floors (Hos 9:1; Ruth 3), where a festive atmosphere generated by the anticipation of plentiful harvests contributed to a general relaxing of morals like the modern Mardi Gras, as did the knowledge that the arduous labor of the agricultural season has finally come to an end. This reference to full granaries (*ûmāleʾû*, Qal perfect stative verb with resultative *waw*) contrasts with the situation described in 1:10–12, where the grain is said to have been ruined. In effect, the statement that the granaries were filled to capacity echoes the promise in 2:19 that YHWH's people will eat to satiety, for there will be no shortage of food. Joel's choice of *bār* in this verse (2:24), whereas elsewhere *dāgān* occurs (1:10, 17; 2:19) along with *tîrôš* and *yiṣhār*, accords with the seeming indiscriminate use of these two nouns for grain in the Old Testament.

spill over. The verb *wehešîqû* (Hiphil perfect with *waw* conjunctive) appears only three times in the Bible (Joel 2:24; 4:13 [3:13]; Ps 65:10 [9]. Essentially, it indicates constriction or narrowness, hence the meaning "being filled to overflowing." The other use in Joel conjures up the idea of judgment necessitated by excessive transgression. The text in Psalms describes YHWH's wonderful generosity in watering the earth and providing grain (*dāgān*, v 10 [9], *bār*, v 14 [13]). The verb *wattešōqeqehā* (Pilpel imperfect with third person singular suffix and with prefixed *waw* consecutive) after a verb indicating YHWH's visiting the earth *(pqd)* suggests divine largesse, which is subsequently specified: abundant water and grain.

Presses in ancient Israel served a dual role, being used to extract both grape juice *(tîrôš)* and olive oil *(yiṣhār)*, as Mic 6:15 states in a typical futility curse.

> *ʾattâ tizraʿ welōʾ tiqṣôr*
> *ʾattâ tidrōk-zayit welōʾ tāsûk šemen*
> *wetîrôš welōʾ tišteh-yāyin*
> You yourself will sow and not reap,
> you yourself will tread olives and not anoint yourself with oil,
> new wine also, and you will drink no wine.

By replacing the anticipated personal pronoun *ʾattâ*, the unexpected *wetîrôš* makes an effective conclusion to this curse, one considerably weakened by the proposed emendation to *tiraš*, although resulting in near-semantic symmetry ("you will tread [grapes]"). The emphasis shifts momentarily away from the person affected by the curse to its content, the lack of newly fermented wine. The subsequent mention of the general term for wine corresponds to the inclusive character of such curses.

new wine and oil. The double object of the verb *wehēšîqû* symbolizes the unlimited quantity of the provisions resulting from divine activity. The brief verse otherwise manifests exact semantic parallelism: verb, subject, object//verb, subject, object. In neither instance do the objects have a preposition, essential in English. The subjects do show gender difference (*haggarānôt*, feminine plural; *hayeqābîm*, masculine plural).

2:25 *I will make up.* The verb *wešillamtî* (Piel perfect) derives from a legal context and designates payment for losses incurred (cf. Exod 21:34, 36–37; 22:1–5, 7, 9, 12–13 [2–6, 8, 10, 13–14]). Naturally, the idea of restitution emerges from the ravages mentioned in 1:4–2:11, now personalized by the addition of *lākem* ("for you"). First person speech returns in v 25, after a lapse of four verses during which the prophet refers to YHWH in the third person (vv 21–24). The divine perpetrator of the offense, already made abundantly clear in the allusion to YHWH's army in 2:11, here promises to compensate the people for their losses. The analogy with Job is instructive; God takes Job's children and possessions from him and subsequently compensates him for the egregious offense.

The object of the verb, *ʾet haššānîm*, is a metonym for the annual harvest (cf. Prov 5:9, *pen-tittēn laʾaḥērîm hôdekā ûšenōteykā leʾakzārî*, "lest you surrender your honor to others and your years to the cruel," where the things accumulated over time are probably intended). The plural implies that the effect of the locusts was felt for a longer duration than one year, which is certainly plausible. The Septuagint reading, *kai antapodōsō humin anti tōn etōn, hōn katephagen hē akris* ("and I will recompense you for the years which the locust . . ."), corresponds to the Masoretic Text, thus offering no support for proposed emendations such as (1) *mišneh*, "double"; (2) *šenîm ʾet*, "double that"; and (3) *hašmanîm* "the rich products" (cf. Gen 27:28). The idea that YHWH will recompense individuals exactly for time allotted to misery also appears in Ps 90:15 ("days"//"years").

the swarming locusts. The sequence of the four terms designating locusts differs from that exhibited in 1:4, making it unlikely that the earlier verse describes stages in the development of the locust infestation. A symbolic use of the verb *ʾkl*, "to eat," occurs in both Jeremiah (15:16, *nimṣeʾû debāreykâ wāʾōkelēm*, "your words were discovered and I ate them") and Ezekiel (3:1–2, *wayyōʾmer ʾelay ben-ʾādām ʾet ʾašer-timṣāʾ ʾekôl . . . wayyaʾakilenî ʾēt hammegillâ hazzōʾt*, "he spoke to me, 'man, eat what you have discovered' . . . and he made me eat this scroll").

my mighty force. The appositional phrase, *ḥelî haggādôl*, returns to the military imagery dominating the similes in 2:4–11 and culminating in the picture of YHWH leading an advancing army. Now Joel has YHWH state categorically that he sent this invading force (*ʾašer šillaḥtî bākem*, "that I dispatched against you"). The similarities with Amos' catalogue of calamities in 4:6–11 show that Joel stands in a line of tradition when interpreting catastrophes as covert divine activity (cf. Amos 4:10, *šillaḥtî bākem deber bederek miṣrayim*, "I sent a pestilence among you in Egyptian fashion").

Verse 25 closes with an echo of its opening words (*wešillamtî lākem . . . šillaḥtî bākem*). Future promise matches past deed, expressed in two verb clauses introduced by the relative pronoun *ʾašer*. The first of these leads one on a tour of locust identification: the swarming locust, the jumper, finisher, and chewer.

2:26 *You will continually consume food*. The verb *weʾakaltem*, when qualified by two infinitives absolute, *ʾākôl weśābôaʿ*, places immense semantic stress on the act of eating and its consequence. The contrast with locusts consuming everything in their path may be intentional, for the situation has reversed itself now and YHWH's people can eat voraciously, their ravenous appetite resulting from severe deprivation. The second infinitive absolute emphasizes the result of such feasting: everyone will always be satisfied. YHWH assures his people in these words: "You will surely eat contentedly," but that is not the last word. They will also praise the name of their God. The verb *wehillēltem* (Qal perfect) occurs frequently in contexts of adoration; the object of human praise recalls Deuteronomic theology of the divine name. Covenantal relationship is reaffirmed in the word *ʾelōhêkem*, your God, which stands in apposition to YHWH.

Full stomachs did not always move people to praise YHWH, an insight embedded within the only prayer preserved in canonical wisdom (Prov 30:7–9). Two extremes, poverty and wealth, are viewed as dangerous in this prayer, so the speaker asks for a happy compromise between them, lest being full he deny YHWH or being starved, he resort to theft, and thereby sully God's reputation. The prophet Hosea joins together the notions of a well-fed people and prideful forgetting of the one who provided the food under conditions of drought (contrast the obligatory response to a full stomach in Deut 8:10, *weʾakāltā weśābāʿetā ûbēraktā ʾet-YHWH ʾelōheykā* ["you will eat, be satisfied, and bless YHWH your God"]; the rest of the chapter warns the people of dire consequences should they forget). Despite the prominence of the "name" in Deuteronomic religion, it does not enter the picture in this verse.

who has worked wonderfully among you. The relative clause in apposition with YHWH, *ʾašer-ʿāśāh ʿimmākem lehaplî*, uses a Hiphil infinitive, best translated adverbially (cf. GKC 114o). The verb *plʾ* ("to do a wonder") came to be used freely to specify YHWH's stupendous deeds *(niplāʾôt)*, and the Hiphil participle even served as a descriptive epithet for him (Judg 13:19; cf. Isa 29:14; 28:29). The verb could also describe extraordinary human achievements (2 Chr 2:8 [9], the temple; 26:15, soldiers' accomplishments).

and my people. In v 18 the prophet spoke of YHWH's land and people (third person pronominal suffix), then he repeated *ʿammô* ("his people," with prefixed *lamedh* indicating indirect object). That mode of address changes to divine speech momentarily in stating the promise of restored food and providing assurance that the nations will not mock them any longer (2:19aβ–b). With the return of divine speech in the first person (vv 25–27), the reference to "my people" contrasts with the liturgical expression referring to YHWH in third person once more ("you will praise the name of YHWH your God who has worked wonderfully among you"), which emits a jarring sound in context.

will never again be shamed. Having reversed the situation pertaining to empty stomachs, YHWH now addresses the problem posed by foreigners making fun of the Judeans whose luck has forsaken them. The answer to that vexing mockery is disarmingly simple: YHWH promises that his people will not be ridiculed again. The verb *yēbōšû*, negated by *lōʾ*, echoes the interplay between *hôbîš* and forms of *ybš* ("to be dry") in 1:10–12, 17, 20. The adverb *leʿôlām* conveys the sense of remoteness approaching eschatology ("unto the ages"). All of 26b is repeated in 27b, but this is not the only instance of exact duplication in the book. The repetition of this assurance actually increases the rhetorical effect of the section, for in both instances a liturgical expression precedes the divine asseveration.

2:27 *Then you will know*. The astonishing answer to the prayer in 2:17 does much more than fill empty stomachs and put songs of praise on the lips of grateful people. It also demonstrates YHWH's presence and uniqueness within the covenant relationship. Joel takes up the so-called formula of recognition and develops it in his own way, making it difficult to determine the exact source of his borrowing. Deutero-Isaiah's formulation includes the essential ideas in Joel's own treatment.

ʾanî YHWH weʾēn ʿôd
I am YHWH and there is no other (Isa 45:5aα).
lemaʿan yēdeʿû
So that you may know (Isa 45:6aα).
lōʾ tēbōšû welōʾ tikkālemû ʿad- ʿôlemê ʿad
[Israel] will not be shamed or confounded until the remote future. (Isa 45:17b)

Because the assertion that YHWH is in the midst of Israel *(kî beqereb yiśrāʾēl ʾānî)* does not occur in Deutero-Isaiah or in Ezekiel's frequent use of the recognition formula (cf. 2:5; 5:13; 6:7, 10, 13–14; 7:4, 9, 27, etc.), Joel may rely on other resources. The assertion appears in Zeph 3:15 (*melek yiśrāʾēl YHWH beqirbēk*, "The king of Israel, YHWH, is in your midst"), Hos 11:9b (*kî ʾēl ʾānōkî welōʾ ʾîš beqirbekā qādôš*, "for I am God, not man, the holy one in your midst"), and Mic 3:11 (*halōʾ YHWH beqirbēnû*, "Is YHWH not in our midst?"). For Zephaniah and for Joel, "Israel" has taken on the sense of later use, corresponding to that of the premonarchical period, to designate all YHWH's people, who happen now to belong to Judah.

The Decalogue has the expression *ʾānōkî YHWH ʾelōheykā* ("I am YHWH your God," Deut 5:6; Exod 20:2), and the declaration that there is no other appears in Deut 4:35, 39, 32:39, and 1 Kings 8:60 (*kî YHWH hûʾ haʾelōhîm ʾēn ʿod milebaddô*, "For YHWH is God; there is none besides him" [Deut 4:35]). The prophet Hosea also stresses YHWH's uniqueness (*weʾanokî YHWH ʾelōheykā meʾereṣ miṣrāyîm weʾlōhîm zûlātî lōʾ tēdāʿ*, "and I am YHWH your God from the land of Egypt; you know none other," 13:4abαβ).

The connection between the statement of recognition and the pouring out of YHWH's spirit occurs in Ezek 39:28–29, the larger context of which strikingly resembles the second chapter of the book of Joel. Wolff has argued persuasively that this statement in Joel does not signal closure but points forward to the outpouring of the spirit in chapter three [2:28–32] (1977:60).

COMMENT

The "perhaps" of 2:14 finds its positive response in this section, 2:18–27. Sorrow has turned to joy (cf. 1:5, 8, 9, 13; 2:13, 17), for YHWH has heard the prayer spoken on behalf of the people by priests (2:17b). The oracle of answered prayer includes hymnic elements, a statement of recognition of YHWH, and an oracle of self-disclosure. Its literary form led C. A. Keller (1982:133–39) to propose that it constituted an antiphonal chant consisting of a prophetic introduction

(2:18), YHWH's response (2:19–20), the prophet's answer (2:21–24), and YHWH's final word (2:25–27). A clear shift in speakers is discernible at 2:20, 21, and 25, but frozen hymnic language complicates matters. The unit consists of three strophes (2:18–20, 21–24, 25–27).

Much debate has taken place over the exact transition point in the book. E. O. A. Merx insisted that the rest of the book from 2:18 on makes up the priestly prayer, but this view required one to ignore the Masoretic vocalization of the verbs in 2:18–19. Bewer (1911:107) and T. H. Robinson (1964:62) did not hesitate to turn the verbs into jussives from 2:15 onward, while Karl Budde saw the decisive change in 2:18 (1919a:104–10). For him, everything prior to 2:18 consists of lament and everything afterward is divine promise. Prinsloo has demonstrated the close connection between what precedes 2:18 and what follows (1985:63–64), making it dubious to emphasize a sharp break in the text. Wolff argued that 2:18 represents the decisive transition, yet he took pains to relate 3:1–5 [2:28–32] with what goes before (1977:57–59). Perhaps the best approach downplays any real break in the text, inasmuch as the lament naturally leads up to the divine answer. On the basis of subject matter alone, the decisive shift takes place in 4:1 [3:1], for the remainder of the book deals with foreign nations. Even that criterion lacks persuasiveness, given the concern over mockery by foreigners expressed in 2:17 and YHWH's corresponding response in 2:19, 26–27. The *setuma* after 2:14 has the advantage of dividing the chapter into two relatively equal parts, each beginning with the imperative *tiqʿû* (2:1, 15).

The assurance oracle in response to a plea is grounded in the turning mentioned in 2:12–17. According to Wolff (1977:58), the communal lament flows into a divine oracle in Pss 60:3–7 [1–5] and 8–10 [6–8]; 85:2–8 [1–7] and 9–14 [8–13]; and 2 Chr 30:6–13 and 14–17. During the postexilic period, such oracles address the people in the second person plural and employ the particle *hinenî* plus a participle (cf. Isa 58:9; 65:1). To some extent, the announcement that YHWH became zealous for his land and took pity on his people (2:18) stands as a separate introductory summation of what will follow, analogous to 1:4 and 1:5–2:17. Nevertheless, the *waw* consecutive on the initial verb in 2:19 links the summary statement with its elaboration, suggesting that 2:18–20 may comprise the summation. Synonymous parallelism characterizes the syntax of this independent preview in 2:18, with the explicit subject receding to a verbal prefix in 2:18b. Otherwise, the symmetry is exact (verb, [subject], prepositional phrase with third person masculine pronominal suffix in each colon). Both verbs, palpably anthropopathic, draw attention to a relationship between YHWH and the two objects of his emotional response. The verse comprises a single bicolon, in sharp contrast with the three bicola that follow (2:19).

Speech about YHWH continues in 2:19 through the first colon, when *hineni*, the characteristic feature of such oracles after the exile, shifts the point of view. Both verses delicately balance this new focus on YHWH with almost equal interest in his people, specifically mentioned in each (cf. the two uses of the second person masculine pronominal suffix and the corresponding verbal prefix). The three bicola in 2:19 lack parallelism, although they take up fixed expressions ("grain, new wine, and oil") and employ hendiadys (*wayyaʿan . . . wayyōʾmer*). The first half of the verse states what YHWH is doing; the second half says what he will not do.

The unusual feature of 2:20 is its length: three short bicola, a long one, and a colon. The semantic emphasis on the direct object matches its enigmatic sense, but "the northerner" undoubtedly functions symbolically to conjure up the excessive anxiety generated by the preceding description of an enemy attack. The twin terms, thirsty and desolate, that modify the land for which this enemy is destined contain a subtle hint of the parched earth it left behind. The additional word about drowning the locusts has a note of irony as well, as does the juxtaposition of stench and grandiose deeds. Semantic parallelism occurs extensively in this verse (additive parallelism in the first two bicola, synonymous parallelism in the third with contrasting content ["face"//"back"; "eastern sea"// "western sea"], and synonymous parallelism in the fourth ("go up"//"go up"; "stench"//"foul odor"). The final colon stands alone, like the proud "northerner" to which the action refers. That arrogance explains YHWH's readiness to turn against his own instrument of punishment.

The second strophe, 2:21–24, registers the divine word of assurance that the time for fear has passed, so majestically has YHWH acted. In ascending order three addressees (land, domestic animals, residents of Zion) hear YHWH's gracious imperative, "Don't be afraid." The three motivation clauses justify the twofold command to be happy and rejoice (2:21, repeated in 2:23 with the additional specification that the exultation has its object in praise of "YHWH your God"). The first two verses are semantically alike, consisting of "fear not," vocative, and a motive clause; v 21 has two additional imperatives after the vocative. The comprehensive motive clause in this verse incorporates all the later ones, while at the same time providing contrast with the arrogant actions of the "northerner." The tenses of the verbs in the motive clauses indicate completed events, at least from the perspective of the speaker. The allusion to the bountiful yield of figs and grapes contains an ironic echo of the threatening army in 2:11 (*ḥêlô* and *ḥêlām*).

The twice-used *lākem* in v 23 reinforces the second person pronominal suffix on *ʾelōhêkem* ("your God"), who has sent rain in abundance. The result of YHWH's generosity, specified in v 24, means that no one need go hungry any longer, for the storage bins for grain overflow like the vats used to extract juice from grapes and oil from olives. These two verses lack parallelism except for the statement, "YHWH has sent you the early rain . . . and caused rain to come down for you" in v 23. The double imperatives, "be happy and rejoice," in this verse are a fixed pair. The entire strophe has less difference as to length of verses:

a single bicolon in vv 21 and 24, two bicola in v 22, and two bicola plus a colon in v 23.

An oracle of divine self-disclosure merges with a statement of recognition to conclude the third strophe, vv 25–27. This divine self-manifestation issues in further declaration (cf. Isa 45:1–7) a promise repeated from v 26, that YHWH's people will never be shamed again. Fixed language from a legal context joins with hymnic phrases to give these verses solemnity and offset YHWH's indirect admission of culpability in sending his mighty army against Judah. Repetition of the four names for locusts recalls 1:4, just as the expression, *ḥêlî haggādôl,* echoes 2:11, and the allusion to shame looks back on various references in chapter one and on 2:19. This entire unit lacks parallelism, although it uses various rhetorical strategies such as repetition of "YHWH your God" and "my people will never again be shamed," extensive specification (the four names for locusts), infinitives absolute, an infinitive used adverbially, and repeated personal pronouns (*ʾanî*). The length of the verses is fairly equal, two bicola in vv 25–26, a colon plus a bicolon in v 27. Wolff remarks that "The confession is not suspended in a vacuum, but rests solidly on YHWH's mighty deeds" and that "Those who eat in plenty must know to praise commensurately" (1977:79).

Signs and Portents (3:1–5 [2:28–32])

3:1 Afterwards I will endow all of you with my vital force,
so that your boys and girls will speak oracles on my behalf;
your old people will discern my will through dreams,
and your young adults will become visionaries.

3:2 On your slaves, too, both male and female,
I will bestow my vital force at that time.

3:3 I will set portents in the sky and on earth—
blood, fire, and mushrooming smoke.

3:4 The sun will be darkened, the moon blood-red,
before YHWH's day dawns—greatly awesome.

3:5 Henceforth everyone who implores YHWH will avoid harm,
for on Mount Zion and in Jerusalem will be an escape
as YHWH promised,
and among survivors whom YHWH calls.

NOTES

3:1 [2:28] *Afterwards*. The anacrusis, *wehāyâ ʾaḥarê-kēn* ("afterwards"), links this divine promise of extraordinary manifestation to what precedes, either 2:24–27 or 2:12–17. The former text emphasizes YHWH's activity in restoring

Judah's ruined crops and lost honor, whereas the latter text places emphasis on human repentance that activates divine compassion. The syntax recalls Isa 2:2, *wehāyâ beʾaḥarît hayyāmîm* ("at some future time"), as if to push the event into the remote—and mythic—future. The rare conjunction, *wehāyâ ʾaḥarê-kēn*, indicates that the current form of 3:1–5 [2:28–32] presupposes something else and therefore cannot be viewed as a separate unit. Of course, the formula may be an editorial means of incorporating alien material into the book, but the criteria for distinguishing such redactional touches often leave much to be desired.

I will endow all of you with my vital force. An inclusio unites 3:1–2 [2:28–29] and sets these verses off from the rest of the unit; v 1 [28] begins with *ʾešpôk ʾet-rûḥî* and v 2 [29] concludes with the same words. The verb *špk* (Qal imperfect) signifies a lavish pouring out and can even indicate accidental spilling of precious liquids. It is used with reference to water, blood, and other liquids, as well as deep emotional feelings (cf. Ps 62:9 [8] and 1 Sam 1:15, where *lēbab* [heart] and *nepeš* [soul] symbolize one's inner disposition). The rejuvenation of despoiled nature through YHWH's spirit is also promised in Isa 32:15.

> *ʿad-yeʿāreh ʿalênû rûaḥ mimmārôm*
> *wehāyâ midbār lakkarmel wakkarmel layyaʿar yēḥašeb*
> Until the spirit is poured out on us from above,
> the wilderness becomes fertile, and is considered a virtual forest.

The affinities between this text and Joel's promise of the spirit would be more significant if the latter associated the gift of YHWH's vital force with the earlier restoration of nature.

The ancient expression of Moses' desire that YHWH would endow everyone with prophetic gifts (Num 11:29) and the subsequent promise of a new heart (Jer 31:33–34) and spirit (Ezek 11:19–20; 36:26–27) have prepared the way for Joel's use of this tradition. The closest text to Joel's promise of YHWH's gift of the *rûaḥ* is Ezek 39:29.

> *welōʾ-ʾastîr ʿôd pānay mēhem*
> *ʾašer šāpaktî ʾet-rûḥî ʿal-bêt yiśrāʾēl neʾum ʾadōnāy* YHWH
> I will never hide my face from them again,
> when I have endowed the Israelites with my vital force.
> An oracle of Lord YHWH.

The implication, that everyone in Israel has direct access to inspiration, accords with that underlying Joel 3:1–2 [2:28–29], which contrasts with Jeremiah's stress on the torah and Ezekiel's similar emphasis in 11:19–20 and 36:26–27. For Joel, the gift of YHWH's spirit has nothing to do with obedience to legal statutes or with moral transformation, nor even with a new creation as in Isa 32:15. The idea of *rûaḥ* does not suggest its opposite, *bāśār* ("flesh"), although this sort of juxtaposition occurs elsewhere (Isa 31:3, *ûmiṣrayîm ʾādām welōʾ-ʾēl wesûsêhem bāśār welōʾ rûaḥ*, "now the Egyptians are human beings, not deity, and their horses flesh, not spirit").

all of you. The expression, *ʿal-kol-bāśār* ("upon all flesh") can also mean "everyone," without ethnic or gender restrictions (cf. Isa 49:26 and Sir 8:19, equivalent to *tout le monde*), but the context indicates that Joel uses it in a more restrictive sense, all Judahites, just as Zech 12:10 limits the outpouring of a compassionate spirit to David's descendants and residents of Jerusalem.

> *wešāpaktî ʿal-bêt dāwîd weʿal yôšēb yerûšālayim rûaḥ ḥēn wetaḥanûnîm*
> I will endow David's descendants and Jerusalem's inhabitants with my gracious and compassionate disposition.

The transference of YHWH's character (cf. Exod 34:6–7) to those who worship him will bring about a desirable change in their attitude to the victim of their fury. For the moment Joel thinks only of the residents of Judah; he will turn to the fate of foreign nations in the final chapter. Cheyne's proposal (see J. A. Bewer 1911:126) that *kol bāśār* is an abbreviation for *kol-bêt yiśrāʾēl* ("all Israel") bears testimony to the power of the context, which speaks of "your sons and daughters, your old people and young."

so that. The *waw* attached to the verb *nbʾ* (*wenibbʾû*, Qal perfect) indicates result. The outpouring of YHWH's vitality will lead to widespread prophecy by the youthful generation (*benêkem ûbenôtêkem*, "your boys and your girls"), unless this is a way of saying that the gift of the spirit will come to a future generation. Further specification of the aged and the mature young men in 3:1b [2:28b] favors the former understanding, "your sons and daughters." In a desire to be comprehensive, the author refers first to little children, then moves to the other extreme, old people, only to return part of the way to mature young people, and finally to transcend social status in v 2 [29]. The significance lies in the immediacy with which all of them relate to YHWH, rather than in the different modes of inspiration (contrast von Orelli's claim [cited from L. C. Allen:1976:99] that "dreams are ascribed to slumbering age, visions to youths with their eager receptiveness"). Whether ecstatic prophecy *(nbʾ)*, dreams *(ḥalōmôt)*, or visions *(ḥezyōnôt)*, the same direct access to YHWH is assumed. No hint of Jeremiah's negative attitude toward dreams as a mode of revelation (23:25, or toward their content, as Overholt, [1970:66–68] believes), appears in this text, which overwhelmingly approves all three kinds of inspiration.

One could view vv 1–2 as a vast merism beginning with all inhabitants of Judah, who are designated by the reference to "your sons and daughters." Since everyone falls into this category, the reference is all-inclusive. The focus then moves to the significant male representatives in society, older men who have the elevated status of decision-makers and younger men who fill military ranks. Similarly, the reference to male and female slaves isolates a group that may be included in the first ("your sons and daughters"), although they may be foreigners and therefore constitute an additional category outside those already mentioned in the comprehensive expression. In this way, the prophet includes the entire community, making everybody a recipient of YHWH's spirit (D. N. Freedman, written communication). For me, however, the inclusive term is *kol bāśār*, and the specification of different groups then follows: boys and girls, old people and valiant warriors, slaves. The verbs for prophesying *(nbʾ, ḥlm, and rʾh)* attached to the first two groups and the repeated statement about an outpouring of YHWH's spirit (this time specifically on slaves) indicate to me that *kol bāśār* is the inclusive term.

your old people will discern my will through dreams. The cognate accusative (*ḥălōmôt yaḥălōmûn*, "they will dream dreams") affirms an ancient tradition according to which YHWH communicated with chosen individuals through dreams, thus completely apart from any human initiative. The reference to young men's visionary powers does not use a cognate accusative, but employs the verb *rʾh*, from which one designation for a "seer" derives, *rōʾeh* (another technical term for seer or diviner, *ḥōzeh*, comes from the verb *ḥzh*; cf. the related noun for vision, *ḥezyōnôt*). The three verbs for prophetic activity are used synonymously here (K. Marti 1904:136), like the editorial equation of *nābîʾ* and *rōʾeh* in 1 Sam 9:9 (cf. also the contrasting use of *ḥōzeh* in Amos 7:12, 14 if *lōʾ nābîʾ* is, as I think, a *lamedh emphatica* instead of the negation, *lōʾ*). The elitism underlying Num 12:6 has completely disappeared in Joel's formulation. Likewise, the expressions for various stages in life show no preference for age over youth, or vice versa (cf. Mal 3:24 [4:6] for mutuality between parents and their children).

The lavish outpouring of YHWH's vital force contrasts with an earlier narrator's assessment of the rarity of visions in Samuel's day (1 Sam 3:1). Joel has YHWH promise that everyone will converse with God—the speaker here is YHWH, who uses the first person singular pronoun. According to 2 Chr 15:1 and 20:14, YHWH's spirit comes upon an individual and serves as a sign of divine presence among the Israelites (cf. Mic 3:8 for an earlier boast of access to YHWH's vital power).

3:2 [2:29] *On your slaves, too, both male and female.* The *wegam* implies that the equality among the generations will *also*—or *even*—be matched by an equality of social status, insofar as access to YHWH's vitality is concerned. Slaves were allowed to participate in the Israelite cult (Exod 20:10; Deut 5:14, rest from labor during the sabbath; Deut 12:12 and 16:11, rejoice before YHWH with tithes and offerings). The absence of a possessive pronoun here (*kem*, "your") struck the translators of the later Greek and Latin texts as strange, resulting in the addition of a first person singular pronominal suffix ("my male and female slaves"). The definite article may have functioned in Hebrew as equivalent to the pronominal suffix. Joel's silence in this regard hardly goes this far, despite its radical concept (cf. Paul's exceptional observation that in Christ all such distinctions as ethnicity, gender, and social status—slave or free person—disappear, Gal 3:28–29).

at that time. The temporal phrase, *bayyāmîm hahēmmâ* ("in those days"), corresponds to the time indicated by the initial "afterwards." The concluding inclusio, *ʾešpôk ʾet-rûḥî*, stresses the divine generosity, verbal amplitude matching the outpouring of vital power. These two verses echo Joel 2:16, where opposites are mentioned (old people and infants) along with special persons (bride and groom).

3:3 [2:30] *I will set portents.* First person divine speech continues, although *wenātattî*, the perfect with *waw* conversive, replaces the imperfect *ʾešpôk* of vv 1 and 2 [28–29]. The primary meaning of the verb *nātan* ("to give") provides subtle irony here as it takes on the secondary sense of "placing" or "setting" something, for these portents augur fearful times for YHWH's enemies. The Hebrew Bible distinguishes three different kinds of signs: (1) *ʾôt*, a sign that does not necessarily refer to something out of the ordinary; (2) *peleʾ*, a wonderful thing that can lack any signative content; and (3) *môpēt*, an extraordinary sign, i.e., a portent. According to Isa 20:3, the prophet walked naked and barefoot for three years as a sign and portent; similarly Isa 8:18 refers to Isaiah and the children YHWH gave him as signs and portents (cf. Ezek 12:6, 11; 24:24, 27 [*ʾôt*]; Zech 3:8 [*môpēt*]). Manoah's awe-inspiring experience in the presence of YHWH's messenger who identifies himself as *peliʾ* and evokes a sacrifice to YHWH *ûmapliʾ laʿaśôt* ("and the one who does wonders" [Judg 13:15–20]; cf. Joel 2:20, 21 *kî higdîl YHWH laʿaśôt*) illustrates the sense of dread and wonder associated with the Israelite notion of *peliʾ*. Of course, the plagues in ancient Egypt best exemplify the idea of extraordinary signs ("portents") *môpetîm* (cf. Pss 78:43, 105:5, 27; 135:9; Neh 9:10).

in the sky and on earth. The normal position of the verb *wenātattî* and the absence of a *nota accusativi* (*ʾet*) strengthen the divine announcement of further demonstration that YHWH, indeed, does mighty works. The objects of his extraordinary signs are none other than the universe, "sky and earth" serving as a merismus for "everywhere." The further elucidation of the portents above and below occurs in chiasmus; those things affecting the earth are mentioned first, then those observable phenomena in the sky. Three items relate to earth, two to sky.

blood, fire, and mushrooming smoke. These three things appear to conjure up terrifying images of warfare. Savage attacks by vicious soldiers spill blood in the streets and within the dubious shelter of houses, as a conquering army sets fire to everything combustible. The unusual expression "mushrooming smoke" (given contemporary relevance by the horrible images associated with an atomic nuclear blast) led S. R. Driver to suggest that the prophet envisioned a powerful desert storm wind, the sirocco (1907:66). Other scholars have suggested that a volcanic eruption best explains the expression, "mushrooming smoke" (*wetîm-arôt ʿāšān*, cf. Cant 3:6), which is related to the word *tāmār*, "date palm," and seems to refer to the resemblance between the shape of these trees and smoke hovering over a devastated city. This association of blood and fire with warfare occurs elsewhere in Ezek 38:22.

> *wenišpaṭtî ʾittô bedeber ûbedām*
> *wegešem šôṭep weʾabnê ʾelgabîš ʾeš wenāperît ʾamṭîr*
> *ʿalâyw weʿal ʾagappāyw weʿal-ʿammîm rabbîm ʾašer ʾittô*
> I will execute judgment on him with pestilence and bloodshed;
> torrential rain, hail, fire and brimstone I will let loose on him,
> his hordes, and his numerous allies.

Kapelrud argues that these allusions to blood and fire signify sacrifice in connection with battle (1948:139–40), whole cities and peoples being offered up to YHWH (cf. Judg 20:40; Isa 34:3–8, especially v 6b, *kî zebaḥ laYHWH bebosrâ wetebaḥ gādôl beʾereṣ ʾedôm* ["for YHWH has a sacrifice in Bozrah, a mighty slaughter in Edom"]).

3:4 [2:31] *The sun will be darkened*. The first two portents of v 3 [30] are confined to earth; the third, mushrooming smoke, provides a superb transition to cosmic manifestations, inasmuch as it takes place in the space between earth and heavenly bodies. Solar eclipses aroused consternation among ancient peoples, as darkness slowly brought with it an eerie sensation. Joel uses this idea in 2:10 as a sign of YHWH's day and in 4:15 [3:15] again, where judgment falls on the nations. In doing so he stands in a venerable prophetic tradition (Amos 8:9; Isa 13:10; 34:4; Ezek 32:7–8; Jer 4:23), one that extends as far back as the Exodus experience (Exod 10:21). This imagery of a darkened sun persists in New Testament eschatology (Rev 6:12; cf. Rev 20:11, which has earth and sky flee from the divine presence).

the moon blood-red. An atmospheric abnormality resulting from raging fires probably provides the imagery for the moon's strange appearance. Zephaniah refers to blood being poured out like dust on that day (1:17), an image that may explain Joel's allusion to a blood-red moon if one imagines dust rising to the sky. The reference to the moon's color may even derive from extraordinary sandstorms that give the moon a reddish appearance.

before YHWH's day dawns—greatly awesome. This entire temporal clause occurs also in Mal 3:23b [4:5b]. Simkins interprets it referentially instead of temporally, yielding "at the coming of YHWH's day, greatly awesome" (1991:210). The combination of greatness and awe, *haggādôl wehannôrāʾ*,

occurs earlier in Joel 2:11, where YHWH's day brought terror for Judah. Now Joel implies that other nations will undergo that same frightening experience, while God's people will escape the divine fury this time. That promise is clearly stated in v 5 [32].

3:5 [2:32] *Henceforth*. The verse begins with the verb "to be" in future tense (Qal perfect with conversive *waw*, "it shall be"), which I translate temporally, "henceforth." The catastrophes lie in the past for Judah; awaiting those who worship YHWH is nothing but bliss.

everyone who implores YHWH will avoid harm. A sort of inclusio opens with the mention of calling on YHWH's name, a synonym for worship in ancient usage (cf. Gen 4:26; 12:8), for the verse concludes with a second specific reference to calling. The initial use of the verb *yiqrāʾ* has indefinite members of Judah as subject, whereas the second one has YHWH as subject of the participle *qōrēʾ*. The indefinite *kol ʾăšer* gives the appearance of universalism that is corrected by the following restrictive specification, *yiqrāʾ bešēm YHWH* ("calls on the name of YHWH"). Only individuals who confess exclusive loyalty to YHWH will escape the terror announced by the aforementioned signs and portents. The verb *yimmālēṭ* (Niphal imperfect) indicates survival in the face of grave danger (cf. Amos 2:14b–15 for a threefold use of the verb with reference to a mighty soldier, a fast runner, and an equestrian). Invoking YHWH's name implied both privilege and responsibility. To come under divine protection in a covenantal relationship meant surrendering to certain obligations of fealty, the worshipper agreeing to keep YHWH's statutes and to render exclusive loyalty to him. In Deuteronomic circles YHWH's name came to stand for the deity, resulting in a theologoumenon concerning the name which YHWH placed in Jerusalem. Later confessional language includes the short formula, *YHWH ṣebāʾôt šemô* ("YHWH of hosts is his name"), often used as a kind of refrain in hymnic texts (J. L. Crenshaw 1969:156–75; 1975). Even a proverbial saying attests to this idea of safety through confessing YHWH ("YHWH's name is a strong tower; the righteous run into it and become inaccessible," Prov 18:10).

for on Mount Zion and in Jerusalem will be an escape. The earlier scene of disaster is here transformed into a safe haven, confirming the presence of YHWH in the midst of his people (2:27). The predicate adjective *pelêṭâ* ("escape") is a frequent parallel word for the verb *mlṭ* (cf. Amos 9:1b, *lōʾ-yānûs lāhem nās welōʾ-yimmālēṭ lāhem pālîṭ*, "none will flee, none escape"). The mention of escapees recalls 2:3, where Joel announces that nobody can escape the locusts' attack, and signals a new era in YHWH's relationship with his people.

as YHWH promised. To what does this allusion refer? Virtually the same words as Joel 3:5bβ [2:32bβ] occur in Ob 17 (*ûbehar ṣiyyôn tihyeh pelêṭâ*, "and an escape will be on Mount Zion"), so Joel could depend on this text, or vice versa. Alternatively, both prophets may rely on an independent tradition, and Joel may actually refer to YHWH's promise in 2:27.

and among survivors whom YHWH calls. The word *śārîd* ("survivor") is often paired with *pelêṭâ* and variants.

wayyakkû ʾôtām ʿad-biltî hišʾîr lô śārîd ûpālîṭ
And they smote them so that no one was left, neither survivor nor escapee.
Josh 8:22 (cf. Ob 14)

welōʾ-yihyeh lāhem śārîd ûpālîṭ mippenê hārāʿâ ʾašer ʾanî mēbî ʿalêhem
There will not be any survivor or escapee from the calamity that I am bringing against them.
Jer 42:17b

welōʾ yihyeh pālîṭ weśārîd lišʾērît yehûdâ
There will be no survivor or escapee for the remnant of Judah.
Jer 44:14a

The syntax of *ûbaśśerîdîm*, although unusual, is not impossible, for *pelêṭâ* carries over to this clause. The meaning is that not only do Jerusalemites escape destruction but also others survive who live outside the city, perhaps even in exile (W. Rudolph 1971:74). If this verse speaks of YHWH's calling these exiled people, 4:7 [3:7] refers to rousing them, as if from slumber. Sellin believed that an original *ûbîrûsālayim śerîdîm* repeated the idea in 3:5b but was eventually corrupted through haplography to *ûbaśśerîdîm* (1929:169, 171). His proposed emendation restores the parallelism, if it ever existed, and removes the awkwardness in syntax. This conjecture probably gives undue weight to the similar text in Ob 17 and overestimates the poetic features of Joel's remarks. The hope that persons in Jerusalem would be spared was not restricted to Obadiah (cf. Isa 1:9; 4:2–3).

COMMENT

These five verses comprise three individual units, 1–2 [28–29], 3–4 [30–31], and 5 [32]. An inclusio (*ʾešpôk ʾet-rûḥî*) links the first two verses, and another one, somewhat flawed (*yiqrāʾ* and *qōrēʾ*), joins the two halves of v 5 [32]. The structural connection between vv 3–4 [30–31] is achieved by means of chiasmus (*baššāmayim ûbāʾāreṣ; dām wāʾēš wetîmarôt ʿāšān* and *haššemeš wehayyāreaḥ*). Poetic parallelism permeates v 1, with three verbs for the act of prophetic inspiration (*nbʾ*, *ḥlm*, and *rʾh*) as well as antithetic expressions (*benêkem // benôtêkem, ziqnêkem // baḥûrêkem*). A linking formula (*wehāyâ ʾaḥarê-kēn*) introduces the unit and isolates it from what goes before. A new unit is signaled by a standard formula for future events in 4:1 [3:1], *kî hinnēh bayyāmîm hāhēmmâ ûbāʿēt hahî.*

The entire unit refers to a time after YHWH's promises recorded in 2:18–27. That is the function of the verb *wehāyâ* and the temporal qualifier, *ʾaḥarê-kēn* ("it will take place at a later time"). The speaker of the first unit, 1–2 [28–29], is YHWH, with the people of Judah addressed frequently in second person pronominal suffixes (and the article with the words for slaves). The second unit also has YHWH as speaker, but no indication of addressee occurs. Moreover, YHWH is said to have used the technical expression *yôm YHWH* (4b [31b]). The speaker in v 5 [32] appears to have changed, the prophet now taking up the divine word and offering a bit of instruction grounded in confessional statements. It follows that vv 1–4 [28–31] consist of a promissory oracle and that v 5 [32] is a prophetic instruction.

The initial unit has YHWH promise an extraordinary happening, the revolutionary pouring out of the divine energy source upon the people of Judah indiscriminately. The fulfilment of Moses' wish for widespread prophetic inspiration will finally come, and that moment will momentarily break down barriers separating people from one another such as sex, age, and social status. This spectacular event will know but one restriction; it will be limited to YHWH's worshippers in Judah. Furthermore, the occurrence will be delayed for Joel's immediate audience, who must be content with the knowledge that their own children (descendants) will experience the outpouring of YHWH's spirit.

The second unit concentrates on extraordinary signs and portents that YHWH promises to set in the sky and on earth as an indication that the terrible day of YHWH is about to dawn. The portents on earth—blood, fire, mushrooming smoke—point to warfare, perhaps also to volcanic eruption and theophanic tradition. Those in the sky—a darkened sun and blood-red moon—also belong to the language of warfare, although approaching eschatological imagery about a conflagration that will usher in God's kingdom on earth. The mood is established by the concluding words, *haggādôl wehannôrāʾ* ("greatly awesome").

The last unit concentrates on the chances for survival during these dreadful manifestations of YHWH's power. The portents will not jeopardize anyone who acknowledges YHWH's sovereignty. The act of allegiance will be met by a mutual calling; everyone who implores YHWH's name will be secure in the inviolable city, and even survivors from afar will experience divine summons. The assurances of 2:27 that YHWH will dwell in the people's midst are once more affirmed; a divine promise made is a promise kept.

The New Testament has Peter cite vv 1–5 [28–32] in Acts 2:16–21 on the day of Pentecost. He understood the remarkable linguistic phenomenon among the Christians in attendance as fulfilment of Joel's prophecy about the pouring out of YHWH's spirit. Peter's rendition of the prophetic text differs in at least two significant respects: (1) it identifies the slaves as YHWH's, and (2) it lacks the second half of v 5 (but he includes part of it in 2:39). Peter widens the scope of those who call upon the name of YHWH to include the Jews of the Diaspora who had come to Jerusalem. In addition, the Greek text on which Peter's speech depends changes the temporal expression "afterwards" to "in the last days" (contrast codex B which has *meta taûta*, "after these things"), adds a preposition ("of, from") to the Greek word for spirit, *pneuma*, specifies that the portents take place "above" and "below," and provides "signs" as a parallel to "portents." The addition of "God declares," the reversal of the order of "old men and young men," the addition of "and they shall prophecy" in 3:2 [2:29] from 3:1a, the substitution of the dative for the cognate accusative "dream dreams" are further minor differences between Peter's version and the Masoretic Text of Joel 3:1–5 [2:28–32]. Oddly, the Old Greek *euangelizomenoi* ("bearers of good news") for *ûbaśśerîdîm* (because of similarity with *ûmebaśśerîm*) is not reflected in Peter's version of the prophecy. In Rom 10:13 the Apostle Paul cites Joel 3:5a [2:32a] as proof that before God there is absolutely no distinction between Jew and Greek, thus giving Joel's statement wider scope. In Acts 2:39 Peter cites the last three words of 3:5b [2:32b], "whom YHWH calls," giving it a universal cast "*pas*" ("everyone"). Significantly, Peter identifies YHWH with Jesus of Nazareth and sees the present moment as already participating in the end time.

YHWH's Reasons for Judging the Nations (4:1–3 [3:1–3])

4:1 [3:1] For in those days
and at that time
when I restore the fortunes
of Judah and Jerusalem

4:2 [3:2] I will gather all nations,
making them descend to the valley of Jehoshaphat
where I will execute judgment on them
because of my people, Israel my inheritance,
whom they dispersed among the nations—
and they apportioned my land.

4:3 [3:3] Casting lots over my people—
they gave a boy for the price of a harlot,
sold a girl for wine and drank it.

NOTES

A divine announcement of judgment against the nations reinforces the promised deliverance of YHWH's chastened people in and around Zion. The only sure way they could dwell in safety was by removing any threat from their powerful oppressors, so the assurance that the nations must now pay for their offenses against Judah and YHWH connects directly with 3:5 [2:32]. The judgment will be universal, just as the offense against Judah is assumed to be inclusive. An eightfold acknowledgment of divine involvement underlines the pathos of the charges leveled against the victorious soldiers from the nations summoned to stand trial in a valley appropriately named "YHWH judges." The eight tokens of YHWH's direct concern are: a pronominal prefix with a verb, three suffixes on verbs, and four pronouns attached to nouns.

4:1 [3:1] The formula *kî hinneh bayyāmîm hahēmmâ ûbāʿēt hahîʾ* occurs elsewhere only in Jer 33:15; 50:4, 20. The context of this unusual linking formula in Jer 33:15a, *bayyāmîm hāhēm ûbāʿēt hahîʾ*, includes the more familiar *hinnēh yāmîm bāʾîm*, "Take note, days are coming," promises a judicial reckoning in the land that results in Jerusalem's security, and designates the city by a new name, "YHWH is our righteousness." The judgment oracle against Babylon in chapter fifty uses this linking formula twice, each time followed by an oracular formula.

Jer 50:4	*bayyāmîm hahēma ûbāʿēt hahîʾ neʾum YHWH*
Jer 50:20	*bayyāmîm hāhēm ûbāʿēt hahîʾ neʾum YHWH*

The source of danger for Babylon is the north, in this respect as in others resembling Joel's use of the linguistic tradition behind this text.

A shift in point of view occurs with *hinnēh* as Joel turns away from describing the divine assurance of safety in Zion to focus on things from the viewpoint of YHWH's antagonists. Adversative *kî* introduces reasons for accepting YHWH's promises with regard to the eradication of danger for the inhabitants of Zion, despite the threatened signs and portents. The double expression, "in those days and at that time," probably uses parallelism of greater precision in which the second temporal phrase telescopes the action, as if stopping time and collapsing a longer period into a single moment. Alternatively, the two temporal expressions are synonymous.

ʾašer. Although missing from a few ancient manuscripts, the relative pronoun conveys the sense of simultaneity, "when." As such it gives definiteness to the following verb and cognate accusative, *ʾāšiwb* (Qʾāšîb) *ʾet-šebût*, lit., "I turn the turning." The twenty-seven occurrences of this idiom do not seem to be used in a unitary manner. The older attempts by E. Preuschen (1895:1–74) and E. Baumann (1929:17–44) to explain the phrase on the basis of its etymology, which they understood as *šbh* ("to make captive") and the exclusively judicial interpretation based on Pss 85:2, 126:4 and Ezek 16:53 ("to abolish a sentence of imprisonment") were opposed by E. L. Dietrich's (1925) explanation from *šûb*, "to return," a view in which W. L. Holladay concurred (1958). R. Borger's caveat (1954:315–16) that the uncertain textual tradition of Kethib/Qere renders a final decision unlikely and M. Bracke's call for a contextual analysis (1985:233–44) discourage sweeping conclusions about this expression. The central idea is undoubtedly restoration, as in Amos 9:14, whether from captivity (Jer 29:14; Ezek 29:14; 39:25, Zeph 3:20) or from calamity (Job 42:10; Ezek 16:53; Ps 126:4, Hos 6:11). Outside the Bible the idiom occurs as early as the eighth century in Sefire stele 3.24 (KAI 224.24).

The addition of "Judah and Jerusalem" identifies the people for whom YHWH intends a reversal of fortune. Concentric circles move ever inward to focus divine favor on the sacred city; together the country and its capital make up the residence of YHWH's covenant community.

4:2 [3:2] The exclusive focus on YHWH's people in 3:1–5 [2:28–32] opens up to include all other nations, although the emphasis falls on Judah's oppressors. An ancient tradition of judgment being executed in a valley near Jerusalem (cf. Isa 10:12–14; Ezekiel 38–39; Zech 9:14–16; 12:1–9) underlies Joel's divine oracle. The gathering of spoil by victorious soldiers, decried in Isaiah's accusation of Assyria, YHWH's instrument of punishment ("For he [Assyria] boasts . . . my hand has discovered, like a nest, the peoples' wealth, and as one gathers abandoned eggs, I have gathered the whole earth" ([Isa 10:13aα, 14a]), contrasts ironically with YHWH's gathering of nations to make them pay for their misdeeds.

The divine decision in Zeph 3:8 to gather all nations and to bring kingdoms together uses the verb *ʾsp* in parallelism with *qbṣ (kî mišpaṭî leʾesōp gôyīm leqobeṣî mamlākôt)*. The latter verb occurs in Joel 4:2 [3:2], *weqibbaṣtî ʾet-kol-haggôyîm*, "I will gather all nations." The notion of gathering guilty people in order to execute judgment on them occurs elsewhere, for example in Isa 66:18 ("I am coming to gather all nations and linguistic groups," reading *bāʾ* with the Septuagint, Peshitta, and Vulgate instead of *bāʾâ*) and in Mic 4:12 ("But they do not comprehend YHWH's thoughts or understand his counsel, that he has gathered them *[kî qibbeṣām]* like sheaves to the threshing floor"). Both texts associate divine gathering of the nations with "thoughts," but the parallel expression in Isa 66:18 is "deeds" whereas Mic 4:12 has "counsel."

making them descend to the valley of Jehoshaphat (wehôradtîm ʾel-ʿēmeq yehôšāpāṭ). According to 2 Chr 20:20–26, King Jehoshaphat of Judah defeated a coalition of soldiers from the Moabites, Ammonites, and Meunites in a valley to which the name "valley of Berakah" was attached from that day forward. The symbolic adjective, "Blessing," resembles several names of valleys in the Bible.

1. the valley of the son of Hinnom (*[be]gêʾ ben-hinnōm*, Jer 7:31)
2. the valley of the travelers (*gêʾ haʿōberîm*, Ezek 39:11)
3. the valley of the horde of Gog (*gêʾ hamôn gôg*, Ezek 39:11)
4. the valley of vision (*gêʾ ḥizzāyôn*, Isa 22:1)

The similar understanding of a valley in Joel 4:14 [3:14] (*hamônîm hamônîm beʿēmeq heḥārûṣ*, "Tumult, tumult! In the valley of decision. . . .") indicates that one need not search for a valley of Jehoshaphat on a map, for it is symbolic rather than topographical. A play on the verb *šāpaṭ*, "to judge," occurs in vv 2 and 12; that pun takes advantage of the meaning of the proper name, "YHWH has judged." This reading of the cipher is found in Theodotion's expression, *chōra tēs kriseōs*, and the Vulgate's *Domini iudicium*. The identification of the valley of Jehoshaphat with Kidron began in the fourth century C.E., according to Eusebius. Technically, Kidron is no valley but a wadi *(naḥal)*; that also goes for other gorges, e.g. Hinnom, in the vicinity of Jerusalem. None of these actually suffices as a wide plain on which the nations could assemble for judgment, although Jer 31:40 uses *ʿēmeq* to designate an area littered with corpses all the way to the wadi Kidron. Rudolph's observation that history began in a valley (Gen 11:2, a plain *[biqeʿâ]* in the land of Shinar) and will also end in one locates this judgment scene in an arena beyond history (1971:79).

The Niphal perfect, *wenišpaṭtî*, when used with the preposition *ʿim* as here *(ʿimmām)*, can have the meaning, "to execute judgment" (2 Chr 22:8, *wayhî kehiššāpēṭ yēhûʾ ʿim-bêt ʾaḥʾab*, "When Jehu executed judgment on Ahab's dynasty"). Alternatively, the verb refers to YHWH's entering into a lawsuit with the gathered nations, the Niphal *tolerativum* indicating the deity's dual role as plaintiff and judge (Wolff 1977:76–77). The legal implications are clear (cf. Jer 25:31aβ, *kî rîb laYHWH baggôyîm nišpaṭ hûʾ lekol-bāśār*, "for YHWH has a lawsuit against the nations; he will judge all mortals"). In Ezek 38:22 *wenišpaṭtî ʾittô bedeber ûbedām* ("and I shall execute judgment against him with pestilence and bloodshed") moves beyond litigation to actual punishment of the offender.

The grounds for a guilty verdict and the two specified offenses relate to YHWH's possessions, which the nations have appropriated. They have dispersed the covenant people and have divided up YHWH's land (*ʿal-ʿammî wenaḥalātî yiśrāʾēl ʾašer pizzerû baggôyim weʾet-ʾarṣî ḥillēqû*, "because of my people, Israel my inheritance, whom they dispersed among the nations—and they apportioned my land"). The priestly prayer in 2:17 identifies the Judeans as YHWH's people *(ʿammekā)* and inheritance *(naḥalātekā)*, whereas the divine response in 2:18 reiterates the former concept *(ʿammô)* in conjunction with the land *(leʾarṣô)*. The same idea occurs in 2:19 *(leʿammô)*, 2:26–27 *(ʿammî)*, 4:3 [3:3] *(ʿammî)*, and 4:16 [3:16] *(leʿammô)*. YHWH's ownership of the land is specified in 1:6, 2:18, and 4:2 [3:2].

The earlier name for YHWH's people, Israel, is applied in this instance to Judah, although the dispersed individuals may include the northern kingdom that was taken captive into Assyria in 731 and 722. Nevertheless, the primary emphasis lies on Judean survivors of the conflicts with Babylonian armies in 605, 597, and 587/86 B.C.E. Joel's choice of the Piel verb *pizzerû* for scattering the exiles occurs mostly in texts with YHWH as subject, e.g. Ps 147:16, *hannōtēn šeleg kāṣāmer kepôr kaʾēper yepazzēr*, "[YHWH] gives snow like wool, scatters frost like ashes". In Esth 3:8 the Pual participles *mepuzzār ûmepōrād* describe Israel as spread out and divided among the peoples in the provinces, whereas Jer 50:17 applies the verb *pezûrâ* to Israel and likens the people to sheep being pursued by lions, that is, by Babylonian kings as successors to equally voracious Assyrians. The actions by Philistines and Arabs during Jehoram's reign as reported in 2 Chr 21:16–17 pale in comparison and cannot offer a plausible background for Joel's remarks. The pathos of losing one's land finds expression in Lam 5:2 (*naḥalātēnû nehepkâ lezārîm bāttēnû lenokrîm*, "our inheritance has been handed over to strangers, our houses to foreigners"). The prophet Amos threatened Amaziah with the loss of his land, among other atrocities associated with invading forces (*weʾadmātekā baḥebel teḥullāq*, "your land will be divided by line," Amos 7:17).

4:3 [3:3] *Casting lots over my people (weʾel-ʿammî yaddû gôrāl)*. The unusual expression for disposing of YHWH's people by lot is elsewhere restricted to Ob 11 and Nah 3:10, both in connection with an oracle against the nations.

> On the day you withdrew, on the day strangers confiscated our property, and foreigners entered his gates and cast lots over (*yaddû gôrāl ʿal*) Jerusalem, you [Edom] were also like one of them (Ob 11).
>
> Even she [Egypt] knew exile, going into captivity; her infants were also smashed at the top of every street, and they cast lots over *(yaddû gôrāl ʿal)* her esteemed ones, binding in ropes all her important citizens (Nah 3:10).

This instance of casting lots had nothing to do with festivities connected with New Year's day but resulted from victory in battle. As late as 1 Macc 3:41, a request was issued to merchants and traders that they come for the purpose of purchasing captives as slaves, and Nicanor is reputed to have offered ninety captives for a talent (2 Macc 8:11).

Such degrading of human beings to objects for sale showed callous disregard for others, an offense that provoked Amos' anger (2:6 and 8:6).

> Thus has YHWH spoken, "For three transgressions of Israel and for four I will not cause it to turn, in that they sold the innocent for silver and the needy for a pair of shoes" (Amos 2:6).
>
> To buy the poor with silver and the needy for a pair of shoes (Amos 8:6a).

The association of abuse of the powerless with drunken debauchery also occurs in Amos 4:1, and the prophet Hosea links drinking with sexual license in 4:11.

they gave a boy for the price of a harlot (wayyittenû hayyeled bazzônâ). The preposition *be* is probably a *bet pretii*, an indication of the sale price (cf.

Peshitta, Septuagint and Targum), although the syntax could indicate that the boy was sold for sexual use. The parallel with the young girl favors the former interpretation, for she was exchanged for a commodity (*wehayyaldâ mākerû bayyayin wayyištû*, "sold a girl for wine and drank it"). The final verb explodes with contempt for those persons who valued human life so little that it merely represented a means of getting drunk. The proposal to read *bammāzôn* ("for food") instead of *bazzônâ* ("for a harlot") does not commend itself. The oft-cited Deut 21:11–14 is not really relevant to the general problem of trivializing human life by selling boys and girls into slavery, for this legal prohibition concerns a special instance involving sexual intimacy under favorable circumstances, the intention of marriage. Having known a captive woman sexually, the law states, one must not then treat her contemptuously by selling her into slavery.

COMMENT

This brief rationale for judging the nations is linked with the preceding announcement of YHWH's empowerment of all Judeans to receive communication from their deity. The awesome signs and portents pose no danger to those persons who pay allegiance to YHWH, but they entail sheer terror for all who acknowledge foreign citizenship. Following a *kî* establishing a connection with 3:1–5 [2:28–32], a rare formula introduces YHWH's promise to bring back those Judeans who had been taken into exile. At a future date, still unspecified, YHWH will reverse the fortunes of the entire country, as well as its capital Jerusalem. Here the general term Judah precedes the more specific reference. Moreover, the linking formula contains redundancy, "For in those days and at that time," in addition to the rhetorical indicator for point of view, the frequent *hinnēh*.

The initial bicolon is continued by a tricolon announcing YHWH's intentions with regard to the nations responsible for the miserable circumstances into which the Judeans have fallen. Just as the fortunes of YHWH's favored ones will be turned around, so will the fate of the nations, who will be assembled in a valley whose name symbolizes the judgment awaiting them. The divine rescue will be comprehensive with respect to all who invoke YHWH, and the punishment will be equally far-reaching, extending to all nations. Escape is anticipated atop the sacred mountain; the nations will be brought down to a valley below. Space thus takes on symbolic meaning for the contrasting peoples. YHWH, an active participant in the moment of deliverance, will assume a similar role in judging guilty offenders. The final adverb "there" may even point beyond its immediate referent, the valley of Jehoshaphat, to Sheol, their ultimate destiny, for the euphemism *šām* sometimes has that ominous sense (Job 1:21).

Six cola enumerate the charges for which the nations must answer. The initial position of verbs now gives way to expressions of relationship, the first one, "my people and my inheritance" being defined more precisely with an apposition, "Israel" (or even "my people," with "my inheritance Israel" as the appositional phrase). The relative pronoun "whom" provides additional specification; it may refer to the distant "my people" or to "Israel." The breakup of families and scattering of individual members in foreign territory comprises an egregious wrong directed against YHWH's devotees. The second breach of relationship concerns the land placed in "Israel's" trust, but always belonging to the deity. Not impressed by the claim of divine ownership of the land, or ignorant of this feature of Israelite faith, foreigners divided it up among alien land-grabbers. This time also the direct object precedes the verb. That pattern continues when the text returns to elaborate further on the crime against YHWH's people, the casting of lots to determine their fate. The initial position of the verb returns momentarily in the fifth colon, the report that these victors disposed of spoil with callous disregard for youthful innocence. In the sixth colon the verb reverts to the dominant pattern here: "They gave a boy for the price of a harlot, *a girl* they sold for the price of wine—and drank it." Nevertheless, the massing of verbs in third person draws attention to the nations' guilt (*pizzerû, ḥilleqû, yaddû, wayyittenû, mākerû, wayyištû*).

Special Instances of Divine Recompense (4:4–8 [3:4–8])

4:4 [3:4] Furthermore,
what are you to me, Tyre and Sidon,
and all regions of Philistia?
Are you paying me back a recompense?
If you are working vengeance on me,
I will very quickly repay your deeds on your heads.

4:5 [3:5] Because you took my silver and gold,
and brought my priceless commodities to your palaces.

4:6 [3:6] Judeans and Jerusalemites
you sold to Ionians
to thrust them beyond their own border,

4:7 [3:7] Look, I am rousing them from the place
to which you sold them,
and I will repay your deed on your heads,

4:8 [3:8] Selling your sons and daughters
by the agency of Judeans,
and they will sell them to Sabeans,

to a distant nation;
for YHWH has spoken.

NOTES

4:4 [3:4] *Furthermore.* The *wegam* introduces a special instance of divine judgment against long-standing enemies, Phoenicians and Philistines. This section interrupts the general announcement that YHWH will execute judgment on all nations; the catchword *mkr* ("to sell") probably attracted the unit to this particular location. Elsewhere *wegam* occurs in 2:3, 12 and 3:2 [2:29], hence the expression does not indicate secondary authorship. It refers to the entire sentence, not just to the pronoun *ʾattem*, "you," and heightens the emphasis as if to exclude any exceptions whatsoever.

What are you to me (mâ-ʾattem lî). A sarcastic question, attributed to YHWH, probes the relationship between Judah's deity and two traditional enemies. The terse expression inquires about actions indicative of relationship, as if to determine intention. It includes both senses of grievance and revenge: what do you have against me and what do you intend to do about it? The people addressed by the personal pronoun *ʾattem* lived along the Mediterranean sea, Philistia to the south and Phoenicia to the north. Two major Phoenician cities, Tyre and Sidon, are singled out for attention, whereas the entire region of Philistia is mentioned, *wekōl gelîlôt pelāšet.* This expression occurs elsewhere only in Josh 13:2, *kol-gelîlôt happelištîm wekol-haggešûrî*, "the entire regions of the Philistines and Geshurites" (cf. Josh 18:17; 22:10–11; Ezek 47:8). At one time a pentapolis existed in Philistia consisting of Gaza, Ashdod, Ashkelon, Gath, and Ekron (Josh 13:3; cf. Judg 3:3; 1 Sam 6:4; Amos 1:6–8 and Zeph 2:4 [these last two omit Gath]). Animosity against Phoenicia persisted despite brief periods of international cooperation resulting from alliances during the reigns of David and Omri. Ahab's marriage with a Phoenician princess, Jezebel, cemented relations between the northern kingdom and Tyre for some time. Resentment lingered as late as Nehemiah's governorship (Neh 13:16) and gave rise to exquisite myths about hubris and its tragic consequences (Ezekiel 27–28).

Are you paying me back a recompense? (haggemûl ʾattem mešallemîm ʿālāy). The question searches for an explanation for the harsh treatment of Judeans by Phoenicians and Philistines. YHWH inquires whether or not they are acting in accord with the principle of *lex talionis*, an exact retribution for every offense. The expression *gml* implies that a person brings a matter to resolution, dealing fully so as to reach an effective conclusion, a full recompense.

welōʾ kigemul ʿālāyw hēšîb yeḥizqiyyāhû kî gābah libbô
But Hezekiah did not respond in kind, for his heart was proud.

2 Chr 32:25a

kemaᶜaśēh yedêhem tēn lāhem hāšēb gemûlām lāhem
According to their deeds, give to them; render to them their recompense.

Ps 28:4

In 2:25 YHWH promised to restore lost years; now that same determination to set things right requires further action, this time directed against nations who have brought suffering to hapless Judeans. The use of the Piel participle *mešallemîm* calls attention to the retribution that will be meted out at this time.

If you are working vengeance on me (weʾim gōmelîm ʾattem ᶜālay). This disjunctive question in 4b explains the obscure *mâ-ʾattem lî* (lit., "what you to me?"). The two rhetorical interrogatives imply that actions grow out of just principles and that an offense demands an appropriate retaliation. The issue is honor rather than greed or meanness, although such generosity in giving the nations the benefit of the doubt is undoubtedly sarcastic. In this way YHWH introduces an outrageous concept, from the deity's perspective, that Tyre and Sidon, along with all Philistia, nurse grudges of a personal nature in which Judah's sovereign has acted wrongly. In 2 Chr 20:11 King Jehoshaphat complains to YHWH that the Moabites, Ammonites, and Edomites are rewarding Israel's kindness in sparing them at an earlier time with its opposite, driving out the favored people from the land YHWH gave them (*wehinnê-hēm gōmelîm ᶜālênû lābôʾ legarešēnû miyyeruššātekā ʾašer hôraštānû*, "they repay us by coming to expel us from your heritage that you bestowed on us").

I will very quickly repay your deeds on your heads (qal mehērâ ʾāšîb gemulkem berōʾšekem). The two terms for quick action, *qal mehērâ*, occur in reverse order in Isa 5:26b (*wehinnê mehērâ qal yabôʾ*, "look, he is coming quickly"). The recoiling of deeds on one's head is also found in Ob 15b (*kāʾašer ᶜāśîtā yeᶜāśeh lāk gemulkā yāšûb berōšekā*, "exactly as you have acted, it will be done to you; your recompense will recoil on your head"). The affinities between this text and Joel 4:4 [3:4] are noteworthy, extending beyond Edom's plundering of Judah during the Babylonian invasion to the notion of YHWH's day. The general concept that God caused wicked deeds to return on the guilty person's head permeated ancient attitudes (cf. Ps 7:17 [16], *yāšûb ᶜamālô berōʾšô*, "his action will recoil on his head"; Judg 9:57, *weʾet kol-rāᶜat ʾanšê šekem hēšîb ʾelōhîm berōʾšām*, "and God caused all the wickedness of the Shechemite men to come back on their heads").

4:5 [3:5] *Because you took my silver and gold*. The relative pronoun *ʾašer* functions causatively in some instances, and that seems to be true here. I translate it like *baʾašer* and understand its causal sense to extend through v 6 ("Because you took . . . brought . . . and sold . . . , I am rousing . . ."). One can read *kaʾašer* ("when"), with v 5b as the main clause, but this reading ignores the conjunctive *waws* at the beginning of 5b and 6a. The causal clause echoes 2 Kings 25:15 and Jer 52:19 (*ʾăšer zāhāb zāhāb waʾăšer kesep kāsep lāqaḥ rab-tabbaḥîm*, "the captain of the guard took what was gold as gold and what was silver as silver"), presumably by melting the precious ore into convenient form for transporting it. Devotional stories from Daniel and elsewhere imply that Babylonians carried off the vessels from the temple at Jerusalem without altering their shape, later using them in a banquet (Dan 5:2–4). The order of the nouns, silver before gold, occurs frequently in the Bible, but the reverse sequence does also. According to Hos 2:8, YHWH is the true source not only of agricultural products such as wine, grain, and oil, but also of silver and gold. YHWH's ownership of these precious metals is explicitly stated in Hag 2:8 (*lî hakkesep welî hazzāhāb neʾum YHWH ṣebāʾôt*, "Mine is the silver, mine the gold, says YHWH of hosts"). The plundering of Judean assets is thus construed as an offense against the deity who owns the land, its inhabitants, and their possessions.

Precisely what did the Phoenicians and Philistines steal? The verb *leqaḥtem* ("you took") implies that these foreigners confiscated valuable treasures belonging to their weaker neighbors. The second colon in v 5 uses another noun in describing the stolen objects (*ûmaḥamadday haṭṭōbîm habēʾtem lehêkelêkem*, "you brought my precious commodities to your palaces"). The basic meaning of the root *ḥmd* is "desire," hence the plural form here connotes valuable items in addition to silver and gold. The adjective "good," while unnecessary, reinforces the divine attachment to the stolen objects which now occupy unaccustomed places.

The Sumero-Akkadian loan-word *hêkāl* refers to a royal palace as well as to a temple, and either meaning suits the context. Precious vessels and ornamentation from the temple in Jerusalem may have been placed in Philistine and Phoenician centers of worship, and valuable items from Judah may have been carried away to stately palaces alongside the Mediterranean Sea. The second person suffix *(kem)* suggests that the conquerors took the treasures to royal palaces, for one would expect something like "for the temples of your gods" or "for Baal" if the text implied religious use. The Philistine capture of the ark, reported in 1 Samuel 4–6, is probably too remote in time from the date of this divine oracle, and its plural form ("my priceless commodities") in all likelihood rules out this particular instance of the plunders of war. Moreover, Judeans had long ago settled that account satisfactorily. The offense mentioned in v 5 must have taken place at a later time, although the biblical record has overlooked it.

4:6 [3:6] *Judeans and Jerusalemites*. Once more, as in the preceding verse, direct objects precede the verb and lack the sign of the accusative. In this instance the general term goes before the more specific one, Judeans incorporating Jerusalemites in its wider scope. The twice-occurring *benê* is generic, referring to males and females, as the threat in v 8 against boys and girls indicates (contrast Wolff 1977:79, who sees the addition of "girls" in v 8 as excessive punishment outside the bounds of exact retribution).

you sold to Ionians. The third use of *benê* in 6a is followed by a rare pleonastic form, "children of *the* Ionians' (cf. 2 Chr 20:19, *min-benê haqqehatîm ûmin-benê haqqorḥîm*, "from the Kohathites and the Korahites," and 1 Kings 20:35, *weʾîš ʾeḥād mibbenê hannebîʾîm*, "a man among the prophets"). Slave trade thrived during wartime, but also in peace time when difficult economic circumstances forced people to adopt dire measures. Amos accused Tyre of an egregious offense in selling slaves to the Edomites (1:9) and, in his view, by doing so they forgot covenantal obligations *(welōʾ zākerû berît ʾaḥîm)*.

Assyrian sources from as early as the eighth century mention the Ionians, who lived on both sides of the Aegean, although all biblical references to these people occur in exilic and postexilic texts (Gen 10:2, 4; 1 Chr 1:5, 7; Isa 66:19; Zech 9:13; Dan 8:21; 10:20; 11:2; Ezek 27:13, 19). In the last of these, Tyre is accused of entering into business transactions with Ionians and other peoples, exchanging commercial products for slaves. The plural *hayyewanîm* occurs only in Joel 4:6 [3:6].

The verb *mekartem* ("you sold") recalls *mākerû* in v 3 and may explain the present location of vv 4–8. A similar phenomenon occurs in Amos 7:10–17, where an oracle announcing the end of Jeroboam's dynasty is interrupted by a biographical sketch in which this vocabulary appears prominently (*baḥereb yāmût yārobʿām*, "Jeroboam will die by the sword"). The priest Amaziah makes a general reference to Jeroboam's dynasty more seditious by applying the words directly to Jeroboam himself ("he will die by the sword"). The practice of linking textual units by means of catchwords is widely attested in the Bible.

to thrust them beyond their own border. The telic sense of *lemaʿan* attributes base intention to the inhabitants of Tyre, Sidon, and Philistia. Greeks, too, participated in activity that resulted in expelling Judeans from their homeland. The Hiphil participle, *harḥîqām*, strengthens the causative force of the sentence. By selling Judean slaves to the Ionians, the guilty Philistines and Phoenicians put considerable distance between the unfortunate slaves and their familiar territory. The twofold third person suffix *ām* calls attention to their miserable status by referring to their former relationship as possessors of land. Now they are owned by others, who buy and sell them at will.

The two charges against the Phoenicians and Philistines, plundering and slave trade, may represent more than a single instance of violating YHWH's property. Memory of their active involvement in slave trade persists as late as 1 Macc 3:41 and 2 Macc 8:11. Although Joel labels the precious metals and commodities as YHWH's personal possessions, the prophet does not designate Judeans and Jerusalemites by endearing terms such as *ʿammî* or *naḥalātî* (contrast 4:2 [3:2]).

4:7 [3:7] *Look, I am rousing them.* The particle *hinenî* often precedes a participle as here; *meʿîrām* (Hiphil participle from *ʿûr* plus third person plural suffix) indicates a rousing from inactivity. The suffix refers to the Judean slaves in remote lands. The power of Joel's deity extends to faraway places, despite appearances to the contrary. A similar statement to v 7 occurs in Isa 13:17, *hinenî mēʿîr ʿalêhem ʾet-māday ʾăšer-kesep lōʾ yaḥšōbû wezāhāb lōʾ yaḥpeṣû bô* ("Look, I am stirring up against them the Medes who do not value silver nor delight in gold").

from the place to which you sold them. The announcement of judgment against the guilty slave traders invokes the principle of *lex talionis*, although with a strange twist. YHWH stirs up the Judeans in a distant land and makes them the agent of punishment. The cumbersome expression, *min-hammāqôm ʾăšer-mekartem ʾōtām šāmmâ*, permits YHWH to mention the offense once more. The referent for the unspecified location ("the place . . . there") is the land of the Ionians. Curiously, the initial charge of plundering YHWH's precious goods does not evoke appropriate response in this context of punishment.

and I will repay your deed on your heads. The Hiphil perfect verb with a *waw* consecutive, *wahašibōtî*, pictures YHWH's active involvement in the resulting turn of fortune. The verb *šûb* appears again, as does the noun for revenge, *gemulkem*. The punishment falls on the heads of the Phoenicians and Philistines, to whom YHWH addresses this oracle. Presumably, the Ionians are exempt from YHWH's ire at this point, having acted merely as buyers of Judeans from their slave traders. In 4:4 [3:4] the threat for unspecified offenses uses virtually identical language, the only difference being the imperfect verb *ʾāšîb* instead of the perfect with *waw* consecutive, *wahašibōtî*.

4:8 [3:8] *Selling your sons and daughters by the agency of Judeans.* The verb *ûmākartî* (Qal perfect first person singular with conversive *waw*, "and I will sell") continues *wahašibōtî* in v 7. YHWH implements the principle of exact retribution, except that in this instance the innocent victim becomes the agent of punishment. Such a mediatorial function of a sufferer is not envisioned elsewhere in statements of *lex talionis*, where the deed itself returns on the heads of violent criminals or YHWH intervenes to assure that sinners get what they deserve. The Phoenicians and Philistines will be forced to watch their own children, both male and female, fall under the control of Judean middlemen in exchanging human beings for commercial gain.

The threefold use of *benê (benôt)* recalls v 6, although here the specification of daughters brings out what was only implicit there. Another graphic difference in v 8 is the use of the accusative particle *ʾet* before "your sons and daughters." Moreover, the general territorial designation *yehûdâ* suffices in v 8, whereas v 6 uses this term as well as its capital, *yerûšālayim*. The expression *beyad*, "by the agency of," functions both literally and symbolically. YHWH appears in the role of a powerful dealer in human flesh who sells young boys and girls to Judeans who turn right around and sell them to others.

and they will sell them to Sabeans. These distant merchants make a cameo appearance in 1 Kings 10:1–2, accompanied by their famous, although unnamed, queen. Ezekiel's lament over Tyre also refers to merchants from Sheba (27:22–23), as does his oracle about the mysterious foreign power Gog (38:13). This latter text mentions plunder, cattle and goods, silver and gold, but it does not specifically refer to slaves. Caravans from Sheba are also mentioned in Job 6:19 (cf. Ps 72:10, *malkê šebāʾ ûsebāʾ*).

to a distant nation. The change from the *le* prefix *(lišebāʾîm)* to *ʾel-gôy rāḥôq* does not imply that Sabeans will then sell the slaves to another nation, one far away (contra Rudolph 1971:77 and Bewer 1911:132). L. C. Allen notes (1976:114, n. 35) the same variation, although in reverse order, in Gen 37:36 ("The Midianites sold him [Joseph] to Egyptians, to Potiphar [*ʾel-miṣrāyim lepôṭîpar*"). "To a distant nation" is in apposition, the slight change in prefix being merely a stylistic variation. In Jer 6:20 Sheba is called a distant land *(mēʾereṣ merḥāq)*. The exact location of Sheba is uncertain, although it probably was in south Arabia. The transfer of seafaring people to the desert corresponds to the earlier sale of Judeans to Ionians on the coast of the Aegean. A previous move to the northwest is matched by one to the southeast (K. Marti 1904:139).

for YHWH has spoken. The formula authenticating a divine address, *kî YHWH dibbēr*, concludes the announcement of judgment against the Philistines and Phoenicians. Isaiah uses the expression to reinforce his initial appeal for a hearing, *šimʿû šāmayim wehaʾazînî ʾereṣ kî YHWH dibbēr* ("Hear, Heaven, listen, Earth, for YHWH has spoken," Isa 1:2a). In Isa 22:25 he uses the only two oracular formulas found in the book of Joel, *neʾum YHWH [sebāʾôt]* and *kî YHWH dibbēr*; here the latter expression concludes the oracles in Joel 4:8 [3:8], to which one may compare Isa 25:8 and Ob 18. A similar formula, *kî pî YHWH [ṣebāʾôt] dibbēr* ("for YHWH [of hosts'] mouth has spoken") occurs in Isa 1:20; 40:5; 58:14; and Mic 4:4.

COMMENT

Verses 4–8 interrupt the announcement of divine judgment on the nations, vv 1–3, 9–14. The verb *mākar*, "to sell," links the two literary units, although other similarities also occur. In v 1 the expressions "Judah and Jerusalem" designate the total Judean populace, just as they do in v 6. The verb *šûb* signified the return of captives in an amazing reversal of fortune akin to that foretold in the verb *wahašibōtî* of v 7. The word for nations, *haggôyīm* (v 2; cf. *baggôyīm* in the same verse) appears in its singular form, *gôy*, in v 8. The reference to male and female youths, *hayyeled wehayyaldâ*, in v 3 corresponds to "your sons and your daughters" in v 8. The particle *hinnēh* in v 1 is matched by *hinenî* in v 7, and the relative *ʾašer* of v 1 recurs in v 5.

Decisive differences between 1–3, 9–14, and 4–8 suggest that the latter unit may not have stood here originally. The following characteristics of 1–3, 9–14 are noteworthy: the focus on all nations rather than specific ones; the use of symbolic terms for a place of divine judgment (the valley of Jehoshapat, the valley of decision); affectionate terms for Judah (my people [twice], my inheritance); mention of the day of YHWH; the displacement of Judeans as an emphasis rather than servitude; the dividing of YHWH's land; the explicit reason for selling Judean youths, that is, for sexual pleasure and for wine; the concentration on an act of judgment in its forensic sense. In each instance 4–8 contrasts sharply with the unit it interrupts. Considerable stylistic differences also occur, particularly the lively rhetorical questions.

This intrusive section comprises a divine interrogation and threat, with Judah's ancient foes, Phoenicia and Philistia, as the imagined audience. Only two cities, Tyre and Sidon, both in Phoenicia, are named in YHWH's sarcastic rhetorical questions. Two additional peoples, the Ionians and Sabeans, play the role of distant agents in causing misery. The notion of remoteness achieves verbal and adjectival expression (*harḥîqām*, Hiphil infinitive plus third person plural suffix, in v 6; *rāḥôq* in v 8).

Tricola prevail over bicola, and an introductory *wegam* and concluding *kî YHWH dibbēr* stand outside this scheme. Verse 4 has three bicola; v 5 consists only of a single bicolon. The next three verses, 6–8, are characterized by tricola. Parallelism rarely occurs in the entire section: Tyre and Sidon // all the regions of Philistia; pay back // get revenge (v 4); silver and gold // previous commodities; you stole // you brought (v 5).

Perhaps the most noticeable feature of the unit is the interplay between the first and second person, which eventually gives way to third person. The initial divine question and threat juxtapose "you" and "me" while introducing a single "I" (4a, *ʾattem lî*; "you," "me" 4b, *ʾattem . . . ʿālāy . . . ʾattem ʿālay*; ["you . . . against me"]; *ʾāšîb gemulkem berōʾšekem* ["I" . . . "you" . . . "your"]). The next verse continues the contrast, now in the opposite order, "my" and "you/your" (*kaspî ûzehābî leqaḥtem ûmaḥamadday . . . habēʾtem lehêkelêkem*, "my . . . my . . . you . . . my . . . you . . . your"). At this point YHWH focuses attention on a third party, "sons of Judah and sons of Jerusalem" (v 6), whom "you" sold to a fourth party, "the Ionians." The second half of v 6 refers to innocent Judeans twice by means of the pronominal suffix *ām (harḥiqām . . . gebûlām)*. Verse 7 opens with a reference to these same people, again in a pronominal suffix *(meʿirām)*, but the attention shifts to an accusatory "you" (*mekartem*, "you sold"), thus reverting to the guilty Phoenicians and Philistines of vv 4–6 and identifying the victims, again by means of the pronominal suffix *(ʾōtām)* with the sign of the direct object. In v 7b the divine "I" returns, along with the opposing "you" ("and I . . . your . . . your"). The final verse continues the divine "I" while introducing a fifth party, "your sons and your daughters" and identifying the former victims in similar language now, "the Judeans," literally "the children of Judah," who have the last word—or deed. The Judeans "will sell them" to a distant people, the Sabeans.

This interplay of actors is energized by a single idea, *lex talionis*. The desire for exact revenge governs the specifics of the divine threat as well as the rhetorical questions. Additional stylistic features are the use of *qal mehērâ* to indicate a superlative, the play on words between *gemul* and *gebûl*, and the appositional use of *ʾel-gôy rāḥôq*, "a distant people."

In short, this section recalls recent offenses by ancient enemies and makes the point that in the great judgment of all nations the specific crimes of lesser powers will not go unseen but will be set right by the one who summons all peoples to the valley of decision. The oracular formula at the end assures readers that such threats as are found here have their basis in YHWH's declared intention, hence nothing can prevent its unfolding in the appropriate time.

YHWH's Judgment Against the Nations (4:9–16 [3:9–16])

4:9 [3:9] Proclaim this among the nations,
"Sanctify a battle.
Rouse the mighty ones.
Let all warriors draw near and go up.

4:10 [3:10] Beat your plowtips into swords,
your pruning knives into spears;
let the weakling boast, 'I am a warrior!'

4:11 [3:11] Hurry and come,
all surrounding nations;
gather there;"
Send down your mighty ones, YHWH.

4:12 [3:12] Let the nations rouse themselves and come up
to the valley of Jehoshaphat,
for there I will sit in judgment
on all surrounding nations.

4:13 [3:13] Put forth the sickle, for the harvest is ripe;
go out and tread, for the wine press is full;
the vats overflow, for their evil deeds are copious.

4:14 [3:14] Tumult! Tumult! In the valley of decision,
for YHWH's day is near in the valley of decision.

4:15 [3:15] Sun and moon have become dark,
stars have withheld their splendor;

4:16 [3:36] then YHWH roars from Zion,
utters his voice from Jerusalem;
heaven and earth tremble,
but YHWH is a refuge for his people,
a fortress for Israelites.

NOTES

The section dealing with a universal judgment on nations other than Judah resumes after a brief digression concerning specific grievances against two ancient enemies, Philistia and Phoenicia. A summons to warfare (vv 9–11) concludes with a momentary prayer for divine action (v 11b); this unexpected petition gives way to a rationale for the call to battle (v 12). A second image for judgment follows, that of harvesting ripe crops (v 13), and evokes terrifying thoughts connected with the day of YHWH (vv 14–16a), as well as comforting ones for Judeans (v 16b).

4:9 [3:9] *Proclaim this among the nations.* Who speaks here, the prophet or YHWH? Presumably, the intended speaker is YHWH, with heavenly heralds as the audience. The Qal imperative, *qirʾû*, thus addresses members of the divine council with an unusual task, that of mustering an army for its own destruction. Elsewhere, the person who called people to battle enlisted them in a cause that, in the eyes of the herald, was in the best interest of those being called into service. The direct object of the imperative, the demonstrative pronoun "this" *(zōʾt)*, anticipates what follows rather than looking back over an earlier comment (cf. 1:2). The summons goes out to the nations, who until now have escaped YHWH's punishment for mocking the Judeans (2:17, 19).

Sanctify a battle. The Piel imperative, *qaddešû* ("sanctify"), alludes to the ancient practice of invoking a deity's will before embarking on a military undertaking. The traditional language attests to an earlier time when Israelites understood their battles as holy wars, but that special sense does not apply here (cf. 1:14; 2:15, "sanctify a fast"). In Isa 13:3 YHWH's warriors are called "consecrated ones," *limquddāšāy*, and Mic 3:5 accuses disreputable prophets of preparing war against persons who refuse to feed them *(waʾašer lōʾ-yittēn ʿal-pîhem weqqidešû ʿālāyw milḥāmâ)*. The language of sanctifying a war even applies to shepherds encamped around Jerusalem (*qaddešû ʿaleyhā milḥamâ*, "prepare war against her," Jer 6:4 aα).

Rouse the mighty ones. The verb *hāʿîrû* (Hiphil imperative from *ʿûr*, "to stir up"), when combined with the earlier *qirʾû* and *qaddešû*, indicates that YHWH's heralds have a threefold task—to announce a conscription, to make appropriate military preparations, and to work the troops into a state of excitement over the prospects of victory. This root, *ʿûr*, often refers to intransitive activity, particularly reflexive rousing of the spirit, but it also can be transitive, e.g. in Hag 1:14 (*wayyāʿar YHWH ʾet-rûʾaḥ zerubbābel* . . . ," YHWH stirred up Zerubbabel") and Jer 51:11a (*hēʿîr YHWH ʾet-rûʾaḥ malkê māday*, "YHWH has stirred up the Median kings"). *haggibôrîm*, the object of the imperative *hāʿîrû*, parallels the subsequent *ʾanše hammilḥāmâ*, "warriors." Both nouns designate persons of considerable strength and courage.

Let all warriors draw near and go up. The brevity of the two jussive verbs, *yiggešû yaʿalû*, without a conjunctive *waw* suggests both haste and disorder as troops quickly respond to commands barked out in rapid succession. The verse provides no point of reference for the verbs—draw near to what? go up where? In Jer 46:3 the verb *nāgaš* indicates soldiers' movements toward the battlefield (*ʿirkû māgēn weṣinnâ ûgešû lammilḥāmâ*, "arrange shield and buckler; draw near for battle"); Jeremiah's choice of the root *ʿrk* probably derives from its essential meaning, "to order, to arrange." It refers to careful attention to battle array; here, too, as in Joel 4:9 [3:9] the warriors advance to their own destruction.

There will be no exclusionary rules in this conflict, for every warrior must take part, regardless of his personal circumstances or psychological state (contrast Judg 7:2–8; Deut 20:5–9; in the latter text the root *qrb* is used for drawing near to battle and *ngš* indicates the approach of the priest who addresses the assembly of warriors). Joel envisions the involvement of every recruit, *kol ʾanšê hammilḥāmâ*.

4:10 [3:10] *Beat your plowtips into swords*. This verse introduces a note of grim irony, although hidden momentarily. It reverses the utopian vision of a time when everyone can relax at home without fear of invasion from soldiers (Isa 2:2–4; Mic 4:1–4). Every conceivable weapon will be forged from whatever implement is available, even agricultural tools like the iron tip of a wooden plow and the cutting device used in vineyards. The unstated speaker of the Qal imperative *kōttû* is either YHWH or the heralds of v 9. The same verb occurs in Isa 2:4b (*wekittetû ḥarbôtām leʾittîm*, "they will beat their swords into plowtips") and Mic 4:3b. Joel's formulation of this activity seems to be parody rather than an original constituent of a summons to battle (contra R. Bach 1962:72, n. 1). The agricultural tool, *ʾittêkem* ("your plowtips"), is cognate with the verb *kātat*, "to beat, hammer out."

your pruning knives into spears. A different word for spear from that found in Isa 2:4b and Mic 4:3b occurs here, *remāḥîm* instead of *ḥanîtîm*. With the exception of Judg 5:8 (*māgēn ʾim-yērāʾeh wārōmaḥ*, "neither shield nor lance was seen"), this expression is found in exilic and postexilic texts such as the Priestly stratum of the Torah, Ezek 39:9, Jer 46:4, 1 Kings 18:28, Nehemiah and the Chronicler. Joel's preference for this word is puzzling if he provides a parody on the tradition preserved in the books of Isaiah and Micah.

Let the weakling boast, 'I am a warrior.' Overcome by excitement associated with the approach of battle, even individuals unsuited for combat are urged to surrender to a form of futile braggadocio. The irony contained in the boast derives from the essential sense of the term for warriors, *haggibôrîm* ("mighty ones"). The nominative sentence, *gibbôr ʾānî* ("I am a warrior"), contains one of Joel's four uses of the personal pronoun *ʾānî;* the others are 2:27 (twice) and 4:17 [3:17]. The restrictive use of this pronoun for YHWH, except for the weakling's boast in 4:10 [3:10], lends further irony, for the dubious soldier, *haḥallāš,* chooses a mode of speech that the prophet otherwise limits to deity. Jer 48:14 emphasizes inappropriateness of a similar boast by Moabites, *ʾêk tōʾmerû gibbôrîm ʾanāḥnû weʾanšê-ḥayil lammilḥāmâ* ("How can you boast, 'We are warriors and valorous in battle'?"). In Zech 12:8 YHWH promises that the Jerusalemite who stumbles "on that day" will be like David, and his house will resemble God—or YHWH's messenger. In short, those Moabites who pretend to be strong like God will fall, whereas YHWH's people who make no pretensions about their strength will experience divine power, directly or indirectly.

4:11 [3:11] *Hurry and come.* The meaning of the hapax legomenon, *ʿûšû,* is unknown, and emendations based on ancient versions or graphic similarity with this verb have failed to solve the problems presented by the entire verse. The Septuagint translates *synathroizesthe* ("gather yourselves together"), with Syriac and Targum following its lead; the meaning thus corresponds to the sense of the later Niphal verb, *weniqbāṣû,* "and gather." The Vulgate's *erumpite* goes its own way, possibly rendering *ḥûšû,* "hurry." Other plausible emendations are *ʿûrû,* "rouse yourselves," or *nûʿû,* "stagger." I translate *ḥûšû* on the basis of context and the remote possibility of an aural mistake by a scribe, ʿ for *ḥ,* but the other suggested emendations serve the context equally well.

all surrounding nations. Just as no potential warrior will escape the call to fight in the approaching battle, no nation will manage to elude the meeting at which their destiny will be decided. This point recurs in v 12, even in identical words, *kol-haggôyîm missābîb.*

gather there. The place for the gathering, *šāmmâ* ("there"), will unfold in due time, like *zōʾt* in 1:2 and 4:9 [3:9]. The Niphal jussive verb, *weniqbāṣû,* indicates the goal and result of the action of the two previous imperatives in the verse. The subsequent form of address, *gibbôreykā,* favors reading an imperative verb form of *qbṣ,* as does the Septuagint's *synachthēte* ("gather yourselves").

Send down your mighty ones, YHWH. Many interpreters consider a prayer in this setting out of place, particularly because of the implied change in speakers. It may constitute a gloss by a later scribe, who wished to activate the ancient promise once more. A similar appeal within a general prayer occurs in Sir 36:6, where the petitioner asks for the restoration of signs and portents that demonstrate YHWH's present deliverance for the elect people. In Ben Sira's prayer the vocabulary comes close to Joel's language, e.g. "all the nations" (v 2), "rouse" (v 8), "hasten" (v 10), and "gather" (v 13). As in Ps 103:20, the "mighty ones" are probably YHWH's heavenly army comparable to the host dispatched against Judah in 2:11. Their descent contrasts with the nations' ascent (W. Rudolph 1971:84).

On the basis of the Targum and Syriac, an emendation to "may YHWH shatter your mighty ones" commends itself (H. W. Wolff 1977:73; R. Simkins 1991:229). The Septuagint differs greatly, *ho praus estō machētēs* ("let the weak be a warrior"). The confused nature of this whole verse, whether deliberate or accidental, matches the events that unfold in chaotic fashion (L. C. Allen 1976:115). By placing the athnach under *weniqbāṣû*, the Masoretes have added to the confusion, agreeing in this respect with the Septuagint *ekei*. On this reading, the petitioner implores YHWH to send his mighty ones thither, with emphasis on the adverb.

4:12 [3:12] *Let the nations rouse themselves and come up.* By repeating the thematic words of the summons to judgment—the verbs "rouse" *(ʿûr)* and "come up" *(ʿālâ)*, the phrase "the surrounding nations" *(haggôyim missābîb)*, the noun "the nations" *(haggôyim)*—this verse brings the initial section to an effective conclusion. In addition, the repetition of "the valley of Jehoshaphat" *(ʾel- ʿēmeq yehôšāpāṭ)*, the verb "judge" (*lišpoṭ*, Qal infinitive), and the adverb "there" *(šām)* link this section with the first three verses in chapter four. The invitation comes close to a dare; YHWH encourages the worldly powers to stir themselves to action and to ascend to the aforementioned site of judgment.

to the valley of Jehoshaphat. The indefinite "there" receives specificity and the stage is set for the final drama.

for there I will sit in judgment on all surrounding nations. In contrast to v 2, where the verb *wenišpaṭtî* does not indicate YHWH's manner of entering into judgment, this verse pictures the supreme judge sitting before the accused and passing out sentences that will be executed on one and all (Pss 9:8–9 [7–8]; 82; 122:5). The dreaded battle, which has dominated the section until now, fades into the background. The implication seems unavoidable—the anticipated encounter between the armies of the nations and YHWH was a monumental mismatch. The victorious YHWH now does what conquering emperors do—decides the fate of the vanquished. Once again the text yields a play on words between the verb "to judge" *(šāpaṭ)* and the place of such activity, "the valley of Jehoshaphat" ("YHWH has judged").

In a related passage, Mic 4:11–13, nations assemble against Zion oblivious to the fact that YHWH has gathered them like sheaves for the threshing floor and commands the inhabitants of Zion to rise up and thresh the peoples, confiscating all their wealth as a gift for YHWH. The verb *wehaḥaramtî*, "I will devote," refers to the ancient practice of dedicating spoil to YHWH through burning *(ḥerem)*, although in this context the sense may connote sacred use rather than complete destruction of the plunder.

4:13 [3:13] *Put forth the sickle, for the harvest is ripe.* YHWH's judgment on the assembled nations now shifts from martial imagery to agricultural symbols, the harvesting of grain and grapes (cf. Isa 17:5 for the former, Isa 63:1–3 for the latter, and Rev 14:14–20 for both images). The rare word for sickle, *maggāl,* occurs elsewhere only in Jer 50:16 and can refer to the vintager's knife. The reason for beginning to harvest the grain, *kî bāšal qāṣîr,* uses an unexpected term, *bāšal* ("to boil"), that applies more readily to grapes bursting in the hot sun than to ripe grain. Some interpreters therefore see only one image here, the harvesting of grapes, but *qāṣîr* normally refers to cereal crops, Isa 18:5 being a significant exception.

The speaker, YHWH, does not specify those addressed, and literary precedent points to Jerusalemites in Mic 4:13 and the heavenly hosts in Zech 14:5b (*ûbāʾ YHWH ʾelōhay kol-qedōšîm ʿimmāk,* "and YHWH my God will come, all your holy ones with you"). These latter beings are probably addressed in v 13 as in v 11. YHWH's mighty ones thus receive their marching orders.

go out and tread, for the wine press is full. In near-perfect symmetry with v 13a, this command reinforces the timeliness of YHWH's judgment. The upper basin of the press, *gat,* is filled to capacity, awaiting someone to walk on the grapes and force the juice to run down into the lower vats, *hayeqābîm.* A second verb breaks the otherwise precise parallelism; this Qal imperative, *redû,* may derive from *rādâ,* "to rule," or from *yārad,* "to go down." The context probably justifies taking it as an extended meaning of dominance, hence "to tread" (cf. the Septuagint, *pateite*).

The military effectiveness of this image of treading grapes achieves near-perfection in Isa 63:1–6, which describes a blood-spattered YHWH who acknowledges, when asked, that lack of companions necessitated his treading the grapes of wrath in Bozrah, Edom's capital. Because the juice from grapes resembled blood, the image of treading grapes was a natural one for pouring out the blood of enemies.

the vats overflow, for their evil deeds are copious. The verb *hēšîqû* (Hiphil perfect from *šûq* probably "to spill over") and its subject, *hayeqābîm,* continue the idea of the second causal clause and provide transition from symbolism to a literal understanding of grievances. A third *kî* clause returns to the actual offenses against Judeans in vv 2–3, labeling their evil deeds abundant *(rabbâ).* The exact referent for the pronominal suffix *ām* ("their") is not made clear; its general nature indicts all Judah's neighbors.

4:14 [3:14] *Tumult! Tumult! In the valley of decision.* The prophet's restraint while observing the decisive events heightens the sense of mystery engulfing these forays and indeed the whole universe. The few details in this concluding section on the judgment of nations, vv 14–16, ignore the actual scenes of fighting. Joel mentions the distant commotion and the growing darkness that provide a sinister background for the decisive encounter, and he refers to powerful tremors that seize earth and sky when YHWH marches forth to do battle. YHWH's assurance that Israelites have nothing to fear draws the unit to a close, at the same time making smooth transition to the book's final section.

The repetition of the plural noun *hamônîm*, which connotes the noise rising from a huge crowd, functions to intensify the impression of din and confusion (GKC 123e), one evoked further by its onomatopoetic capacity. A similar expression occurs in Isa 13:4 (*qôl hāmôn behārîm demût ʿam-rāb qôl šeʾôn mamlekôt gôyīm neʾesāpîm*, "a commotion on mountains like a multitude, a din of kingdoms like nations gathered together") and 17:12 (*hôy hamôn ʿammîm rabbîm kahammôt yammîm yehemayûn ûšeʾôn leʾummîm kišʾôn mayim kabbîrîm yišāʾûn*, "Oh, the noise of numerous people, they thunder like the Sea's roaring; oh, the tumult of peoples, they roar like the sound of powerful waters").

The finality of the divine decision, its irrevocable fixedness, is underscored by an alternative symbolic name for the site of judgment, the valley of decision. The adjective *heḥārûṣ* derives from the cognate verb *ḥāraṣ*, "to decide" (cf. 1 Kings 20:40 and Isa 10:22–23 for its negative sense). Amos 1:3 refers to threshing sledges of iron, *baḥaruṣôt habbarzel*, with which Syrians mutilated the corpses of Gilead or desecrated corpses. A dual sense for the word *heḥārûṣ* is therefore possible—a place of decision and of threshing (G. W. Ahlström 1971:81).

for YHWH's day is near in the valley of decision. Poetic license is operative here, inasmuch as that dreaded day has finally arrived. Its nearness earlier terrified YHWH's people, but their prayer and divine compassion gave them a reprieve (1:15; 2:1, 11, 13–14, 18–19). The association between tumult and YHWH's day already occurs in Isa 13:4–6 (cf. v 6, *kî qārôb yôm YHWH*) and Joel 1:15; 2:1.

4:15 [3:15] *Sun and moon have become dark, stars have withheld their splendor*. This verse is identical with 2:10b and a variant of 3:4a [2:31a].

4:16 [3:16] *Then YHWH roars from Zion*. The *waw* attached to YHWH, the subject of the verb *yišʾāg*, is best translated "then," for it indicates an event subsequent to the darkened heavens. The reversal of normal order for verb and subject places the emphasis on the subject, YHWH, who charges forth from Zion (*miṣṣiyyôn*), the sacred city, to lead an army against the assembled warriors from surrounding lands. The image of roaring either derives from the sound of a lion as it begins to devour its prey or from thunder associated with a weather deity (cf. Job 37:2, 4–5). In 2:11a YHWH raises a battle cry at the head of his army, a shout also preceded by darkened heavens.

The apparent contradiction between YHWH's sitting in the valley of Jehoshaphat to judge the nations and setting out from Zion to attack the same group need not indicate secondary tampering with the text. Instead, two different understandings of YHWH's judging the people, judicial and military, have given rise to the dual renderings of the deity's scene of activity. Poetic imagination can picture complementary visual images without quibbling about the actual contradiction. According to Isa 52:12, YHWH will lead the exiled Judeans on their return to Jerusalem and he will also bring up the rear. The idea that YHWH supplies both a vanguard and a rearguard is the poet's way of announcing that the people will be protected both from ambush and from pursuit.

The expression *miṣṣiyyôn* may be an attribute of YHWH, the one from Zion, similar to attributes of Canaanite deities: *bʿl ṣdn, bʿl lbnn, bʿlt gbl* (Andersen/Freedman, 1989:224). This conclusion rests on the order of the phrase in Joel 4:16 [3:16], subject-locative-verb, and on extra-biblical parallels, now also attested at Quntillet Ajrud (*YHWH šmrm, YHWH tmn*—YHWH of Samaria, YHWH of Teman).

utters his voice from Jerusalem. This clause stands in synonymous parallelism with the previous one, the subject carrying over and the verb taking an object to complete its meaning *(ûmîrûšālayim yittēn qôlô)*. Here also the preposition and the place from which YHWH departs precede the verb. Sentence order so far stresses the actor and the location of the activity—YHWH, from Jerusalem. The idiom, *yittēn qôlô,* often refers to thunder, whence it becomes a metaphor for loud speech.

This bicolon is also found in Amos 1:2a, where the sequel mentions the devastating effect of the thunderous roar on the environment. Shepherds' pastures mourn, and the tip of [Mount] Carmel withers. Elsewhere Amos alludes to the lion's roar and identifies it with YHWH's irresistible call of the prophet (3:8). It is impossible to determine which prophet influenced the other, given the difficulty of establishing a date for Joel. Both Joel and Amos probably took the sentence from a floating tradition, each one investing it with his own application to the historical situation.

A related text in Jer 25:30 speaks of YHWH's roaring from a dwelling place on high.

> *YHWH mimmārôm yišʾāg ûmimmeʿôn qodešô yittēn qôlô šāʾog yišʾag*
> *ʿal-nāwēhû hêdad kedōrekîm yaʿaneh ʾel kol-yōšebê hāʾāreṣ*
> YHWH roars from the height and utters his voice from his holy abode;
> he roars loudly from his habitation, like those treading [grapes]
> he sings out a shout to all earth's inhabitants.

The context of this announcement resembles Joel's allusion to YHWH's resounding voice, for it mentions a judgment against the nations and uses the image of treading. The judging (*nišpāṭ,* Niphal perfect) of all flesh *(kol-bāśār)* in v 31 echoes Joel 3:1 [2:28].

heaven and earth tremble. In 2:10 the order of "heaven and earth" is the opposite of 4:16 [3:16] and two verbs express the idea of "shaking," *rāgaz* and *rāʿaš*. In addition, an adverbial phrase, *lepānāyw* ("before him") introduces the clause. The overall sequence in 2:10–11a is (1) the trembling of earth and heaven, (2) the darkening of heavenly luminaries, and (3) YHWH's mighty shout. The order in 4:15–16 is (1) the darkening of the celestial lights, (2) YHWH's loud shout, and (3) the shaking of heaven and earth.

but YHWH is a refuge for his people. Neither the cosmic reverberations nor YHWH's loud shout pose any danger for Judeans, who experience their protector as a haven in the midst of peril. Joel here uses psalmic language, to which one may compare

ʾelōhîm lānû maḥaseh wāʿōz
God is for us a refuge and fortress.

Ps 46:2a (46:1a)

The absolute noun *maḥaseh* occurs three times, and its shortened form *(maḥseh)* occurs six times. Both are used in Psalms, usually with a pronominal suffix (14:6; 46:2 [1]; 61:4 [3]; 62:8–9 [7–8]; 71:7; 73:28; 91:2, 9; 94:22; 142:6 [5]; *māʿōz* is used seven times (27:1; 28:8; 31:5 [4]; 37:39; 52:9 [7]; 60:9 [7]; 108:9) (cf. also Nah 1:7, *māʿôz* // the verb *ḥāśâ* [*ṭôb YHWH lemāʿôz beyôm ṣārâ weyōdēaʿ ḥosê bô,* "YHWH is good, a stronghold in a time of difficulty; and he knows those who trust him"] and Isa 25:4 [*kî-hāyîtā māʿôz laddāl māʿôz laʾebyôn baṣṣar-lô,* "for you have been a fortress to the weak, a stronghold to the poor in their affliction"]). Only this latter verse has *maḥaseh* and *māʿōz* together (*maḥseh mizzerem ṣēl mēḥōreb,* "a shelter from the storm and a shade from the heat"; cf. Isa 4:6).

a fortress for Israelites. The parallelism between this phrase and 4:16b is exact, except for the explicit subject in the initial one. Naturally, the subject, YHWH, carries over: "YHWH is a refuge for his people, a fortress for Israelites." The people of YHWH are identified here as "children of Israel" instead of "children of Judah" or "Zionites." Israel refers in this instance, as also in 2:27 and 4:2 [3:2], to the people of Judah, not to inhabitants from the northern kingdom. The form of the expression here, *benê yiśrāʾēl,* is unique for Joel.

COMMENT

This section, 4:9–16 [3:9–16], invites foreign nations to prepare for war, commands an opposing army to overwhelm the gathered militia, and promises Judeans a secure place during the conflict. The summons to battle is full of irony, and the description of the engagement on the battlefield uses images of harvesting crops. For one brief moment the prophet implores YHWH to dispatch a mighty force against the nations. The end of the unit is ambiguous; most interpreters extend the thought unit through v 17, despite the obvious change in speakers here.

Who speaks in this unit? The answer is complicated by abrupt shifts in verb forms and in addressees. The initial imperatives in v 9 are presented as divine speech, but the command, "proclaim this," implies that a herald has been enlisted in YHWH's service. Accordingly, this spokesperson may then mock the nations by urging them to place into use every conceivable weapon and by encouraging bravado (v 10). The same speaker gives precise instructions about the location for the gathering of warriors—there in the valley of Jehoshaphat. That the adverb *šāmmâ* refers to the earlier juridical language of vv 1–3 is confirmed by the mention of this valley once more in v 12.

A change in addressee certainly occurs in v 11b, where the prophet interjects a brief prayer for decisive action against the gathered warriors. Perhaps the herald and prophet are identical. The next verse reverts to divine speech once again, and the jussives suggest that even vv 10–11a may also derive from this same speaker. That possibility is strengthened by the continuation of divine speech in v 13, but imperatives recur here. The herald's (prophet's?) voice returns in v 14, which introduces the idea of YHWH's day into this portrayal of eschatological judgment, and continues through v 16.

Imperatives suggest the urgency of action (*qirʾû, qaddešû, haʿîrû*, v 9; *kōttû*, v 10; *ʿûšû wābōʾû, hanḥat*, v 11; *šilḥû, bōʾû redû, hešîqû*, v 13), while jussives reinforce this impression (*yiggešû yaʿalû, yoʾmar*, v 10; *weniqbāṣû*, v 11; *yeʿôrû weyaʿalû*, v 12). Vocatives stress the immediacy of direct address (*kol-haggôyim missabîb, YHWH*, v 11), and *kî* clauses provide the rationale for conduct (vv 12, 13 [three times], 14). A rare nominative sentence catches the irony of a weakling's boast, expressed without a verb and in language imitating YHWH (v 10, *gibbôr ʾānî*). Another nominative sentence gives the impression of breathless dread (v 14) as repetition of *hamônîm* increases the power of this onomatopoetic jewel. A single infinitive indicates YHWH's purpose in assembling the foreign peoples (v 12, *lišpōṭ*, "to judge"). This divine intention gave rise to symbolic names for the place designating the great arraignment ("the valley of Jehoshaphat," "the valley of decision"). Exquisite symbols also portray the final judgment as the harvesting of crops and treading of grapes (v 13).

Parallelism occurs sporadically in this section ("plowtips" // "pruning knives"; "swords" // "spears," v 10; "put forth the sickle" // "go out, tread," "the harvest is ripe" // "the winepress is full," v 13; "sun and moon" // "stars," "have become dark" // "have withheld their splendor," v 15; "from Zion" // "from Jerusalem," "YHWH roars" // "utters his voice," "a refuge" // "a fortress," "for his people" // "for Israelites," v 16).

The verses vary in length considerably. Two bicola in v 9 are followed by tricola in vv 10–11, with v 12 reverting to two bicola. Three short bicola make up v 13, and v 14 has two short bicola. The next verse, 15, has only one bicolon, while v 16 compensates for such brevity by having a tricolon and a bicolon.

This whole section echoes 2:10–11, 24. The earlier invasion by a vast locust horde as a prelude to YHWH's day is here mirrored by YHWH's warriors who attack an equally vulnerable foe. In both texts YHWH's mighty shout brings terror to those who must bear the brunt of such unleashed power, and in each unit the language of full harvest occurs. One decisive difference exists, however, for the excess of wine (and oil) in 2:24 is a sign of divine favor, whereas the image connotes judgment in 4:13 [3:13].

A transitional verse (17) serves as a threshold piece, marking the end of the section dealing with YHWH's judgment of the nations, as the Masoretes noted with the S indicating closure. This verse also inaugurates a positive promise for YHWH's people. The complete restoration of Judeans will take place now, for the threat from surrounding peoples has been removed and the assurance of divine residence in the sacred city vindicates those who previously endured mockery because their deity had, to all appearances, abandoned them.

Judah's Security Is Assured (4:17–21 [3:17–21])

4:17 [3:17] Then you will know that I YHWH your God
dwell in Zion, my sacred mountain;
and Jerusalem will be (a place of) holiness,
foreigners no longer traversing it.

4:18 [3:18] On that day
mountains will drip sweet wine,
hills will course with milk,
and all channels of Judah will flow with water,
a stream rushing from YHWH's house,
watering the valley of Shittim.

4:19 [3:19] Egypt will become a waste,
Edom a desolate steppe;
because of violence against Judeans,
the spilling of innocent blood in their land.

4:20 [3:20] Judah will be inhabited from now on,
Jerusalem for untold generations.

4:21 [3:21] I shall avenge their blood, yet unavenged,
and YHWH will dwell in Zion.

NOTES

4:17 [3:17] *Then you will know*. YHWH interrupts the prophetic description of cosmic disturbances to confirm the conclusion drawn from the terrifying events, specifically that the people of Judah will experience YHWH as refuge and fortress. The traditional identification of YHWH's people as "children of

Israel" ("Israelites") in v 16 invites Judeans to claim age-old promises of divine favor, which YHWH here reaffirms. The formula of recognition or acknowledgment, *wîdaʿtem*, picks up the previous statement in 2:27, where YHWH asserts that the return of a bountiful harvest will persuade Judeans that their deity is in their midst and there is no other; in that context YHWH twice promises Judeans that they will not be shamed again. Now YHWH elaborates on the hymnic language in 4:16b [3:16b] and comments on the implications of such protection. Any doubt the people of Judah may have harbored as a result of want and mockery by foreigners will be banished from their minds by incontrovertible proof in the sky and on earth.

that I YHWH your God dwell in Zion, my sacred mountain. The earlier "in your midst" (2:27) gives way to a staggering thought: that YHWH actually resides in Jerusalem. This bold reassertion of an element of the tradition about Zion's inviolability, despite plain evidence to the contrary in 586 B.C.E., uses the language of tabernacling (*šāken*, "to pitch a tent," "to dwell"). The object of the statement of recognition, *kî*, governs three things, the first of which refers to YHWH's choice of a sanctuary. Undoubtedly polemical, this identification of a divine dwelling excludes similar sanctuaries such as Baal's Mount Saphon. The god of Judah has chosen to pitch a tent in Zion, thus making the site holy (cf. Ezek 43:12 and Ob 17). The notion of Zion as YHWH's dwelling place occurs in Isa 8:18 (*mēʿim YHWH ṣebāʾôt haššōkēn behar ṣiyyôn*, "from YHWH of hosts who dwells on Mount Zion"). For Joel, Zion has actually become YHWH's sanctuary, and its cultic significance overshadows everything else. A similar comment occurs in Zech 2:14 [10].

> *rānnî weśimḥî bat-ṣiyyôn kî hinnenî-bāʾ wešākantî*
> *betokēk neʾum YHWH*
> Sing and rejoice, daughter Zion, for I am coming and I will dwell in your midst. YHWH's oracle.

Zechariah emphasizes YHWH's actual residence among the populace as proof that his prophetic message is authentic.

and Jerusalem will be holiness. The second thought governed by *ki* concerns the extraordinary result of YHWH's dwelling in the sanctuary. Holiness is dispersed throughout the entire city of Jerusalem, now the ultimate embodiment of holiness, *the* holy place. This remarkable observation stops short of Zechariah's claim that holiness attaches to bells worn by horses and to virtually everything in the land that could be used in the cult, even ordinary cooking pots in Judah and Jerusalem (14:21). The designation of Jerusalem as a holy city is found in Isa 52:1 (*ʿûrî ʿûrî libšî ʿuzzēk ṣiyyôn libešî bigedê tipʾartēk yerûšālayim ʿîr haqqōdeš*, "Wake up. Wake up. Put on your strength, Zion. Put on your attractive apparel, Jerusalem, the city of [the] holiness). Here and in Zech 14:21

this elevation of Zion to a sanctuary is associated with a promise that the city will no longer be subjected to those who would desecrate it, specifically the uncircumcised and the unclean (Isa 52:1) or Canaanites (Zech 14:21). According to Nah 2:1 [1:15], all worthless persons *(beliyyaᶜal)* will be excluded from wandering about in the city (*laᶜabōr*, reading Qere').

foreigners no longer traversing it. The city will be declared off limits to everyone outside the religious community who worships YHWH. The choice of the verb *ᶜābar*, "to cross over," in the third idea governed by the preceding *kî* carries heavy irony, in that the word for Hebrews *(ᶜibrîm)* comes from the same verb. By excluding foreigners from the city, persons responsible for maintaining a holy environment in the cult will finally succeed in their mission. The sustained purity will result in permanent favor from their deity. This attitude toward strangers or foreigners as unclean resembles that of Ezra and Nehemiah, for whom non-Judeans constituted a strong threat to the purity of worship.

The statement of recognition in 2:27 shows certain affinities with two observations of this kind in Ezekiel 39, a chapter that, as earlier noted, shares several ideas with Joel (YHWH's zeal, the people's shame, return from exile, and the outpouring of YHWH's spirit, vv 22, 25–29).

4:18 [3:18] *On that day.* An eschatological formula, *wehāyâ bayyôm hahûʾ*, links v 18 with the preceding promise that YHWH will reside in Jerusalem. The allusion to an unspecified day echoes numerous prophetic texts, e.g. Isa 7:18; 24:21; Jer 4:9; 30:8; Ezek 38:10, 18; 39:11; Hos 1:5; Amos 8:9; Mic 5:9 [10]; Zeph 1:10; Zech 12:3, 9; 13:2, 4; 14:6, 8, 13, among others. This formula frequently links supplementary material with what precedes it. In 4:1 [3:1] Joel varies the wording appreciably, *kî hinnēh bayyāmîm hāhēmmâ ûbāᶜēt hahîʾ*, "for in those days and at that time." Joel's use of *wehāyâ bayyôm hahûʾ* introduces ideas resembling those in Zechariah 12–14, where the linking formula also occurs. Its presence in Ezekiel 38 and 39 is noteworthy, inasmuch as the content of these chapters coincides with that of Joel in several respects (cf. also the so-called apocalypse of Isaiah, especially chapters 24 and 27).

mountains will drip sweet wine (yiṭṭepû hehārîm ᶜāsîs). Under the impact of locusts and a severe drought, Judeans had to endure a complete loss of sweet wine (1:5, 9, 12), but Joel promises that in the restored community blessed by YHWH's permanent presence the nearby hills will produce an abundant supply. This vision of plentiful sweet wine echoes the optimistic ending to the book of Amos, 9:11–15, where the following words appear:

wehiṭṭîpû hehārîm ᶜāsîs wekol-haggebaᶜôt titmôgagnâ
And the mountains will drip sweet wine,
all the hills will flow (with it).

Amos 9:13aβ

The chiastic sequence of verb-subject-verb, the balancing of the object with the adjective *kol*, which like *ʿāsîs* carries over to the other colon, and the complete parallelism enhance the poetic quality of this verse. The intensive Hiphil verb, *wehiṭṭîpû* (from *nāṭap*), conveys the image of a mighty torrent of juice from newly pressed grapes. Joel's language is more reserved; sweet wine drips, as opposed to its cascading down the mountainside in Amos. Joel's introductory formula also differs from that in Amos, where one finds *hinnê yāmîm bāʾîm neʾum-YHWH*, ("Look, days are coming, an oracle of YHWH").

hills will course with milk (wehaggebāʿôt telaknâ ḥālāb). A Canaanite text mentions the consequence of Baal's return to life as follows: *šmn šmn tmṭrn nḫlm tlk nbtm*, "the heavens rain oil, the valleys flow with honey" (CTA 6, 3:6–7, 12–13). Similarly, Joel thinks of the benefits derived from YHWH's residence in Zion. The depletion of sweet wine reported in 1:5 will be generously corrected, for the surrounding hills will always have an abundant supply of it. This vision of plenty exceeds the expectation in 2:19–26, which made up for earlier lack, and the language abounds in hyperbole. The idea seems to be that cattle will have adequate grass so they will produce a constant supply of milk (contrast 1:18). The ancient description of the land flowing with milk and honey may have given rise to this observation in Joel, although the omission of "honey" is strange (Exod 3:8; Lev 20:24; Num 13:27; Deut 6:3; Josh 5:6). Job's reminiscence about an earlier time when Shaddai's presence brought blessings indicates that the idea was widespread.

> *birḥōṣ halîkay beḥēmâ weṣûr yaṣûq ʿimmādî palgê-šāmen*
> When my feet were washed with cream and a rock poured out streams of oil for me.
>
> 29:6

and all channels of Judah will flow with water (wekol-ʾapîqê yehûdâ yēlekû māyim). Whereas 1:20 mentions dry channels, Joel here envisions perennial streams flowing throughout the land, providing water for cattle and people, whose age-old struggle against drought will come to an end at last. The nouns, prominently placed, obscure the verb *hālak*, despite its twofold use in 4:18a; [3:18a]. The structure of the last two verbal clauses emphasizes the continuity of thought: "hills will course with milk" and "channels will flow with water" (subject-verb-object and subject-verb-object).

a stream rushing from YHWH's house (ûmaʿyān mibbêt YHWH yēṣēʾ). This idea of a stream flowing from the sanctuary appears elsewhere in Ps 46:5 [4], Ezek 47:1–12, and Zech 14:8 (cf. also Ps 65:10 [9], Gen 2:10–14; Isa 33:21). Joel's description of the life-giving stream is closer to Ezekiel 47 than to Zechariah 14, which mentions two rivers, one flowing eastward, the other westward. The river referred to in Ezekiel 47 flows from the south of the temple eastward to the Arabah, emptying into the Dead Sea and bestowing life on its waters. The miraculous nature of this water will be evident from its healing effect, extending even to the trees flourishing along the banks of the river. The initial position of the subject in this clause highlights the stream, with the verb *yēṣēʾ* appearing last.

watering the valley of Shittim (wehišqâ ʾet-naḥal haššiṭṭîm). Like the waters of Shiloah in the area of the temple that extend their reach a short distance in the Kidron valley, the stream that Joel envisions flows all the way to the arid region where only acacias can grow. If an actual valley is intended, the most likely candidate is the Wadi ʾen-Nar, a continuation of the Kidron valley that passes through the Judean wilderness and ends at the Dead Sea. The problem with the alternative site, the Wadi ʾes-Sant, is that this naturally fertile valley runs westward from Bethlehem toward Ashkelon. The importance of acacia wood in making some cultic items (Exod 25:10, 23–24; 26:15; 27:1; 30:1) may have occasioned Joel's choice of language, but the expression may also have a symbolic meaning like the "valley of Jehoshaphat" and the "valley of decision," thus implying that even the thirstiest valley will have flowing water. The word *naḥal* indicates a deep gorge between two hills, whereas *ʿēmeq* in 4:2, 12, 14 [3:2, 12, 14] refers to a much wider area. The depression on the east side of the Jordan opposite Jericho, called Shittim in Num 25:1; 33:49; Josh 2:1; 3:1, can hardly be meant, for that would require the stream from Zion to flow through the Jordan river.

4:19 [3:19] *Egypt will become a waste, Edom a ruin (miṣrayim lišmāmâ tihyeh weʾedôm lemidbar šemāmâ tihyeh).* Judah's prosperity can only be complete if her foes are discomfited; hence Joel mentions two ancient enemies, Egypt and Edom, who will suffer desolation comparable to what Judeans endured as a result of the locusts (2:3). In contrast with Judah and Israel, Egypt, the gift of the Nile, was blessed with an abundant supply of water. Joel's depiction of Judah's existence under optimal conditions, namely YHWH's permanent residence in Zion, reverses that situation. Now Judah enjoys a copious water supply and Egypt is changed into a desolate waste. Edom, never so fortunate as Egypt with regard to water, will find itself even harder pressed to discover enough of it for survival. Such predictions as this one find their inspiration in earlier prophecies about YHWH's day, particularly Ezek 29:9–10, 12, and 32:15 (for Egypt) and 35:3, 4, 7, 9, 14, 15 (for Edom). The expression "desolation" functions thematically in these oracles (cf. Zeph 1:13; 2:4, 9, 13). YHWH had promised to deliver Judah's tormentor, the locust horde, into a desolate land (2:20); now a similar fate awaits Egypt and Edom.

because of violence against Judeans (meḥamas benê yehûdâ). The rationale of YHWH's punishing these southern enemies lacks specificity, although using a term for extreme cruelty, *ḥamas*. Judeans were the objects of violence, not its perpetrators—*benê maqqeph yehûdâ* is objective genitive, hence the phrase refers to atrocities committed against Judeans. A similar expression occurs in Ob 10,

> *mēḥamas ʾaḥîkā yaʿakōb tekassekā bûšâ wenikratā leʿôlām*
> Because of violence against your brother Jacob, shame will cover you and you will be cut off forever.

Because Edom equals Esau, Jacob's twin brother, the mistreatment of Judeans by the people of Edom was especially irksome.

the spilling of innocent blood in their land (ʾašer šāpekû dām-nāqîʾ beʾarṣām). Syntatically difficult, this clause accuses Egyptians and Edomites (the implicit subject of the Qal perfect verb *šāpekû*, "they poured out") of killing innocent victims in their land, that is, Judah. Syntax favors reading *beʾarṣām* with reference to the preceding *benê-yehûdâ*. The unusual spelling of *nāqîʾ* occurs elsewhere only in Jonah 1:14; normally it takes the form *nāqî*. Egyptians invaded Judah on more than one occasion; the biblical record includes attacks by Sheshonk I (1 Kings 14:25–26; 2 Chr 12:2–12), Osorkon I (2 Chr 14:9–15; 16:8), and Neco in 609 B.C.E. (2 Kings 23:29–34). Given the Deuteronomistic exaltation of King Josiah, his death at the hands of Pharaoh Neco may easily have been viewed as the shedding of innocent blood. If "in their land" actually refers to Egyptians (and Edomites), one thinks immediately of Exod 1:15–22.

Although Edomites refused to let the Israelites pass through their land during their flight from bondage in Egypt, the real source of bitter animosity was the shabby treatment Judeans received while fleeing from Babylonian soldiers in 586 B.C.E., perhaps also Edomite association with Moabites and Ammonites in attacking Jehoshaphat. Biblical testimony to the resulting hatred of Edomites is widespread (cf. Ob 1–21; Lam 4:21; Ps 137:7; Mal 1:3–4; Sir 50:26). According to ancient belief, innocent blood cried out to YHWH, who acted to avenge wrongdoing (Gen 4:10).

> *wayyōʾmer meh ʿāśîtā qôl demê ʾaḥîkā ṣōʿaqîm ʾēlay min-hāʾadāmâ*
> He [YHWH] said, "What have you done? Listen! The sound of your brother's blood is crying out to me from the ground."

Edom's close ties with Israel in ancestral tradition adds poignancy to this particular expression of violence against innocent victims and its punishment.

4:20 [3:20] *Judah will be inhabited from now on, Jerusalem for untold generations (wîhûdâ leʿôlām tēšēb wîrûšālayim ledôr wādôr).* The verb *tēšēb* (Qal imperfect from *yāšab*, "to sit") applies to Judah and Jerusalem in this verse characterized by synonymous parallelism.

Judah	//	Jerusalem
from now on	//	for untold generations
will be inhabited	//	will be inhabited (implied)

Although Judah is normally construed as masculine, exceptions occur (cf. Lam 1:3); Joel's use of the feminine verb with Judah may be influenced by its proximity with Jerusalem, cities always being feminine. If *tēšēb* is masculine, one could read "Judah, you will be inhabited from now on." The extended meaning for the verb *tēšēb*, "to be inhabited," is otherwise attested in several prophetic texts.

lōʾ tēšēb lāneṣaḥ welōʾ tiškōn ʿad-dôr wādôr
It will never again be inhabited nor occupied (Isa 13:20).

wešākan harērîm bammidbār ʾereṣ meleḥa welōʾ tēšēb
They will dwell in scorched places of the wilderness, an uninhabited salt flat (Jer 17:6, cf. v 25).

weʾašqelôn lōʾ tēšēb
And Ashkelon will not be inhabited (Zech 9:5).

weyāšebâ yerûšālayim ʿôd taḥteyhā bîrûšālāyim
And Jerusalem will again be inhabited in its site, in Jerusalem (Zech 12:6).

Emphasis in Joel 4:20 [3:20] falls on the unbroken habitation of YHWH's city. Now that YHWH's presence there has been effected, Joel imagines Jerusalem's citizens finally at rest from their enemies. This security will, in his view, last into the distant future, a point he makes by using two temporal expressions, *ʿôlām* and *dôr wādôr* with prefixed *lamedh* (cf. 2:2, where different prepositions precede the terms, *min* ["from"] and *ʿad* ["unto"]).

4:21 [3:21] *I shall avenge their blood, yet unavenged (weniqqamtî dāmām lōʾ niqqamtî)*. Although in 2:13 Joel uses the ancient expression about YHWH's compassionate attributes (cf. Exod 34:6–7), he omits the divine traits in v 7, unless this final verse alludes to one of them, punishing guilty persons. The expression *wenaqqēh lōʾ yenaqqeh* ("and by no means declares innocent") differs markedly, however, from the grammar in Joel 4:21, where two finite verbs occur rather than an infinitive absolute followed by a negated finite verb. A lone negating particle can apply to both verbs, and the withholding of the negation until the second verb can have a dramatic purpose, so that the reading in the Masoretic Text cannot be ruled out entirely. It seems to me, nevertheless, that the correct solution to this difficult verse must be sought elsewhere. I have changed the initial *weniqqêtî* (Piel perfect from *nāqâ*, "to consider or declare innocent") to *weniqqamtî* (Qal perfect from *nāqam*, "to avenge"), which appears to be what the Septuagint translator read (*kai ekzetēsō to aima autōn kai ou mē athōōsō* ("and I will make inquisition for their blood and will by no means leave it unavenged"); cf. also the Peshitta *w*ʾ*tb*ʿ *dmhwn wl*ʾ ʾ*ḥs*ʾ, both of which seem to have read *weniqqamtî dāmām welōʾ ʾanaqqeh*). Another possibility is to construe the first verb as a question: "Shall I leave their blood unpunished? I shall not," for which a comparable text exists, Jer 25:29, although the Niphal of *nāqā* rather than Piel occurs there. A third possibility is to follow the Septuagint and the Peshitta in their rendering of two different verbs, which yields the following translation: "I shall avenge their blood that I have declared innocent" (reading the verb *nāqam* in the first clause, *nāqā* in the second). Another option is to understand the negative *lōʾ* as a *lamedh* emphatica, yielding "I will surely. . . ."

Regardless of how one resolves the difficulty of these verbs, the reference to "their blood" presents a problem because of the verse that intervenes between it and the earlier mention of innocent blood (v 19). The natural conclusion to v 19 is v 21a, and the logical sequel to v 20 is v 21b.

Egypt will become a waste, Edom a ruin; because of violence
done to Judeans, the spilling of innocent blood in their land (v 19).
I shall avenge their blood, yet unavenged (v 21a).
Judah will be inhabited from now on,
Jerusalem for untold generations (v 20).
And YHWH will dwell in Zion (v 21b).

This juxtaposition of the various parts of vv 19–21 improves the sense in yet another way, for it removes the abrupt transition from one speaker to another in v 21. As the Masoretic Text stands, YHWH speaks in v 21a and the prophet Joel returns in v 21b. The transposition also provides the rationale for v 20; YHWH's residence in Zion will make it possible for Judeans to live safely in Jerusalem.

and YHWH will dwell in Zion (waYHWH šōkēn beṣiyyôn). The book of Joel closes with the declaration that YHWH has taken up permanent residence in the sacred city. A similar observation concludes the book of Ezekiel,

> *wešēm-hāʿîr miyyôm YHWH šāmmâ*
> And the city's name from that day will be, "YHWH is there" (48:35).

The conjunction in v 21b may be asseverative: "as surely as YHWH resides in Zion."

COMMENT

The final five verses of the book take up the matter of Judah's future in light of the continued existence of two ancient enemies, Egypt and Edom. The other great powers, Assyria and Babylon, had already paid for their crimes, but the present threat from Egypt and Edom must be removed before Judeans can rest confidently. This section, vv 17–21, addresses that problem and promises utter destruction for these hated foes. A transitional verse, 17, brings the previous unit to a close and introduces the final theme of the book: YHWH's permanent dwelling in the sanctuary and the benefits of divine presence. The next verse, 18, identifies the era of YHWH's residence in Zion as the long-awaited day of YHWH, now viewed positively insofar as Judeans are concerned, and describes the miraculous results of YHWH's presence—a life-giving fountain issuing from the temple and fructifying everything in its path. The next verse, 19, mentions the negative effects of YHWH's residence in Jerusalem on two enemies, Egypt and Edom, who will be made desolate because of their crimes against innocent Judeans. The discomfiture of Egypt and Edom will naturally enable Judeans to dwell securely, v 20, inasmuch as YHWH has avenged their murdered victims and thereby demonstrated the truth of the promise to reside in Zion, v 21.

The divine self-declaration in v 17 uses the statement of acknowledgment for a second time (cf. 2:27), and v 18 appeals to the traditional expectation of a decisive day when YHWH overcomes his enemies in battle. A divine oracle, presumably spoken by the prophet Joel, makes up vv 17–20, 21b; this prophetic address in YHWH's name is interrupted in v 21a, where YHWH speaks in the first person. The initial statement of acknowledgment is thus matched by a divine asseveration in v 21a, as if to say that these promises are entirely reliable.

Structurally, vv 18aβ, 19–20, resemble one another in their near-exact parallelism.

18	mountains // hills	*hehārîm // wehaggebaʿôt*
	wine // milk	*ʿāsîs // ḥālāb*
	drip // drip [implied]	*yiṭṭepû // [yiṭṭepû]*
19	Egypt // Edom	*miṣrayim // weʾedôm*
	waste // ruin	*lišmāmâ // lemidbar*
	will become // will become	*tihyeh // tihyeh*
20	Judah // Jerusalem	*wihûdâ // wîrûšālayim*
	from now on // for untold generations	*leʿôlām // ledôr wādôr*
	will be inhabited // will be inhabited [implied]	*tēšēb // [tēšēb]*

The unequal length of these verses stands out. Two bicola make up v 17, while the next verse has a colon, a tricolon, and a bicolon. Two bicola return in v 19, with vv 20 and 21 having one bicolon each.

The position of the verb varies throughout the section, with nouns coming first in vv 19–20. The sequence is as follows:

17a Verb + object (a nominative clause introduced by *ki* and containing a participle)
17b Verb + subject + predicate adjective, followed by subject + negated verb + locative and adverb
18a Verb + prepositional phrase, followed by verb + subject + object and subject + verb + object, followed by subject + verb + object
18b Subject + prepositional phrase + verb and verb + object (with a sign of the accusative)
19 Subject + predicate adjective prefixed by *lamedh* + verb, followed by subject + predicate adjective with *lamedh* + verb
20 Subject + adverb + verb, followed by subject + adverb
21 Verb + object + negated verb, and subject + participle + prepositional phrase

The participles in vv 17 and 21, a sort of inclusio, emphasize continuity; the repetition of *šōkēn* with YHWH as subject serves as divine assurance that the holy sanctuary will not be threatened again and that Judeans can live in security. The ordeal of the past has come to an end, for YHWH dwells in his sacred mountain, in Zion. Where YHWH resides, one need not fear locust plagues, drought, fire, or foreign armies. That message in Joel 4:17–21 [3:17–21] provides an effective conclusion to a book in which ominous threats play such a prominent role.

INDEX OF SUBJECTS

Index of Authors

Rosenzweig, F. 50
Rostovzeff, M. I. 25n.25
Rothstein, J. W. 29
Rudolph, W. 24n.23, 31, 87, 95, 100, 109, 117, 121, 128, 141, 150, 155, 169, 175, 184, 190

Schmid, H. H. 155
Schneider, D. A. 22n.19
Schoors, A. 26n.28, 124
Schunck, K. D. 48n.86
Sellers, O. R. 88
Sellin, E. 133, 151, 170
Shapiro, H. 40n.59
Simkins, R. 40n.65, 90, 92, 96, 100, 102–4, 108, 111–12, 122, 124, 146, 168, 190
Skehan, P. W. 12n.3
Smith, S. 53
Sternberg, M. 15n.9

Taylor, A. 90
Thompson, J. A. 39, 91, 96

VanderKam, J. C. 25n.26
van der Meer, W. 31
Vanoni, G. 42n.69
Vernes, M. 29
Vogels, W. A. 31n.42

Wanke, G. 146
Watts, J. D. W. 100
Weinfeld, M. 133
Weiser, A. 141, 144
Weiss, M. 48n.86
Wenham, G. 98
Whitley, C. F. 123
Whybray, R. N. 12n.2
Wilson, R. R. 40n.63
Wolfe, R. E. 22n.20
Wolff, H. W. 22, 22n.20, 26n.27, 30–31, 84, 89–90, 96–97, 99, 105, 119, 122, 124–25, 129, 133, 138–39, 146, 152, 155, 160–62, 175, 182, 190
Wright, A. D. G. 12n.3

Zimmerli, W. 36n.53
Zimmerman, F. 97

Index of Hebrew Words

unvocalized b

vocalized b

dôr wādôr 130, 202
derek 124, 131
diršûnî wiḥyû 144
deše᾿ 154
dāše᾿û 153

unvocalized h

hyll 97
hnht 23n.21
hṣpṣpny 151
hry῾w 118

vocalized h

ha᾿azînû 85
hā᾿elōhîm 42
ha᾿arbeh 88–89
hôbîš 37n.55, 100, 102, 109, 112, 114, 159
hôbîš tîrôš 39, 99, 114
hôbîšâ 37n.55, 101
hōbîšû 101, 109
haggibôrîm 188–89
haggādôl 128
haggādôl wehannôrā᾿ 128, 168, 171
haggāzām 88–89
haggôyīm 184, 190
haggôyim missābîb 189–90, 195
haggepen 109
haggarānôt 157
hāh 106
hehāgāb 89
hehārîm 204
hû᾿ 145
hazzeqēnîm 86
haḥallāš 189
heḥāsîl 88–89
haḥargōl 89
heḥārûṣ 192
hôy 106
hāyâ 79
hayyewanîm 182
hayyeled wehayyaldâ 184
hayyeleq 88–89
hayeqābîm 157, 191
hayyat haśśadeh 111
hāyetâ 121
hakkōhanîm 99
hêkal 23n.21, 181
hokrat 98, 104
hālak 199
hêlilû 100–1, 103, 106, 114
hemma 53
hammāzôn 155
hamônîm 38, 53, 192, 195
hammôreh 155
hammôreh liṣdaqâ 155
hammaśśā᾿ 81
hannebālâ 98
hinnēh 173, 177, 185
hinnēh yāmîm bā᾿îm 173
hanḥat 29, 195
hinenî 150, 161, 183, 185
hassāle῾am 89
hā῾îrû 187–88, 195
haṣṣepônî 150–51
hāqîṣû 95
harḥîqām 182, 185
haśśatan 18n.13
haššelaḥ 26, 124, 131
hašmanîm 158
hēšîqû 191, 195

vocalized v

we 101
we᾿edôm 204
we᾿aḥarāyw 120, 130, 138, 152
we᾿akaltem 158
we᾿im 23n.21, 26, 87
we᾿al-bigedĕkem 135
we᾿emet 42, 136

unvocalized z

vocalized z

unvocalized ḥ

vocalized ḥ

unvocalized y

vocalized y

unvocalized m

vocalized m

unvocalized š

vocalized š

unvocalized t

vocalized t

INDEX OF OTHER LANGUAGES

AKKADIAN

ARABIC

ARAMAIC

EGYPTIAN

GREEK

LATIN

POST-BIBLICAL HEBREW

PROTO-SEMITIC

SUMERIAN

SYRIAC

UGARITIC

Index of Scripture References

HEBREW BIBLE

Genesis

Exodus

Hosea

Joel

Amos

Job

NEW TESTAMENT

Matthew

Acts

Romans

Galatians

Revelation

APOCRYPHA AND PSEUDEPIGRAPHA

1 Esdras

2 Esdras

1 Maccabees

2 Maccabees

Judith

Martyrdom and Ascension of Isaiah

Sirach